Collectible
Drinking
Glasses

Identification & Values

Mark E. Chase & Michael J. Kelly

COLLECTOR BOOKS
A Division of Schroeder Publishing Co., Inc.

The current values in this book should be used only as a guide. They are not intended to set prices, which vary from one section of the country to another. Auction prices as well as dealer prices vary greatly and are affected by condition as well as demand. Neither the Authors nor the Publisher assumes responsibility for any losses that might be incurred as a result of consulting this guide.

Searching For A Publisher?

We are always looking for knowledgeable people considered to be experts within their fields. If you feel that there is a real need for a book on your collectible subject and have a large comprehensive collection, contact Collector Books.

On the cover:
- Upper left: Slow Poke Rodriguez
  (Pepsi-Warner Bros., 1973). $30.00 – $50.00.
- Upper right: Underdog
  (Pepsi-Leonardo TTV). $15.00 – $20.00.
- Lower left: Snidely Whiplash
  (Pepsi-P.A.T. Ward). $10.00 – $15.00.
- Lower left over one: Howard the Duck
  (7- Eleven). $15.00 – $18.00.
- Lower left over two: Bugs Bunny
  (Pepsi-Warner Bros., 1973). $5.00 – $7.00.
- Bottom of page far right: Tasmanian Devil
  (Pepsi-Warner Bros., 1973). $15.00 – $20.00.
- Center of page: Two Davy Crockett glasses.
  $4.00 – $6.00.

Cover Design: Sherry Kraus
Book Design: Benjamin R. Faust

Additional copies of this book may be ordered from:

COLLECTOR BOOKS
P.O. Box 3009
Paducah, KY 42002-3009

@ $17.95. Add $2.00 for postage and handling.

Contents

About the Authors

Mark E. Chase is the director of Learning Technology User Services at Slippery Rock University, Slippery Rock, PA. He holds an Ed.D from the University of Pittsburgh in Instructional Design and Technology (1994).

Michael J. Kelly has been teaching English at Slippery Rock University since 1967. He holds a Ph.D. in English from the University of Massachusetts (1968) and a Master of Arts in Technical and Professional Writing from Carnegie Mellon University (1989).

Special thanks go to Melva Davern
who inspired and started this project.

Overview and Brief History of the Glass Collecting Hobby

Most glass or tumbler collectors will agree that the origin of this phenomenon can be traced to the jam, cheese, dairy, and food product glasses of the 1930s and 1940s; to soft-drink companies which printed their trade-marks and product designs on glasses, jars, and milk bottles to stimulate sales and to capture public awareness; and to newspaper comics such as Li'l Abner, Popeye, and Dick Tracy. Manufacturers, hoping to increase the sale and popularity of their products, offered limited edition character designs on the sides of their glass containers. In time, sets and series evolved, and because so many different colors and designs were available, collectors discovered the fun and challenge of putting together sets of their favorite glasses which could, after all, be used in the kitchen and dining room.

The Disney cartoon character glasses which were offered by food product manufacturers were extremely popular because of the success and popularity of Disney's films — *Fantasia, Snow White, Pinocchio, Sleeping Beauty,* just to name a few — in the 1930s and 1940s. The multiplicity of Disney characters naturally encouraged the production and distribution of sets and series of glasses. Collectors — a good number of them children — simply had to have them all, and parents found that it was easier to get stubborn children to drink all their milk or juice if Mickey's or Donald's or some other cartoon character's image appeared on the side of the glass. Thus, food packagers and manufacturers found an interesting way to stimulate sales, and consumers had something of permanent utilitarian and aesthetic value left after the product was used. After all, an attractive tumbler with a nice, colorful design or cartoon character was clearly superior to an empty, ugly tin can. And what about the educational benefits? With nursery rhymes, brief poems, the alphabet, songs, and other juvenile fare on glasses, children sitting at the breakfast or dinner table could practice their reading skills and take in some worthwhile information, sometimes in advance of actual schooling.

With the precedent for decorated series of food product glasses so well established in the 1930s and 1940s, it is no wonder that today there are so many different kinds of glasses out there to collect. Today's glasses primarily promote restaurants and soft drinks, and the subject matter found on glasses ranges from movies to personalities to places and historical and contemporary events. Advertisers and manufacturers have always been aware of the commercial possibilities and the obvious fact that there is no other substitute for a simple drinking glass. As a result, plain, unadorned and undecorated drinking glasses are virtually the exception rather than the rule today.

It becomes slightly easier when we get to the late 1940s and early 1950s to follow the evolution of collectible drinking glasses. With television came popular children's shows like Howdy Doody, and Welch's jellies and jams were successfully promoted and sold in small 7½ ounce glasses featuring the Doodyville characters with catchy little rhymes praising Welch's products. In the mid 1950s, similar small food glasses bearing Davy Crockett lore, jingles, and adventures corresponding with the popular television serial appeared. Then the early 1960s brought a second wind for jam glasses when Welch's began to issue its Flintstone series with a seemingly endless number of color and bottom embossment combinations. This Welch's jam glass phenomenon continued into the 1990s with The Archies, Warner Brothers, and NFL sets. And who can forget the Saturday morning Hanna-Barbera cartoons of the 1960s and 1970s (as well as the re-runs today!), the Jay Ward cartoon characters, MGM's Tom and Jerry, the Harvey Cartoon cast, and others — they are all on glass!

During the 1960s gasoline companies even got into the collectible drinking glass act by issuing glasses with their logos on them, as well as glasses with regional attractions, sports teams and players, and famous American Indians. Glasses commemorating various World's Fairs and even the United States' space missions also found favor with the public. The idea was — buy something, and get a free (or cheap) glass to keep the experience in your mind.

In the early 1970s fast-food restaurants began to offer cartoon or comic character tumblers to patrons who purchased a soft drink or packaged meal. Soon, the major national franchises adopted this successful promotion technique, usually with the sponsorship of a soft-drink manufacturer. The 1973 Pepsi Collector Series of eighteen glasses featuring Warner Brothers cartoon characters was one of the earliest and most popular large-scale promotions. This success led to other promotions which soon spread to a large number of chains, especially those which were committed to a specific soft drink. The results are quite apparent now: there is hardly an existing cartoon character who hasn't been publicized and immortalized on the panels of a drinking glass!

It is safe to say that our country's bicentennial year, 1976, and the accompanying review and re-appreciation of our country's history, were mainly responsible for an accelerated production and issuance of collectible drinking glasses. This surge in glass production essentially began in 1974 when Libbey Glass, the National Flag Foundation, and Herfy's Restaurants distributed their Historic Flags sets, and it continued with Bicentennial commemorative sets issued by franchises such as Arby's, Burger Chef, Burger King, and Wendy's and by soft-drink companies such as Coca-Cola.

Another phenomenon which popularized collectible drinking glasses in the 1980s and 1990s were the Hollywood film, television series, and the video revolution. The James Bond movies, King Kong, the Star Wars trilogy, Indiana Jones, Battlestar Galactica, The Goonies, Star Trek, Superman, Batman, The Flintstones — these are names and titles which come to mind when movie-glass tie-ins are mentioned.

Looking back, we are now able to see that the chunk of years from 1975 to 1980 was the peak production period for collectible drinking glasses. (For collectors with foresight, it was a golden opportunity.) The cost for such promotions has increased from the twenty-two cents per glass that the 1976 Arby's Bicentennial Series and the 1976 Pepsi-Warner Brothers Interaction Series originally cost the distributor to something nearly twice that; with minimum case order requirements and other cost-of-doing-business complications, many franchises simply do not want to go to the trouble of running an extended promotion, even though it is an established fact that such promotions significantly stimulate and increase business. Rising costs have no doubt been responsible for a greater number of plastic drinking container promotions, and collectors are sure to have noticed that in the past few years the restaurants that are still issuing glasses from time to time (McDonald's, Arby's, and Pizza Hut) are charging more for them. Perhaps increased business at restaurants which use glass promotions, books such as this one, collectible drinking glass clubs and the publicity which such organizations could potentially generate, and articles on collectible drinking glasses in collectors' publications will combine to create a climate in which collectible drinking glass promotions are regular, and much anticipated events. We strongly feel that these glasses have now firmly established themselves as part of our popular culture and that they deserve to be treated with serious regard because of their commercial, historical, and cultural relevance. Of all the major franchises, McDonald's has proved to be the most consistent over the years when it comes to glass promotions, most recently with the 1994 Flintstones movie set of four mugs and the summer of 1995 Batman mug set.

Collectors have a wealth of kinds of glasses to choose from and to collect, and collecting boundaries are limited only by the collector's personal preferences and tastes. They can extend to gasoline and oil company premiums, sports teams, popular cartoon characters, a specific restaurant chain, the American Bicentennial or Revolution, the American space effort, a certain soft-drink manufacturer, or any other cohesive category or area of interest. It is our experience that realistic collectors make a point of narrowing their collecting interests simply because the variety of glasses is simply too vast for comprehensive collecting. And eventually, as most collectors will readily admit, storage and display become issues that have to be faced.

In fact, it is the sheer variety of glasses that is available that has played a large part in determining the contents of this book.

Systematic gathering of information on all the different types and variations of glasses has only seriously begun in the last ten years. There have always been collectors, but it was not until fairly recently that a large number of them actually began to coordinate, compile, exchange, and examine information about the glasses. It is a sad fact that many, perhaps most, glass manufacturers kept few or poor records on the types and quantities of glasses manufactured and distributed. It is no doubt true also that promoters, advertisers, and food product manufacturers originally considered their designed or otherwise decorated glasses to be relatively ephemeral; that is, they probably expected most of the glasses to be broken or discarded fairly soon after distribution, and they probably never dreamed that people would be building permanent collections of these glasses, prizing them, and passing them on to future generations. It is equally likely that they could never have foreseen books dedicated to cartoon character, fast-food, or Kentucky Derby glasses.

Modern collectors who want to know as much as possible about the glasses they are collecting have much to do and many obstacles to overcome. People are already beginning to forget when and where they got certain unsponsored and undated glasses or sets of glasses. Even restaurant managers and employees tend to forget when certain promotions were held or indeed, if they were held. Parent companies and national headquarters kept poor records and are unable or unwilling to provide collectors with the kinds of information they want. However, persistence frequently pays off, and we have found that information can be gathered if collectors do their homework, ask the right questions, and network at antique shows, glass conventions, and flea markets.

Truly reliable information is precious and often extremely difficult to collect and verify. This is the case for many reasons, one of the most obvious being the regional nature of many glass promotions. Glasses that are in abundance in a certain state or area of the country may never have been heard of in other states or areas of the country, even when they were distributed by franchise giants like McDonald's or Arby's. Many promotions were extremely limited, and some simply failed or were cut short or canceled. Other promotions, like many of McDonald's, were national, and huge numbers of glasses were involved, too many, evidently, for the corporations themselves to keep track of. Certain specific glasses or cartoon characters met with disfavor or, even worse, public indifference. And sets which were planned and only reached the prototype stage, never to be released to the public, further complicate the modern glass historian's job and frustrate the avid collectors who know about these glasses but can never hope to obtain them for their collections. And then there are the glasses, both singles and sets, that are quite simply rare because large numbers of them were never produced. All of these factors contribute to the essential appeal and challenge of glass collecting.

Today, the successful collector is a person who travels widely to flea markets, thrift shops, yard sales, and collectible shows; who corresponds and trades with a good number of other collectors from all parts of the United States; and who literally exhausts all channels in an attempt to find glasses for his or her collection as well as information about them. We have heard countless stories about fabulous glass discoveries, and the bottom line on almost all of them has something to do with a collector who takes the time to talk with people about his or her interests, who doesn't mind spending some money on telephone calls, and who reads and advertises in national collectible publications. Because collectible drinking glasses haven't yet entered the roaring collectible mainstream, awareness of them is spotty, but we have found that all it takes is a little communication to pry both information and glasses loose.

PRICING AND NOTES ON CONDITION

As with most any collectible, condition is a key factor in determining value and collectibility. Most collectors want only the best specimens available and, after they have seen the best, the second or third best has little or no appeal. With collectible drinking glasses, brightness of color is absolutely desirable. Color is the first quality that the viewer notices when examining a collectible drinking glass. Close to color in importance is strong, clear lettering. Imperfect or missing letters detract significantly from the value and appeal of a glass because they are almost always immediately apparent. Finally, on a top quality glass, colors are always within their outlines and nicely registered, there is no missing paint, and there are no scratches or rim chips.

The automatic dishwasher and its detergent are a glass collector's worst enemy. One trip through the dishwasher and a "mint" glass becomes a "good" glass. Repeated trips through a dishwasher result in "a" glass. In other words, the high gloss that is evident on new ("mint") glasses is very susceptible to the detergent and hot water action of today's efficient dishwashers, and serious collectors will not buy or trade such glasses, nor will they want them in their own collections unless they happen to be extremely rare and unusual. With a fairly constant supply of mint or near-mint glasses still available, it makes little sense to bother with faded glasses. Of course, with older glasses from the 1930s and 1940s, it is not as easy to find pristine examples, so most knowledgeable collectors will gladly settle for glasses that show a little dullness. Personal preferences, collecting experience, and price will kick in and determine for each collector where the line is when it comes to gloss.

We attempt to provide realistic price ranges for collectible drinking glasses. Besides condition, discussed above, several other factors determine the actual buying and selling prices for glasses. These factors include the popularity or regional availability of a particular series, the sponsor or distributor of a particular series and, of course, the rareness or scarcity of a particular issue. Basically, universal economic laws of supply and demand operate in the glass collecting field. What is difficult to find in one area may be easy to find in another. Individual collectors ultimately decide what a glass or set of glasses is worth to them based on their own interests and collecting goals. Through extensive contacts with other collectors throughout the United States and through our own experience buying, selling, auctioning, and trading, we have arrived at realistic price ranges for the glasses we list in this book. Naturally, there are going to be anomalies, exceptions, and discrepancies in a field as new as this one. We are fully aware that on any given day at any given flea market or yard sale, a collector may be lucky enough to purchase a given amount of rare collectible drinking glasses for practically nothing, but such happy events are fairly uncommon and not especially significant when it comes to influencing general trends and everyday buying and selling prices. If you are a serious collector and you need or want any of the glasses we have listed in this book, you will not be far off the glass's "real" value if you buy somewhere within the price ranges we suggest. If you have a chance to buy it for less — congratulations! That happens frequently in every collectible field, and everyone loves a bargain and deserves one once in a while.

CARE AND STORAGE OF GLASSES

We have already cautioned collectors to refrain from running their glasses through dishwashers. If glasses must be washed, it is best to use a mild pH-balanced dishwashing solution and warm water. Glasses should then be dried with a cotton polishing cloth for that extra sparkle. It is best not to wash glasses too often. We all know the old saying about taking the pitcher to the well: eventually, the unexpected or the inevitable will happen. It is also wise to keep glasses out of direct and prolonged sunlight which will eventually subdue the colors.

The storage of collectible drinking glasses presents its own special problems. Most collectors are proud of their collections and want to display them, but such displays are often impractical for several reasons. For one thing, even a "fair" or "good" collection may easily contain from 500 to 600 different glasses, and an "excellent" one might comprise 1,200 to 1,500 glasses. Since a collector would want to show off each individual glass, it would not be effective to arrange glasses more than one deep on a shelf. The good news is that each linear foot of shelving can accommodate four glasses so, for example, an eight foot wide by five foot high shelf system with seven inches between shelves can accommodate 256 glasses. Larger shelf systems could be built, depending on the availability of wall space.

Some collectors find it necessary to store their glasses, and there are several safe options for doing this. Probably the most convenient and safest way to store glasses is in cardboard, twelve-compartment liquor boxes. Glasses housed in these boxes do not need to be wrapped, and if the fronts of the boxes are clearly labeled (we suggest taping a piece of 8½" x 11" paper to the box and labeling it with a marking pen), it is an easy matter to locate and examine glasses when necessary. Being able to locate glasses quickly is important when comparing new acquisitions to old ones. Collectors who wrap their glasses in newspaper and pack them in boxes cannot easily locate a specific glass, and the kind of handling that newspaper wrapping and unwrapping requires often leads to accidents and breakage. In addition, we have found that newspaper tends to make the glasses dirty. Finally, if the glasses are wrapped up and unsystematically stored, it will be extremely difficult for you to show them off to interested friends and fellow collectors.

While storing glasses in sturdy compartmentalized liquor boxes is convenient, there is one drawback: space. Boxes take up substantial room, and if a collector has a thousand glasses in his collection, he will need to have room for 83 boxes. Duplicates, which every serious collector has on hand, compound the storage problem. Many collectors' homes are not spacious enough to accommodate quantities, and we know from experience that many collectors' spouses therefore demand that the glasses go outside to the barn or to the garage, or in some lucky cases, to the basement. If there is an up side to such blatant discrimination, it is that glasses are rarely affected by freezing temperatures and they can be safely stored in unheated buildings in boxes in the coldest climates. Needless to say, storage and display problems must be solved by the individual collector.

SHIPPING OF GLASSES

Shipping is an unavoidable evil for collectors who trade with or sell to geographically distant fellow collectors. It would be wonderful if we didn't have to commit our precious glasses to the temporary care of package handlers and conveyors, but this is the only practical way for most collectors to add to their collections. This fact admitted, there is only one solution to the shipping problem: pack as if your glass's "life" depended on it — because it does! We recommend double boxing a smaller box inside a larger one, and further that the two boxes be separated and insulated from each other with Styrofoam pellets, crushed newspaper, or large bubble wrap. We advise that the inner box be a sturdy one with dividers; twelve-compartment liquor boxes are excellent to use for inner boxes. Put a layer of Styrofoam pellets in the bottom of each compartment, and then insert each bubble-wrapped glass (the small

bubbles are ideal for glasses packed this way) into a compartment and fill the remaining space with Styrofoam pellets or crushed newspaper. Do not pack the glasses into the compartments too tightly; it is important that they have some room to move. If they do not have some space to move in, a blow to any outside glass is sure destruction for its inner companions, since there will be a chain reaction inside the box. Next, tape this box up with filament or clear sealing tape, and cover its top with a two to three-inch layer of Styrofoam pellets and a piece of bubble wrap for good measure. Finally, tape the outside box shut with filament or clear sealing tape. When you shake the box, you shouldn't feel much movement within it, and you shouldn't hear any either. You'll know when you have packed the boxes just right; and, as you pack more and more boxes, you'll find ways to improve on your strategies to ensure safe delivery of your glasses.

WHERE TO FIND MORE INFORMATION

Newsletter

Collectors can gather and exchange information about glasses, from a small but increasing number of sources. The first (established in 1988) and still the only regularly published glass collectors' newsletter is our publication, *Collector Glass News* (P.O. Box 308, Slippery Rock, PA 16057), a bimonthly newsletter (28 to 32 pages) with informative articles on a variety of glass collecting issues and topics. We are interested in hearing from collectors who have information to share or questions to ask about collectible drinking glasses, and we can be contacted by writing to P. O. Box 308, Slippery Rock, PA 16057. We can also be reached at this telephone number: 412-946-2838. Our fax number is: 412-946-9012. Subscription: $15 per year, 6 issues. Sample copies $3.00.

Organizations/Associations/Shows

Another source for information is the recently founded Promotional Glass Collectors Association. Its President is Carl Sehnert, and its address is 4595 Limestone Lane, Memphis, TN 38141. This organization sponsors regional meetings around the United States and disseminates information about glasses in its occasional mailings. Its annual meeting and elections occur the first Saturday in December in the Grayslake, Illinois, area in connection with the Great Lakes Toy and Collectible Show. This show, which takes place the first Sunday in December, is organized by Tom Hoder and features a "glass alley" where glass collectors from all over the United States assemble to buy, sell, trade, and share information about glasses. For more information about this show, watch for information in *Collector Glass News* or contact Tom Hoder at 444 S. Cherry St., Itasca, IL 60143.

Books/Price Guides

Our first book, *Contemporary Fast-Food and Drinking Glass Collectibles* (Wallace-Homestead Book Company, 1988), is now out of print, but there may be some copies of it sitting on bookstore shelves somewhere, and it can be found in many public libraries. Another book that many collectors find useful is *Tomart's Price Guide to Character & Promotional Glasses*, Revised and Expanded 2nd Edition (1993), by Carol Markowski. (Inquire: Tomart Publications, 3300 Encrete Lane, Dayton, OH 45439.) Collectors looking for glass prices can also find selected listings in many collectible price guides including *Schroeder's Collectible Toys Antique to Modern Price Guide* (Collector Books, P.O. Box 3009, Paducah, KY 42002-3009; 800-626-5420).

Auctions

In addition to the other channels for acquiring glasses, collectors can bid on and buy glasses at auction. We recommend the following auctions:

Collector Glass News Auction. Auction listing appears in regular issues of *Collector Glass News*. Six auctions per year, no fee for participation, but bidders must be subscribers to *Collector Glass News* (P.O. Box 308, Slippery Rock, PA 16057; $15.00 per year).

Ho-Mar Auctions. Three auctions per year. $3 auction booklet charge per auction. Contact: Tom Hoder, 444 S. Cherry St., Itasca, IL 60143.

Glasses, Mugs & Steins. Several auctions per year. Bidders must buy auction booklet. Contact: Pete Kroll, P.O. Box 207, Sun Prairie, WI 53590.

ABOUT THIS BOOK

In this book we have attempted to show a wide variety of collectible glasses. Our selection does not pretend to be comprehensive, but we believe that it is representative of the kinds of glasses that collectors will encounter wherever they look. We have made every effort to present accurate, interesting, and useful information about the glasses. For glasses that are not pictured, our policy has been to list and/or make reference to only those glasses that we have absolutely confirmed the existence of. We have been careful to avoid rumor and hearsay. The pricing information that we furnish should be considered realistic and in accord with today's glass collecting market. In other words, knowledgeable collectors are buying and selling glasses within the price ranges we suggest. Our prices are based on our personal experience and our knowledge of glass auction trends. We realize, of course, that particular glasses here or there, in this antique mall or at that flea market, may sell for less or more than the figures we quote in this book. Supply and demand will pretty much take care of that for all of us. In general, the prices of most modern "common" glasses are coming down and/or leveling off, while the prices of earlier, less common, or special interest exotic glasses are rising steadily.

Artists and Producers

PLATE 1

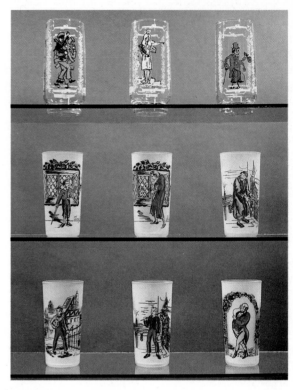

PLATE 2

Currier & Ives

Row 1: Kraft cheese containers
These containers were sold with Kraft cheese spreads in the 1970s.
1. The Old Homestead in Winter . . . .$1.00 – 3.00
2. American Winter Scene . . . .$1.00 – 3.00

Row 2: Currier & Ives frosted tumblers
This is a set of eight frosted tumblers depicting nineteenth century life in America. These were probably sold as a set through department stores in the late 50s or early 60s.
1. Lady in carriage . . . .$1.00 – 3.00
2. Man and woman strolling . . . .$1.00 – 3.00
3. Cutting ice . . . .$1.00 – 3.00
4. Hunters . . . .$1.00 – 3.00

Row 3: Currier & Ives frosted tumblers, continued
1. Locomotive . . . .$1.00 – 3.00
2. Ice skating . . . .$1.00 – 3.00
3. Front porch social scene . . . .$1.00 – 3.00
4. Steamboat . . . .$1.00 – 3.00

Charles Dickens

Row 1: Subway Limited Edition — *A Christmas Carol*
A set of four glasses issued in the early 1980s as a promotion by the Subway Limited franchises.
1. Tiny Tim & Bob Cratchit . . . .$4.00 – 6.00
2. Ghost of Christmas Past/Ghost of
   Christmas Present . . . .$4.00 – 6.00
3. Ebenezer Scrooge . . . .$4.00 – 6.00
Not pictured:
Bob Cratchit . . . .$4.00 – 6.00

Row 2: Dickens' characters frosted tumblers
This set of eight Federal glasses comes in two sizes. The 5" version is shown, but there is also a shorter cocktail glass. These were probably purchased as sets from a department store.
1. Tiny Tim . . . .$3.00 – 5.00
2. Scrooge . . . .$3.00 – 5.00
3. Fagin . . . .$3.00 – 5.00

Row 3: Dickens' characters frosted tumblers, continued
1. David Copperfield . . . .$3.00 – 5.00
2. Oliver Twist . . . .$3.00 – 5.00
3. Mr. Pickwick . . . .$3.00 – 5.00
Not pictured:
Fat Boy . . . .$3.00 – 5.00
Mr. Micawber . . . .$3.00 – 5.00

PLATE 3

The Walt Disney Company

Row 1: Donald Duck

Glasses number 1 and 3 are part of a set of six Donald Duck food container glasses issued in 1942. They can be found in some slight size variations. Glass number 2 is a late 60s or early 70s issue which promoted Donald Duck Cola.

1. Donald Duck on burro . . . .$25.00 – 35.00
2. Donald Duck Cola . . . .$15.00 – 20.00
3. Donald Duck and Goofy sled riding . . . .$25.00 – 35.00
Not pictured:
Donald playing golf . . . .$25.00 – 35.00
Donald & nephews cooking . . . .$25.00 – 35.00
Donald & nephews as scouts . . . .$25.00 – 35.00
Donald riding a bicycle . . . .$25.00 – 35.00

Row 2: Disney First Dairy Series

These glasses were part of one of the first true glass promotions. These Disney characters were featured on sour cream and cottage cheese containers in the mid-1930s. The promotion proved to be very successful and led to a number of other Disney-related dairy products promotions over the next fifteen years. These glasses can be found with several variations in the size and shape of the tumbler as well as differences in the size of the printed image. Prices for the variations do not differ significantly from the glasses pictured. A second dairy series of glasses was distributed shortly after the first; it included Elmer, 1st Pig, 2nd Pig, 3rd Pig, and Big Bad Wolf.

1. Donald Duck . . . .$40.00 – 60.00
2. Minnie Mouse . . . .$40.00 – 60.00
3. Mickey Mouse . . . .$40.00 – 60.00

Row 3: Disney First Dairy Series, continued

1. Horace Horsecollar . . . .$40.00 – 60.00
2. Pluto . . . .$40.00 – 60.00
3. Clarabelle Cow . . . .$40.00 – 60.00
Not pictured:
Funny Bunny . . . .$40.00 – 60.00

PLATE 4

Walt Disney, continued

Row 1: Disney Pinocchio Series (1940)

Another of the Disney dairy promotions, this twelve-glass set is probably the most common of the early Disney glasses. Each glass has a rhyme on the reverse, telling its part of the story of Pinocchio. Again, there are variations in the glass sizes — at least three, maybe four — for this series. Look for bright glossy colors on the glasses. A good many of the Pinocchio glasses found today show varying degrees of dullness because they were used and washed frequently.

1. Pinocchio . . . .$15.00 – 20.00
2. Cleo (the goldfish) . . . .$15.00 – 20.00
3. Stromboli . . . .$15.00 – 20.00
4. Monstro the Whale . . . .$15.00 – 20.00

Row 2: Disney Pinocchio Series, continued

1. Geppetto . . . .$15.00 – 20.00
2. Gideon . . . .$15.00 – 20.00
3. Figaro . . . .$15.00 – 20.00
4. Jiminy Cricket . . . .$15.00 – 20.00

Row 3: Disney Pinocchio Series, continued

1. Lampwick . . . .$15.00 – 20.00
2. J. Worthington Foulfellow . . . .$15.00 – 20.00
3. Blue Fairy . . . .$15.00 – 20.00
4. Coachman . . . .$15.00 – 20.00

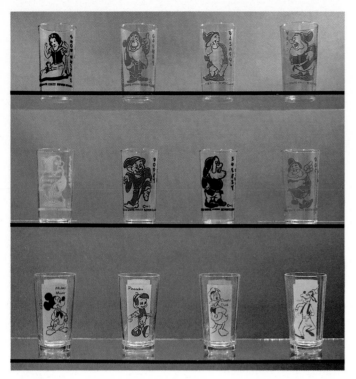

PLATE 5

PLATE 6

Walt Disney, continued

Row 1: Snow White and the Seven Dwarfs, set of eight (1938)
Walt Disney's first animated feature film was immensely popular, and there were an enormous number of commercial spinoffs — not the least of which were glass tumblers. The Snow White & the Seven Dwarfs set we show here comes in a variety of sizes and colors. This set was produced in the late 1930s, and the glasses contained dairy products. (There are several other Snow White sets which were produced in the late 30s; among the most collectible are the Second Dairy or "Musical Notes" Series [1938] and the Bosco chocolate drink set which originated as a premium in 1938.)

1. Snow White . . . .$15.00 – 20.00
2. Grumpy . . . .$15.00 – 20.00
3. Bashful . . . .$15.00 – 20.00
4. Happy . . . .$15.00 – 20.00

Row 2: Snow White and the Seven Dwarfs, continued
1. Sleepy . . . .$15.00 – 20.00
2. Dopey . . . .$15.00 – 20.00
3. Sneezy . . . .$15.00 – 20.00
4. Doc . . . .$15.00 – 20.00

Row 3: Disney double character color block, set of four
The four tumblers shown in this row were food containers from the 50s or early 60s. Each glass has a natural Disney pair of characters on it. They can be found in both 5" and 6" versions.
1. Mickey Mouse/Minnie Mouse . . . .$12.00 – 15.00
2. Pinocchio/Jiminy Cricket . . . .$12.00 – 15.00
3. Donald Duck/Daisy Duck . . . .$12.00 – 15.00
4. Goofy/Pluto . . . .$12.00 – 15.00

Walt Disney, continued

Row 1: Disney double character color block set (reverse of Plate 5: Row 3)

Row 2: 1939 Disney All Star Parade, set of 10
This dairy promotion was issued in 1939, and the complete set contains 10 two-color and, we might add, extremely attractive glasses. Four of the glasses are more difficult to find and therefore command a higher price. As with most of these early Disney sets, there are size variations to be found, at least two for this set.
1. Snow White and the Seven Dwarfs . . . .$30.00 – 50.00
2. Ferdinand the Bull . . . .$30.00 – 50.00
3. The Ugly Duckling . . . .$30.00 – 50.00
4. Mickey, Minnie, Pluto . . . .$30.00 – 50.00

Row 3: 1939 Disney All Star Parade, continued
1. The Greedy Pig and Colt . . . .$50.00 – 75.00
2. The Big Bad Wolf and Three Little Pigs . . . .$30.00 – 50.00
3. Donald Duck and nephews . . . .$30.00 – 50.00
4. Goofy and Wilbur . . . .$55.00 – 65.00
Not pictured:
Wally Walrus and Penguins . . . .$50.00 – 75.00
Raccoon, turtle, fawn & rabbit . . . .$50.00 – 75.00

PLATE 7

Walt Disney, continued
Row 1: Cinderella, set of eight
The glasses in this set dating from the late 1950s to the early 1960s were originally food containers. There are eight numbered glasses in the set, and the Cinderella story appears in short installments on the backs of the glasses. These glasses come in two size variations that we know of: 4⅝" and 5¼", and there are also two Canadian versions with slightly different colorings (green and yellow; and yellow, black, light blue, dark blue). Add 25% to 50% for the 5¼" version and for the Canadian versions.
1. #1 Cinderella with dog and cat . . . .$8.00 – 12.00
2. #2 Cinderella attending stepsisters . . . .$8.00 – 12.00
3. #3 Godmother appears . . . .$8.00 – 12.00
4. #4 Godmother creates dress . . . .$8.00 – 12.00

Row 2: Cinderella, continued
1. #5 The coach and horses . . . .$8.00 – 12.00

2. #6 Cinderella dances with the prince . . . .$8.00 – 12.00
3. #7 The clock strikes twelve . . . .$8.00 – 12.00
4. #7 The clock strikes twelve (reverse)
5. #8 The slipper fits . . . .$8.00 – 12.00

Row 3: Sleeping Beauty, set of six
This six-glass set was also a food container promotion of the late 1950s. There's also a Canadian set of twelve glasses which was issued at about the same time; prices for this set are steeper than for the American set.
1. Maleficent . . . .$10.00 – 14.00
2. The good fairies bestow their gifts . . . .$10.00 – 14.00
3. Briar Rose and her friends . . . .$10.00 – 14.00
4. Sleeping Beauty touches the spindle . . . .$10.00 – 14.00
5. Prince Phillip to the rescue . . . .$10.00 – 14.00
6. Samson, Prince Phillip's horse . . . .$10.00 – 14.00

13

PLATE 8

Walt Disney, continued

Row 1: Wonderful World of Disney Collector Series, set of six
Each glass in this attractive set shows a scene from one of Disney's most famous animated films. Pepsi-Cola was the co-sponsor of this set which was issued in the early 1980s. The set can be found more frequently on the west coast, and prices for mint examples with good registration have gone up in response to demand.

1. *Snow White & the Seven Dwarfs* . . . .$15.00 – 25.00
2. *Pinocchio* . . . .$15.00 – 25.00
3. *Alice in Wonderland* . . . .$15.00 – 25.00
4. *Lady & the Tramp* . . . .$15.00 – 25.00
5. *Bambi* . . . .$15.00 – 25.00
6. *101 Dalmatians* . . . .$15.00 – 25.00

Row 2: Pepsi-Cola Collector Series, set of six
This set of round-bottom glasses — referred to by collectors as the single character Disney set — was another late 70s early 80s Pepsi-Cola promotion. Identical static poses of the characters appear on both sides of the glass. On rare occasions these images can be found on Brockway style sample tumblers which were produced in limited quantities but never distributed.

1. Mickey . . . .$8.00 – 12.00
2. Minnie . . . .$8.00 – 12.00
3. Donald . . . .$8.00 – 12.00
4. Daisy . . . .$8.00 – 12.00
5. Goofy . . . .$8.00 – 12.00
6. Pluto . . . .$8.00 – 12.00

Row 3: Pepsi-Cola/Walt Disney Collector Series, set of six
This Pepsi-Cola set of six is sometimes referred to as the Texas set because it was heavily distributed in Texas or as the Picnic Set since it features the major Disney characters in a picnic context. Two complete cases of these glasses were found at a Pennsylvania flea market in the late 1980s which suggests that they may have been distributed in other areas as well. The Goofy and Pluto glasses were not issued to all the restaurants, and therefore they command premium prices because they are in rather short supply and harder to find. These glasses were distributed in 1979 or 1980.

1. Mickey . . . .$8.00 – 12.00
2. Minnie . . . .$8.00 – 12.00
3. Donald . . . .$8.00 – 12.00
4. Daisy . . . .$8.00 – 12.00
5. Goofy . . . .$45.00 – 65.00
6. Pluto . . . .$45.00 – 65.00

PLATE 9

Walt Disney, continued
Row 1: McDonald's Disneyland, set of four (1989)
This set of four colorful glasses was a test market promotion done in 1989 at several McDonald's restaurants in the Joplin, Missouri, area. These glasses were readily available right after the promotion began, but supplies have dried up and recent prices have been higher.
1. Minnie in Fantasyland . . . .$8.00 – 12.00
2. Goofy in Adventureland . . . .$8.00 – 12.00
3. Donald Duck in Critter Country . . . .$8.00 – 12.00
4. Mickey in Tomorrowland . . . .$8.00 – 12.00

Row 2: Disney Canadian movie series, set of four
This set, which features four of Disney's most successful animated movies, was distributed by McDonald's in Canada and co-sponsored by Coca-Cola. The titles of the films are in French and English. This appealing set has been expensive in the past, but lately a

plentiful number of sets have been migrating to the U.S. from Canada, and prices have gone down.
1. *Cinderella* . . . .$8.00 – 15.00
2. *Fantasia* . . . .$8.00 – 15.00
3. *Peter Pan* . . . .$8.00 – 15.00
4. *Snow White and the Seven Dwarfs* . . . .$8.00 – 15.00

Row 3: Mickey Through the Years, set of six (1988)
In 1988, Sunoco gas stations in Canada offered this set of six glasses showing Mickey's evolution through the years.
1. 1928 Steamboat Willie . . . .$5.00 – 7.00
2. 1938 Magician Mickey . . . .$5.00 – 7.00
3. 1940 Fantasia . . . .$5.00 – 7.00
4. 1953 Mickey Mouse Club . . . .$5.00 – 7.00
5. 1983 Christmas Carol . . . .$5.00 – 7.00
6. 1988 Modern Mickey . . . .$5.00 – 7.00

PLATE 10

PLATE 12

Walt Disney, continued
Row 1: The Rescuers collector series (1977), set of eight
This 1977 set of eight Brockway tumblers features characters from the Disney film *The Rescuers*. It was issued during the heyday of the Pepsi-Cola promotions of the mid and late 70s. The photographs show the front and the reverse of the glasses. Madame Medusa and Rufus tend to bring slightly higher prices than the others although the distribution of all the glasses was the same.

According to the advertising representative who developed the promotion, Disney insisted that Pepsi-Cola promote some of the current Disney films in order to gain licensing rights to use "The Big Guys" (Mickey & friends). The Rescuers promotion was one of the activities that was done to satisfy that commitment.
1. Madame Medusa . . . .$25.00 – 30.00
2. Bianca . . . .$10.00 – 12.00
3. Penny . . . .$10.00 – 12.00
4. Rufus   . . . .$25.00 – 30.00

Row 2: The Rescuers, continued
1. Bernard . . . .$10.00 – 12.00
2. Orville . . . .$10.00 – 12.00
3. Evinrude . . . .$10.00 – 12.00
4. Brutus and Nero . . . .$10.00 – 12.00

Walt Disney, continued
Row 1: Happy Birthday Mickey Pepsi-Cola collector series
This set of eight glasses, issued to commemorate the 50th anniversary of Mickey Mouse's creation by Walt Disney, can be found with 1977 or 1978 copyright dates. The 1977 set was issued in the St. Louis area on a test-market basis. Its success led to much wider distribution the following year. The 1977 images tend to be larger and more detailed than the images of the 1978 glasses, and there are other small differences. The 1977 glasses are more difficult to find and tend to bring about 25% more than their 1978 counterparts. The Daisy & Donald and the Horace & Clarabelle glasses in both sets usually bring slightly higher prices due to their more limited distribution. We show the front and reverse of each glass here. At least two sets of seven 1977 glasses have been found (lacking Horace & Clarabelle) without the *Happy Birthday Mickey* graphic; these were sample glasses which were never distributed.
1. Minnie . . . .$6.00 – 8.00
2. Mickey . . . .$6.00 – 8.00
3. Daisy & Donald . . . .$12.00 – 15.00
4. Donald . . . .$6.00 – 8.00

Row 2: Happy Birthday Mickey, continued
1. Goofy . . . .$6.00 – 8.00
2. Pluto . . . .$6.00 – 8.00
3. Horace & Clarabelle . . . .$15.00 – 20.00
4. Uncle Scrooge . . . .$6.00 – 8.00

PLATE 11   **Reverse of Plate 10**

PLATE 13   **Reverse of Plate 12**

PLATE 14

Walt Disney, continued

Row 1: Disney Jungle Book, Pepsi-Cola collector series

This set of eight glasses sponsored by Pepsi-Cola is a favorite of many collectors and fairly difficult to complete. Issued in the second half of the 70s, probably in connection with a re-release of *Jungle Book* movie, the attractive colors and images coupled with the limited distribution make it a highly desirable set. This is another of the sets that Pepsi-Cola agreed to do for Disney in order to use Mickey and his friends on future promotions. These glasses are found primarily in the Midwest or on the West Coast where they were most heavily distributed. Disney's *Jungle Book* film was issued in 1967, but there is no date on these glasses, and *Jungle Book* doesn't appear on them either. Familiarity with the

Disney movie and/or Kipling's story is assumed. The front and reverse of each glass are shown here.

1. Bagheera . . . .$60.00 – 90.00
2. Mowgli . . . .$40.00 – 50.00
3. Rama . . . .$45.00 – 60.00
4. Shere Kahn . . . .$60.00 – 90.00

Row 2: Jungle Book, continued

1. King Looie . . . .$50.00 – 65.00
2. Baloo . . . .$50.00 – 65.00
3. Kaa . . . .$50.00 – 65.00
4. Colonel Hathi . . . .$50.00 – 65.00

PLATE 15   **Reverse of Plate 14**

PLATE 16

Walt Disney, continued

Plate 16

Row 1: Disney Jungle Book, set of six, short (4⅞") version
The two sets of Jungle Book glasses shown below bear 1966 copyrights, and they were probably issued at about the same time the Disney Jungle Book film was released in 1967. Each glass is numbered, and there is some informative text, for example: "Inspired by Walt Disney's *The Jungle Book* based on Rudyard Kipling's Mowgli Stories, Number 1 of a Series of Six Jungle Book Glasses © Copyright 1966 Walt Disney Productions." Each set has its admirers, and the short set seems to be a little more difficult to find than the taller one. Collectors will immediately notice differences between the American and Canadian versions. One small difference that perplexes us is the different spellings: Shere "Kahn" in the American set and Shere "Khan" in the Canadian set.
1. Mowgli (Number 1) . . . .$40.00 – 60.00
2. Baloo (Number 3) . . . .$40.00 – 60.00
3. Bagheera (Number 4) . . . .$40.00 – 60.00
4. King Louie (Number 6) . . . .$40.00 – 60.00
Not pictured:
Shere Khan (Number 2) . . . .$40.00 – 60.00
Flunkey (Number 5) . . . .$40.00 – 60.00

Row 2: Disney Jungle Book (continued), set of six, tall (6½") version
1. Mowgli (Number 1) . . . .$30.00 – 50.00
2. Shere Khan (Number 2) . . . .$30.00 – 50.00
3. Baloo (Number 3) . . . .$30.00 – 50.00
4. Bagheera (Number 4) . . . .$30.00 – 50.00
5. Flunkey (Number 5) . . . .$30.00 – 50.00
6. King Louie (Number 6) . . . .$30.00 – 50.00

Disney Character Tumblers and Mugs

Plate 17

Row 1: Disney frosted juice glasses
A set of six glasses sold in the late 1980s at department stores. These are also available in a taller tumbler.
1. Mickey . . . .$2.00 – 4.00
2. Minnie . . . .$2.00 – 4.00
3. Donald . . . .$2.00 – 4.00
4. Daisy . . . .$2.00 – 4.00
5. Uncle Scrooge . . . .$2.00 – 4.00
6. Goofy . . . .$2.00 – 4.00

Row 2: Miscellaneous Disney mugs and juice tumblers
Decal cheese containers (numbers 2 and 4) — In the 1960s, some food containers were sold with decals of Disney characters applied to the glass. From a distance these glasses look like they were printed, but close inspection reveals that the image is a decal stuck to the outside of the glass. Condition is all-important on these glasses.
1. Disney school house mug . . . .$2.00 – 4.00
2. Mickey Mouse . . . .$3.00 – 5.00
3. Mickey Mouse . . . .$4.00 – 6.00
4. Donald . . . .$3.00 – 5.00
5. Mickey Mouse mug . . . .$2.00 – 4.00

Row 3: Mickey Through the Years clear mugs
These mugs, which highlight some of Mickey's most famous roles, were available as a set at department stores in the early 1990s.
1. 1928 Steamboat Willie . . . .$3.00 – 5.00
2. 1937 Magician Mickey . . . .$3.00 – 5.00
3. 1940 Fantasia . . . .$3.00 – 5.00
4. 1955 Mickey Mouse Club . . . .$3.00 – 5.00

PLATE 17

PLATE 18

Disney Tumblers and Mugs, continued

Plate 18

Row 1: Disney Pedestal milk glass mugs
These mugs were marketed at the theme parks. There are probably others in this series.
1. Minnie Mouse . . . .$3.00 – 5.00
2. Pluto . . . .$3.00 – 5.00
3. Mickey Mouse . . . .$3.00 – 5.00

Row 2: Pepsi-Cola Disney Single Character Collectors Series milk glass mug
This set of four Anchor Hocking ovenproof mugs was promoted by Pepsi-Cola. The Pepsi collector series logo appears in black on the side of each mug. Periodically, discussion about mugs with differently positioned logos surfaces, but these out-of-the-way variations should not concern the average collector.
1. Mickey . . . .$8.00 – 10.00
2. Minnie . . . .$8.00 – 10.00
3. Donald . . . .$8.00 – 10.00
4. Daisy . . . .$8.00 – 10.00

Row 3: Pepsi-Cola Mickey Through the Years Collector Series milk glass mugs (1980)
This 1980 Pepsi-Cola four-mug promotion reviews Mickey Mouse's career from 1928 to 1980, and the mugs sometimes give the appearance of being much older than they are because of the historical dates on them. The Pepsi-Cola logo is the clue to accurate dating. Some unaware dealers try to pass the Steamboat Willie mug off as being from 1928. It is not! And they also try to pass the "1955" Mickey Mouse Club mug off as being from the mid 50s. It is not! The date on the fourth mug is the date of the set. Occasionally there are reports of mugs with varying logo configurations, but we find the differences quite academic.
1. 1928 Mickey Mouse as Steamboat Willie . . . . . .$8.00 – 10.00
2. 1940 Mickey Mouse in Fantasia . . . .$8.00 – 10.00
3. 1955 The Mickey Mouse Club . . . .$8.00 – 10.00
4. 1980 Mickey Mouse Today . . . .$8.00 – 10.00

Disney Tumblers and Mugs, continued

Plate 19

Row 1: Mickey Mouse Club, set of six
An attractive set of six glasses showing the Disney characters in action. The Mickey Mouse Club logo appears on the reverse of each of these glasses.
1. Mickey waving . . . .$8.00 – 12.00
2. Minnie with bathtub . . . .$8.00 – 12.00
3. Mickey on pogo stick . . . .$8.00 – 12.00

Row 2: Mickey Mouse Club, continued
1. Donald building a brick wall . . . .$8.00 – 12.00
2. Goofy fishing . . . .$8.00 – 12.00
3. Donald with a hoe . . . .$8.00 – 12.00

Row 3: Disney World souvenir, set of six
This set, which comes in two sizes, was available from the theme park in the early 1970s. The complete set contains six glasses. The Mickey Mouse Club glass shown in the center is not actually part of the set but is printed on the same size glass and fits in well with the group. The Goofy glass is not easy to find, and the Winnie the Pooh glass (not shown) was available for only a limited time due to an exclusive arrangement made by Sears to merchandise Pooh-related items. The glass was withdrawn after a brief appearance and consequently is the most difficult to locate and the most expensive.
1. Minnie Mouse . . . .$5.00 – 7.00
2. Mickey Mouse . . . .$5.00 – 7.00
3. Mickey Mouse Club (not part of this set) . . . .$5.00 – 7.00
4. Donald Duck . . . .$5.00 – 7.00
5. Goofy . . . .$10.00 – 15.00
Not pictured:
Pluto . . . .$5.00 – 7.00
Winnie the Pooh . . . .$15.00 – 25.00

PLATE 19

Miscellaneous Disney Tumblers and Mugs, continued

Plate 20

Row 1: Miscellaneous Disney souvenir mugs
There's a veritable plethora of mugs from the Disney marketing machine that look much like these mugs and others shown. It's difficult to keep abreast.
1. Walt Disney World mug . . . .$6.00 – 8.00
2. Mickey Mouse mug . . . .$6.00 – 8.00

Row 2: Disney World souvenir mug set
The images on these mugs are the same as the images on the Disney World juice set pictured in Plate 19, Row 3. The date and production history are the same also. A complete set consists of six mugs. Goofy and Pooh are the toughest ones to find.
1. Donald Duck . . . .$8.00 – 10.00
2. Winnie the Pooh . . . .$20.00 – 30.00
3. Pluto . . . .$8.00 – 10.00
Not pictured:
Mickey Mouse . . . .$8.00 – 10.00
Minnie Mouse . . . .$8.00 – 10.00
Goofy . . . .$8.00 – 10.00

Row 3: Miscellaneous Disney souvenir mugs
1. Big Al mug from Disney World Theme Park . . . . .$5.00 – 7.00
2. Pinocchio mug . . . .$7.00 – 10.00

Plate 21

Row 1: Mickey Mouse juice set
This set was available in department stores in the late 1980s. The four glasses are identical.
Complete set with box . . . .$15.00 – 20.00

Plate 22

Row 1: Mickey Mouse birthday and bicentennial celebrations
1. Happy Birthday Mickey (Mickey's 50th Birthday) $8.00 – 10.00
This glass, which shows Mickey lighting candles on his birthday cake, was available at the theme parks in the late 1970s.
2. America on Parade, Bicentennial Glass, 1976 . . .$8.00 – 10.00
An unusual size and shape of this famous parody of Archibald Willard's "Spirit of '76."
3. Coca-Cola, America on Parade, Bicentennial
   Glass, 1976 . . . .$5.00 – 7.00
Archibald Willard's famous painting, parodied again in a larger format.

Row 2: These are all Anchor Hocking department store glasses that feature Mickey and Minnie in various activities.
1. Mickey and Minnie dancing . . . .$2.00 – 4.00
2. Mickey dancing . . . .$2.00 – 4.00
3. Mickey and Minnie in a convertible . . . .$2.00 – 4.00

Row 3: Disney plastic cups
A sampling of some of the plastic issues that are available. Plastic cups are increasingly popular with collectors. Some reasons: they don't break, they are easy to store, and because they are routinely thrown away, they may very well be tomorrow's most wanted collectible.
1. Donald . . . .$1.00 – 2.00
2. Goofy . . . .$1.00 – 2.00
3. Mickey . . . .$1.00 – 2.00
4. Mickey (variation) . . . .$1.00 – 2.00

PLATE 20

PLATE 21

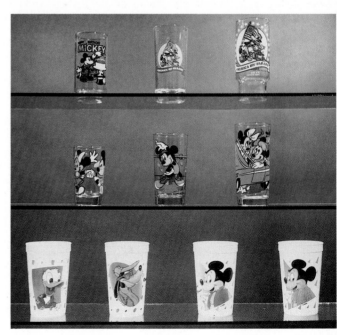

PLATE 22

Hanna-Barbera

Hanna-Barbera Productions, Inc. have been responsible for many of America's most popular cartoon characters and personalities. In fact, several generations have been raised on them, and their popularity shows no signs of abating. Hanna-Barbera collectibles are, in general, hot.

Row 1: 1960s food containers from Hanna-Barbera, set of five
These jam glasses from the early 1960s are very difficult to find, especially in fine condition. This set probably represents the earliest use of the Hanna Barbera characters on glass. There is only one collector that we're aware of who has a complete set. These glasses tend to be pricey because of their age and scarceness.
1. The Flintstones . . . .$50.00 – 90.00
2. Yogi Bear . . . .$50.00 – 90.00
3. Quick Draw McGraw . . . .$50.00 – 90.00
Not pictured:
Cindy Bear . . . .$50.00 – 90.00
Huckleberry Hound . . . .$50.00 – 90.00

PLATE 23

Row 2: Pizza Hut Flintstone Kids, set of four, (1986)
A set of four glasses promoted through the Pizza Hut chain in the mid-1980s.
1. Freddy . . . .$2.00 – 4.00
2. Wilma . . . .$2.00 – 4.00
3. Barney . . . .$2.00 – 4.00
4. Betty . . . .$2.00 – 4.00

Row 3: Pepsi-Cola Hanna-Barbera collector series, (1977)
This attractive set of six glasses features the most popular of the Hanna-Barbera cartoons from the late 1970s. Prices for these classic Brockway tumblers continue to climb because they are a favorite of Pepsi-Cola collectors and cartoon collectors. Only true baby boomers will remember the catchy Josie & the Pussycats theme song.
1. Huck & Yogi . . . .$15.00 – 25.00
2. Mumbly . . . .$15.00 – 25.00
3. Josie & the Pussycats . . . .$15.00 – 25.00
4. Scooby Doo . . . .$15.00 – 25.00
5. The Flintstones . . . .$15.00 – 25.00
6. Dynomutt . . . .$15.00 – 25.00

PLATE 24   **Reverse of Plate 23**

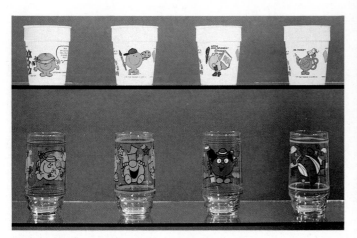

PLATE 25

PLATE 26

Roger Hargreaves

Roger Hargreaves is a contemporary artist/illustrator.

Row 1: Wendy's Roger Hargreaves plastic set
1. Little Miss . . . .$1.00 – 2.00
2. Mr. Happy . . . .$1.00 – 2.00
3. Little Miss Splendid . . . .$1.00 – 2.00
4. Mr. Tickle . . . .$1.00 – 2.00

Row 2: Roger Hargreaves Mr. Men & Little Miss tumbler set
1. Little Miss Sunshine . . . .$3.00 – 5.00
2. Mr. Silly . . . .$3.00 – 5.00
3. Little Miss Neat . . . .$3.00 – 5.00
4. Mr. Bump . . . .$3.00 – 5.00

Harvey Cartoons

The Pepsi-Cola promotions of the late 70s produced a number of different glasses using the Harvey Cartoon characters. The glasses were not issued as the sets shown here, but were mixed with other characters from other artists to put together a stable of offerings to restaurants for promotions. Collectors have segregated the glasses by artist in their collections, and that organization makes the best sense in inventorying and displaying a collection. Some color variations in the lettering on these glasses are noted. The Harvey Cartoons family of cartoon characters occupies a special place in American cartoon lore.

Row 1: Pepsi-Cola Harvey Cartoons 5" Action Series
1. Big Baby Huey . . . .$8.00 – 12.00
2. Wendy . . . .$8.00 – 12.00
3. Casper . . . .$8.00 – 12.00
4. Hot Stuff . . . .$8.00 – 12.00

Row 2: Pepsi-Cola Harvey Cartoon 5" Static Pose Series
1. Big Baby Huey . . . .$12.00 – 15.00
2. Wendy . . . .$12.00 – 15.00
3. Casper . . . .$12.00 – 15.00
4. Hot Stuff . . . .$12.00 – 15.00

Row 3: Pepsi-Cola Harvey Cartoon 6" Static Pose Series
1. Sad Sack (hardest one in set to find) . . . .$25.00 – 30.00
2. Big Baby Huey . . . .$12.00 – 15.00
3. Wendy . . . .$12.00 – 15.00
4. Casper . . . .$12.00 – 15.00
5. Hot Stuff (also available in white lettering) . . . .$12.00 – 15.00
6. Richie Rich . . . .$15.00 – 20.00

PLATE 27

Miscellaneous: Terrytoons, Callahan's, Domino's, Walter Lantz, Leonardo TTV, and MGM

Row 1
This row contains a grouping of miscellaneous character glasses that will interest most collectors. The first glass is the famous Pepsi-Cola Terrytoons Mighty Mouse glass made by Brockway. It was the only glass from the Terrytoons series that was actually distributed (see Miscellaneous Chapter: "Sample Glasses," pages 126 & 127, for others). Relatively few Mighty Mouse glasses were distributed, and the other Terrytoons characters exist only as samples or prototypes in very limited quantities. The value of this glass has been climbing in recent years, but there are indications that its price is leveling off and stabilizing.

The next three glasses are part of a set of four with Pepsi-Cola/Callahan's Hot Dogs sponsorship; their distribution was, as far as we know, limited to New Jersey. They are very colorful and tough to find. *Callahan's/So Big! So Good!* appears on each glass along with *©El Friede Monaco*. On the basis of glass style, we estimate this set's date to be early 1980s, probably 1982; the glasses very closely resemble the Pepsi-Cola/Popeye's 10th Anniversary set of four.

The last glass in this row is a Domino's Pizza Dick Tracy made by Brockway and distributed in the mid-1970s. A Gravel Gertie glass

is known to exist but only as a sample glass. Domino's probably planned a larger set; obviously something went wrong, and Dick Tracy is the only one from the set that most collectors will be able to find.

1. Mighty Mouse . . . .$500.00 – 600.00
2. The Blues Burgers! . . . .$100.00 – 125.00
3. Hot Diggity! . . . .$100.00 – 125.00
4. The Pop Stars! . . . .$100.00 – 125.00
5. Domino's Pizza Dick Tracy . . . .$100.00 – 125.00
Not pictured: The Fried Pipers! . . . .$100.00 – 125.00

Row 2: Walter Lantz/Pepsi-Cola, set of six characters
The Walter Lantz set of six characters in this row is one of Pepsi-Cola's most popular sets. It was distributed sometime between the mid and late 1970s, and seems to have had greater exposure in the west than elsewhere. Space Mouse is especially sought by collectors and is in relatively short supply; it commands a hefty price for those reasons. Andy Panda isn't far behind Space Mouse when it comes to price and availability. Woody Woodpecker comes in both black and white letter versions and seems to be more frequently encountered than the others.

1. Andy Panda . . . .$100.00 – 125.00
2. Chilly Willy . . . .$35.00 – 55.00
3. Cuddles . . . .$40.00 – 60.00
4. Space Mouse . . . .$150.00 – 200.00
5. Wally Walrus . . . .$35.00 – 55.00
6. Woody Woodpecker . . . .$10.00 – 20.00

Miscellaneous continued

Row 1: Walter Lantz double character, set of six
This set was distributed at restaurants in the late 70s or early 80s. The set comes in two sizes: a tall 6⅛" version and a shorter, heavier, and wider 5⅝" version.
1. Andy Panda/Miranda . . . .$20.00 – 30.00
2. Chilly Willy/Smedly . . . .$20.00 – 30.00
3. Wally Walrus/Homer Pigeon . . . .$20.00 – 30.00
4. Buzz Buzzard/Space Mouse . . . .$25.00 – 35.00
5. Cuddles/Oswald . . . .$20.00 – 30.00
6. Woody/Knothead and Splinter . . . .$15.00 – 20.00

Row 2: Leonardo TTV Pepsi-Cola collector series
These are more glasses from the Pepsi-Cola promotion that combined major cartoon characters into one large promotion. All of the glasses have the Pepsi-Cola logo on the side except for the blue-lettered Underdog.
1. Underdog, 6" (also available in white) . . . .$15.00 – 20.00
2. Underdog, 5" action . . . .$8.00 – 12.00
3. Underdog, 6" blue lettering, logo or no logo . . .$20.00 – 25.00
4. Go-Go Gophers, 6" . . . .$15.00 – 20.00

Row 3: Leonardo TTV Pepsi-Cola collector series, continued
1. Sweet Polly, 6" (also available in white lettering) $15.00 – 20.00
2. Sweet Polly, 5" . . . .$8.00 – 12.00
3. Simon Bar Sinister, 6" (white letters) . . . .$15.00 – 20.00
4. Simon Bar Sinister, 5" . . . .$8.00 – 12.00
5. Simon Bar Sinister, 6" (black letters) . . . .$15.00 – 20.00

Row 1: Pepsi-Cola MGM 5" action set of two (1975)
The MGM characters were also part of the Pepsi-Cola promotions (long before Ted Turner got a hold of them). The 5" action glasses come only in black lettering.
1. Tom (chasing Jerry into mousehole) . . . .$6.00 – 10.00
2. Jerry (catching Tom's tail in mousetrap) . . . .$6.00 – 10.00

Row 2: Pepsi-Cola MGM 6" Collector Series (1975)
All of the 6" characters come in black and white lettering.
1. Tuffy . . . .$10.00 – 12.00
2. Tom . . . .$10.00 – 12.00
3. Jerry . . . .$10.00 – 12.00

Row 3: Pepsi-Cola MGM 6", continued
1. Barney . . . .$10.00 – 12.00
2. Droopy . . . .$10.00 – 12.00
3. Spike . . . .$10.00 – 12.00

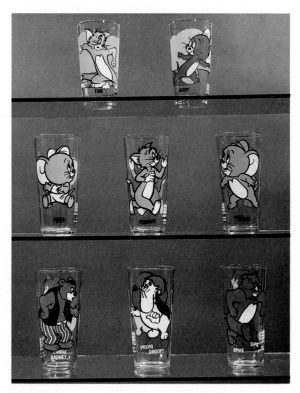

PLATE 29

PLATE 28

PLATE 30   **Norman Rockwell**

PLATE 31

Norman Rockwell's artwork is prolifically represented on glassware, and this collecting field alone would keep even the most aggressive collector busy. Many collectors find his optimistic, nostalgic, and humorous depictions of American life and history irresistible.

Row 1: Coca-Cola Reproductions of original Rockwell paintings
A set of three glasses reminiscent of life on the Mississippi, featuring the companionship of a boy and his dog. This set comes in two different glass styles.
1. Boy with hoe and a Coca-Cola . . . .$3.00 – 5.00
2. Boy with a sandwich and a Coca-Cola . . . .$3.00 – 5.00
3. Boy with a fishing pole and a Coca-Cola . . . .$3.00 – 5.00

Row 2: Country Time Lemonade Saturday Evening Post covers, set of four
A mail premium from Country Time Lemonade. When these glasses are found, they are usually found in sets. And there are two slightly different sets. One is differentiated by the presence of a Saturday Evening Post Authorized Reproduction logo; the colors on this set are more vivid than those on the other no-logo set. Add 50% for glasses from the authorized logo set.
1. Grandpa's Girl (SEP, February 3, 1923) . . . .$5.00 – 7.00
2. The Big Moment (SEP, January 25, 1936) . . . . . .$5.00 – 7.00
3. Low and Outside (SEP, August 5, 1916) . . . .$5.00 – 7.00
4. The Rocking Horse (SEP, September 12, 1933) . . .$5.00 – 7.00

Row 3: Arby's Norman Rockwell Summer Scenes, set of four, (1987)
In the summer of 1987, Arby's restaurants featured these glasses. This was a national promotion, but not all of the restaurants participated making this set a little more difficult to complete than some of the others. Glasses not sold the first summer resurfaced at many Arby's the following summer!
1. Gone Fishing (1930) . . . .$3.00 – 5.00
2. Sunset (1926) . . . .$3.00 – 5.00
3. Gramps at the Plate (1916) . . . .$3.00 – 5.00
4. No Swimming (1921) . . . .$3.00 – 5.00

Norman Rockwell, continued
Row 1: Saturday Evening Post pedestals, set of four
A set of Norman Rockwell glasses available through department stores in boxed sets.
1. Sunstruck . . . .$2.00 – 4.00
2. After the Prom . . . .$2.00 – 4.00
3. Old Friends at Trail's End . . . .$2.00 – 4.00
4. Washington at Valley Forge . . . .$2.00 – 4.00
    (add $5.00 – 7.00 for original box)

Row 2: Arby's Norman Rockwell Saturday Evening Post covers, set of six
This set of six was distributed by Arby's in the early 1980s. Each glass is numbered One of Six, Two of Six, etc. These glasses are very prone to scratching because the artwork consists of a thin applied decal (which is difficult to detect unless you look closely). Hold the white images up to bright light and if there are scratches, you will be able to see them clearly. It is difficult to find these glasses in truly mint condition and equally difficult to account for their low value. We predict that they will have their day.
1. Knuckles Down (One of Six) . . . .$1.00 – 3.00
2. No Swimming (Two of Six) . . . .$1.00 – 3.00
3. Catching the Big One (Three of Six) . . . .$1.00 – 3.00
4. The Champ (Four of Six) . . . .$1.00 – 3.00
5. The Spooners (Five of Six) . . . .$1.00 – 3.00
6. Leapfrog (Six of Six) . . . .$1.00 – 3.00

Norman Rockwell, continued

Plate 32

Row 1: Arby's/Pepsi-Cola Norman Rockwell Winter Scenes, set of four, (1979)
1. A Boy Meets His Dog (One of Four) (1959) ......$3.00 – 5.00
2. Downhill Daring (Two of Four) (1949) ....$3.00 – 5.00
3. Chilling Chore (Three of Four) (1963) ....$3.00 – 5.00
4. Snow Sculpturing (Four of Four) (1952) ....$3.00 – 5.00

Row 2: The Four Seasons mug collection
All four of these mugs are entitled *A Boy and His Dog.* The art-work bears a 1956© by Brown & Bigelow, but there is also a 1984© by the Norman Rockwell Museum, Inc. The mugs appear to have been available in the mid-1980s.
1. Boy and dog on the bank ....$3.00 – 5.00
2. Boy pouring medicine ....$3.00 – 5.00
3. Boy with puppies ....$3.00 – 5.00
4. Boy with dog in a box ....$3.00 – 5.00

PLATE 32

PLATE 33

Norman Rockwell, continued

Plate 33

Row 1: Norman Rockwell *Good Old Days* (1982)
These mugs were made in Japan and say ©HMI 1982, USA and title on bottom.
1. *Blasting Off* ....$3.00 – 5.00
2. *Kitchen Capers* ....$3.00 – 5.00
3. *Thirsty Bunch* ....$3.00 – 5.00
4. *A Dog's Life* ....$3.00 – 5.00

Row 2: Rockwell Mugs, ©HMI 1981, Made in Japan
1. *Sour Note* ....$3.00 – 5.00
2. *Vacation's Over* ....$3.00 – 5.00
3. *The Music Maker* ....$3.00 – 5.00
4. *Party Time* ....$3.00 – 5.00

Row 3: Rockwell Mugs ©1985, The Norman Rockwell Museum, Inc., Made in Japan
1. *Braving the Storm* ....$4.00 – 6.00
2. *For a Good Boy* ....$4.00 – 6.00
3. *Looking Out to Sea* ....$4.00 – 6.00
4. *River Pilot* ....$4.00 – 6.00

PLATE 34

P.A.T. Ward Collector Series

All of the glasses on this page were part of the Pepsi-Cola promotions of the late 1970s. Jay Ward's famous characters need no further comment.

Row 1: Pepsi-Cola P.A.T. Ward 5" Action Series
1. Dudley Do-Right in canoe . . . .$8.00 – 10.00
2. Rocky as circus performer . . . .$8.00 – 10.00
3. Bullwinkle with balloons . . . .$8.00 – 10.00

Row 2: Pepsi-Cola P.A.T. Ward 5" Static Pose Series
1. Boris Badenov . . . .$10.00 – 15.00
2. Natasha . . . .$10.00 – 15.00
3. Mr. Peabody . . . .$10.00 – 15.00
Not Pictured:
Dudley Do-Right . . . .$15.00 – 20.00
Bullwinkle . . . .$25.00 – 30.00

PLATE 35

P.A.T. Ward Collector Series, continued

Row 1: Pepsi-Cola P.A.T. Ward 6" & 5" static pose characters
1. Rocky, 6" (also available with black lettering) . .$15.00 – 20.00
2. Rocky, 5", static pose . . . .$20.00 – 25.00
3. Rocky, 6", brown lettering, no Pepsi-Cola logo .$20.00 – 25.00

Row 2: Pepsi-Cola P.A.T. Ward 6" & 5" static pose characters
1. Snidely Whiplash, 6" (also available in black lettering) $15.00 – 20.00
2. Snidely Whiplash, 5" static pose . . . .$10.00 – 15.00
3. Snidely Whiplash, 6" . . . .$15.00 – 20.00

Row 3: Pepsi-Cola P.A.T. Ward 6" static pose characters
1. Dudley Do-Right (also available in black lettering
   and with red lettering with no Pepsi-Cola logo) $15.00 – 20.00
2. Bullwinkle (also available with black lettering) .$15.00 – 20.00
3. Bullwinkle, brown lettering (no Pepsi-Cola logo)$20.00 – 25.00
4. Boris & Natasha
   (also available with white lettering) . . . .$20.00 – 25.00

PLATE 36

PLATE 37

P.A.T. Ward Collector Series, *continued*

Row 1: Holly Farms Fried Chicken & Seafood and Pepsi-Cola Rocky

The first four glasses in Row 1 were distributed by Holly Farms restaurants in 1975 and are marked with the Holly Farms logo rather than a Pepsi-Cola logo. These glasses received a very limited regional distribution, primarily in the southeast. The last glass in Row 1 is the unusual Pepsi-Cola gray Rocky variation which also had a very limited distribution.

1. Holly Farms Boris Badenov . . . .$60.00 – 80.00
2. Holly Farms Bullwinkle . . . .$60.00 – 80.00
3. Holly Farms Natasha . . . .$60.00 – 80.00
4. Holly Farms Rocky . . . .$60.00 – 80.00
5. Pepsi-Cola/P.A.T. Ward Rocky — gray . . . . .$100.00 – 125.00

Row 2: Pizza Hut/P.A.T. Ward/Leonardo TTV, set of six

The set shown in Row 2 is referred to by collectors as the CB Lingo set because it features popular Ward and Leonardo TTV cartoon characters using CB radio language to describe humorous situations. The glasses, made by Brockway, are undated, but they probably came out in the mid to late 70s. Four of the glasses are referred to by collectors according to the color of the truck on them. Five of the glasses feature Ward characters; one features Underdog, a Leonardo TTV character. It is extremely difficult to find these glasses with perfect registration, so fussy collectors will have to make some compromises.

1. Bullwinkle and Boris: *Tijuana Taxi* . . . .$45.00 – 65.00
2. Bullwinkle and Rocky: *Coat rack to fat tail!*
   How's the tide, good buddy? . . . .$45.00 – 65.00
3. Bullwinkle and Dudley Do-Right . . . .$45.00 – 65.00
4. Boris, Rocky, and Bullwinkle: *Is it clear...?* . . . .$45.00 – 65.00
5. Underdog: *Breaker 10! This is big U!* . . . .$45.00 – 65.00
6. Simon Bar Sinister and Dudley . . . .$45.00 – 65.00

Warner Brothers

Pepsi-Cola Warner Brothers Interaction Series, 1976

This set of twenty-four glasses which show a spectrum of Warner Brothers characters in humorous interaction was issued over a period of time in groups of six glasses. The glasses do not have any of the characters' names on them as do other Warners Brothers/Pepsi-Cola glasses. Twelve of these glasses are relatively easy to locate because they were widely distributed by fast-food restaurants. Twelve others are more difficult to find because promotion headquarters required restaurants to commit to ordering at least 1,800 dozen (21,600) glasses. Therefore, fewer restaurants ordered the last twelve glasses. One group of Taco Bell restaurants in California was the only restaurant group which ran all twelve of these (now) "tough" glasses. Most of the "tough twelve" show up on the West Coast, but according to the market representatives, they were distributed in pockets throughout the country. A complete set of these glasses is by itself a nice collection or a beautiful addition to a collection. Prices for the easy glasses have been low and stable. The tough twelve continue to go up in price. The scenes on some of these glasses were carried over to vinyl-plastic placemats.

Row 1: 1976 Warner Brothers interactions
1. Beaky Buzzard/Cool Cat/kite . . . .$8.00 – 10.00
2. Bugs Bunny/Elmer Fudd/shotgun . . . .$5.00 – 7.00
3. Foghorn Leghorn/Henery Hawk/tennis/bomb . . . . .$5.00 – 7.00
4. Daffy Duck/Pepe Le Pew/garden hose . . . .$5.00 – 7.00
5. Porky Pig/Petunia Pig/lawn mower . . . .$5.00 – 7.00
6. Road Runner/Wile E. Coyote/catapult . . . .$5.00 – 7.00

Row 2: 1976 Warner Brothers Interactions, continued
1. Tweety/Sylvester/saw/limb . . . .$5.00 – 7.00
2. Daffy Duck/Tasmanian Devil/hot dog/firecracker . .$5.00 – 7.00
3. Porky Pig/Tasmanian Devil/fishing pole . . . .$8.00 – 10.00
4. Sylvester/Tweety/Marc Antony/net . . . .$5.00 – 7.00
5. Bugs Bunny/Yosemite Sam/cannon . . . .$10.00 – 15.00
6. Yosemite Sam/Speedy Gonzales/panning gold . .$10.00 – 15.00

PLATE 38

1976 Warner Brothers Interactions, continued

Plate 38

Row 1

1. Bugs Bunny/Marvin Martian/mirror/ray gun . . . . .$45.00 – 65.00
2. Cool Cat/Colonel Rim fire/coconuts . . . .$35.00 – 40.00
3. Daffy Duck/Elmer Fudd/Bugs Bunny/hunting sign . . .$35.00 – 40.00
4. Daffy Duck/Elmer Fudd/marching band . . . . . .$40.00 – 50.00
5. Foghorn Leghorn/Marc Antony/doghouse/bomb $40.00 – 50.00
6. Pepe Le Pew/girlfriend/perfume . . . .$45.00 – 65.00

Row 2: 1976 Warner Brothers Interactions, continued

1. Porky Pig/Daffy Duck/cooking pot . . . .$35.00 – 40.00
2. Speedy Gonzales/Slow Poke Rodriguez/
   Sylvester/mallet . . . .$45.00 – 65.00
3. Granny/Sylvester/Tweety/birdbath . . . .$35.00 – 40.00
4. Hippity Hop/Sylvester/boxing . . . .$35.00 – 40.00
5. Road Runner/Wile E. Coyote/sailplane . . . . . .$45.00 – 65.00
6. Wile E. Coyote/Ralph/sheep . . . .$35.00 – 40.00

PLATE 39

1973 Pepsi-Cola Warner Brothers Series

This is probably the most familiar of all cartoon glass sets. Characters in this large family of glasses were offered in both the United States and Canada. The advertising group that coordinated the promotion with Pepsi-Cola estimates that 14 to 15 million of these glasses were produced. The promotion began in 1975 with Carroll's restaurants in upstate New York (later to become Burger King). At first, 5" and 6" glasses were available. As word of the success of the promotion spread, more and more restaurants that sold Pepsi-Cola participated. The increased demand also resulted in new production runs and the need for more than one glass company to help meet the demand. The eighteen characters can be found in both Brockway Glass Company (the heavy style) and Federal Glass Company (the thin style) tumblers. Later in the promotion, the characters' names were changed to white lettering because with the black lettering, the characters' names could not be read when the glasses were filled with Pepsi-Cola.

These glasses were distributed throughout the country (to a much lesser extent in Canada), but not all restaurants distributed all the characters or all the glass styles. Most signed on for at least the six original characters but did not offer all eighteen. Therefore, in various areas, some of the characters are harder to find than others, and this fact influences prices.

There are five different tumbler sizes that were offered: (1) 16 oz. Brockway (heavy glass shell); (2) 16 oz. Federal (thin glass shell); (3) 15 oz. Federal (LUN); (4) 12 oz. Brockway (heavy glass shell) logo under name; and (5) 12 oz. Federal (thin shell), logo under name. Not all the characters can be found on all the glass types. There are a number of glass style variations as well. For instance, Plate 38: Row 1 and Plate 39: Row 1 show the Pepsi-Cola logo under the name of the character rather than on the side. All of the 12 oz. and 15 oz. glasses are found with the logo under the name (sometimes referred to as LUN — Logo Under Name). The six glasses in Plate 40: Row 1 are the only 16 oz. LUN examples.

Plate 39

Row 1: 12 oz. Brockway Warner Brothers logo under name, 1973. (The Federal versions of these glasses are very similar in appearance and value. These glasses also come in a 12 oz. side logo version which is harder to find and more expensive.)

1. Daffy Duck . . . .$10.00 – 15.00
2. Bugs Bunny . . . .$10.00 – 15.00
3. Tweety . . . .$10.00 – 15.00
4. Porky Pig . . . .$10.00 – 15.00
Not pictured:
Sylvester . . . .$10.00 – 15.00
Road Runner . . . .$10.00 – 15.00

Row 2: 16 oz. Federal Warner Brothers logo on side, 1973
In this set, all eighteen of the characters can be found with black lettering, but only fourteen of them can be found with white lettering. The four that were apparently not produced in white are: Foghorn Leghorn, Cool Cat, Slow Poke Rodriguez, and Henery Hawk.

1. Bugs Bunny (white lettering) . . . .$6.00 – 10.00
2. Speedy Gonzales (black lettering) . . . .$6.00 – 10.00
3. Elmer Fudd (white lettering) . . . .$5.00 – 8.00

Row 3: 16 oz. Federal Warner Brothers logo on side, 1973, continued
1. Henery Hawk (black lettering) . . . .$25.00 – 40.00
2. Petunia Pig (black lettering) . . . .$5.00 – 8.00
3. Cool Cat (black lettering) . . . .$8.00 – 12.00

PLATE 40

Notes:

Cool Cat, Foghorn Leghorn, Henery Hawk, and Slow Poke Rodriguez are not available on Federal 16 oz. side logo glasses in white lettering.

Regarding the 15 oz. Federal Logo Under Name set — we know of no collector who has the entire set, and therefore we cannot confirm the existence of all eighteen characters. We do know that Petunia Pig, Tasmanian Devil, and Henery Hawk are extremely difficult to find, and as a result, most collectors do not have all these glasses in their collections. No one really knows if there are 15 oz. LUN versions of Slow Poke Rodriguez and Beaky Buzzard. Time will tell.

The Federal glasses, because of their thin, rather delicate appearance, tend to be valued a bit more highly than their Brockway counterparts which seem, in comparison, rather clunky. This is our perception, and it is not necessarily true in all cases, since individual collectors have their own preferences.

1973 Pepsi-Cola/Warner Brothers Series, continued

Row 1: 1973 Warners Brothers set of six Brockway 16 oz.
Rows 1 through 3 shows all Brockway Glass Company Warner Brothers characters 16 oz. examples. Row 1 shows the six Brockway 16 oz. glasses that can be found with the logo under the name (LUN); Row 2 shows examples of white lettering; Row 3 shows examples of black lettering.
1. Bugs Bunny . . . .$10.00 – 15.00
2. Porky Pig . . . .$10.00 – 15.00
3. Tweety . . . .$10.00 – 15.00
4. Sylvester . . . .$10.00 – 15.00
5. Road Runner . . . .$10.00 – 15.00
6. Daffy Duck . . . . : . . . .$10.00 – 15.00

Row 2: 1973 Warner Brothers characters, continued
1. Elmer Fudd . . . .$3.00 – 5.00
2. Petunia Pig . . . .$6.00 – 8.00
3. Tasmanian Devil . . . .$15.00 – 20.00
4. Pepe Le Pew . . . .$7.00 – 10.00
5. Beaky Buzzard . . . .$7.00 – 10.00
6. Yosemite Sam . . . .$3.00 – 5.00

Row 3: 1973 Warner Brothers characters, continued
1. Henery Hawk . . . .$25.00 – 40.00
2. Wile E. Coyote . . . .$3.00 – 5.00
3. Speedy Gonzales . . . .$3.00 – 5.00
4. Slow Poke Rodriguez . . . .$30.00 – 50.00
5. Cool Cat . . . .$7.00 – 10.00
6. Foghorn Leghorn . . . .$7.00 – 10.00

Price Ranges For 1973 Warner Brothers Glasses

	16 oz. Brockway/Federal (Side Logo)	15 oz. Federal (LUN)	12 oz. Federal/Brockway (LUN)
1. Bugs Bunny	$5.00 – 7.00	$15.00 – 20.00	$10.00 – 15.00
2. Porky Pig	$3.00 – 5.00	$15.00 – 20.00	$10.00 – 15.00
3. Tweety	$3.00 – 5.00	$15.00 – 20.00	$10.00 – 15.00
4. Sylvester	$3.00 – 5.00	$15.00 – 20.00	$10.00 – 15.00
5. Road Runner	$3.00 – 5.00	$15.00 – 20.00	$10.00 – 15.00
6. Daffy Duck	$3.00 – 5.00	$15.00 – 20.00	$10.00 – 15.00
1. Elmer Fudd	$3.00 – 5.00	$15.00 – 20.00	
2. Petunia Pig	$6.00 – 8.00	$50.00+	
3. Tasmanian Devil	$15.00 – 20.00	$100.00+	
4. Pepe Le Pew	$7.00 – 10.00	$15.00 – 20.00	
5. Beaky Buzzard	$7.00 – 10.00	(existence questionable)	
6. Yosemite Sam	$3.00 – 5.00	$15.00 – 20.00	
1. Henery Hawk	$25.00 – 40.00	$150.00+	
2. Wile E. Coyote	$3.00 – 5.00	$15.00 – 20.00	
3. Speedy Gonzales	$3.00 – 5.00	$15.00 – 20.00	
4. Slow Poke Rodriguez	$30.00 – 50.00	(existence questionable)	
5. Cool Cat	$7.00 – 10.00	$15.00 – 20.00	
6. Foghorn Leghorn	$7.00 – 10.00	$15.00 – 20.00	

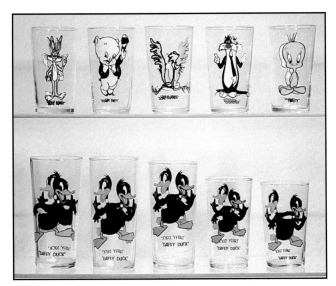

PLATE 41

PLATE 42

Warner Brothers Series, continued

These glasses are 4¹³⁄₁₆" high, while their American Brockway and Federal counterparts are 5⅛". Two sets are available with the same characters. One set is dated 1975, and the other is dated 1977. The sixth glass to the set (Daffy Duck) is shown in Row 2 position 5. Another thing that makes these glasses different are the words *Serie De Collectioneur* above the Pepsi-Cola logo.

Row 2 shows the same character on different glass styles to help collectors visualize the different sizes of glasses available.

Row 1: Canadian Warner Brothers, set of six, (1975 & 1977)
1. Bugs Bunny . . . .$20.00 – 25.00
2. Porky Pig . . . .$20.00 – 25.00
3. Road Runner . . . .$20.00 – 25.00
4. Sylvester . . . .$20.00 – 25.00
5. Tweety . . . .$20.00 – 25.00
Last one in this set is in second row, number 5.

Row 2: Warner Brothers Collectors Series in five different sizes, Daffy Duck
1. 16 oz. Brockway tumbler
2. 16 oz. Federal tumbler
3. 15 oz. Federal LUN tumbler
4. 12 oz. Brockway LUN tumbler
5. 10 oz. Federal (Canadian) . . . .$20.00 – 25.00

Warner Brothers Series, continued

Row 1: Arby's Looney Tunes Adventures, set of four, (1988)
In the summer of 1988, Arby's carried out a brief and limited promotion of four Warner Brothers Looney Tunes Adventures glasses in the Louisville, Kentucky area. These glasses are quite colorful and fairly hard to find, and they are in demand by collectors.
1. Bugs Bunny in *Diving for Carrots* . . . .$15.00 – 20.00
2. Daffy Duck in *Jungle Jitters* . . . .$15.00 – 20.00
3. Porky Pig in *Lunar Launch* . . . .$15.00 – 20.00
4. Sylvester & Tweety in *Anchors Away* . . . .$15.00 – 20.00

Row 2: Pepsi-Cola/Warner Brothers/Tim Horton Donuts (Beignes), set of six, (1978)
The set of six Pepsi-Cola/Warner Brothers glasses shown below in Row 2 was distributed by Tim Horton (the hockey player) Donut Shops in Canada in 1978. The glasses, which are 4¹³⁄₁₆" high, have a *D* on the bottom and were made in Canada. *Serie De Collectioneur* appears above the Pepsi-Cola logo. This is the only set of small glasses that these characters appear on. A set of these glasses is difficult to complete.
1. Elmer Fudd . . . .$20.00 – 25.00
2. Foghorn Leghorn . . . .$20.00 – 25.00
3. Pepe Le Pew . . . .$20.00 – 25.00
4. Speedy Gonzales . . . .$20.00 – 25.00
5. Wile E. Coyote . . . .$20.00 – 25.00
6. Yosemite Sam . . . .$20.00 – 25.00

PLATE 43

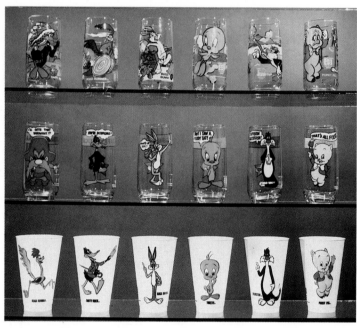

PLATE 44

Warner Brothers Series, continued

Plate 43

Row 1: Ultramar Looney Tunes series, set of six, (1989)
This set of six glasses was distributed by Ultramar gasoline stations in Canada in 1989. These attractive glasses are thin-shelled and fragile, and they have small but detailed depictions of the characters. The names of the characters do not appear on these glasses, and the character's image appears on only one side of the glass.
1. Wile E. Coyote . . . .$5.00 – 7.00
2. Daffy Duck . . . .$5.00 – 7.00
3. Bugs Bunny . . . .$5.00 – 7.00
4. Tweety . . . .$5.00 – 7.00
5. Sylvester . . . .$5.00 – 7.00
6. Road Runner . . . .$5.00 – 7.00

Plate 44

Row 1: Pepsi-Cola/Warner Brothers Looney Tunes Collector Series, set of six, (1979)
This Pepsi-Cola promotion from 1979 featured six glasses with Warner Brothers characters in humorous interaction.
1. Daffy Duck . . . .$7.00 – 10.00
2. Road Runner . . . .$7.00 – 10.00
3. Bugs Bunny . . . .$7.00 – 10.00
4. Tweety . . . .$7.00 – 10.00
5. Sylvester . . . .$7.00 – 10.00
6. Porky Pig . . . .$7.00 – 10.00

Row 2: Pepsi-Cola/Warner Brothers Star and Banner, set of seven, (1980)
Collectors have adopted the name *Star and Banner* for this set because of its design. The reverse side of these glasses has a large color star with the featured character's head inside of it along with a colored banner across the top with the character's name. The complete set contains seven glasses. Not shown is the Road Runner glass, which is the toughest glass to find due to a more limited distribution. The Daffy Duck glass bears a 1980 copyright (date of issue of the set), and the other six glasses have 1966 copyrights which confuses some collectors and dealers into assuming that these glasses were issued in 1966. They were not! The basic set of six (without Road Runner) was also issued by Arby's in 1980 with an Arby's logo. The Arby's glasses are worth a little less than the Pepsi-Cola's.
1. Yosemite Sam . . . .$5.00 – 7.00
2. Daffy Duck . . . .$5.00 – 7.00
3. Bugs Bunny . . . .$5.00 – 7.00
4. Tweety . . . .$5.00 – 7.00
5. Sylvester . . . .$5.00 – 7.00
6. Porky Pig . . . .$5.00 – 7.00
Not pictured:
Road Runner . . . .$15.00 – 20.00

Row 3: Warner Brothers single character (plastic), 1973
These plastic glasses, which bear a 1966 copyright, are similar to their glass counterparts. Some of the poses are different, but they were distributed during the mid-1970s. These are hard to find and even harder to find in good condition. Many Pepsi-Cola collectors consider plastic glasses like these to be the next collecting wave's sleepers.
1. Road Runner . . . .$3.00 – 5.00
2. Daffy Duck . . . .$3.00 – 5.00
3. Bugs Bunny . . . .$3.00 – 5.00
4. Tweety . . . .$3.00 – 5.00
5. Sylvester . . . .$3.00 – 5.00
6. Porky Pig . . . .$3.00 – 5.00

Characters and Personalities

Davy Crockett

Davy Crockett enjoyed an immense popularity in the 1950s — a period when Disney programs and related merchandising boomed. As a result, there is a large variety of types, sizes, and styles of glasses available.

Most Davy Crockett glasses were originally container-jars for a variety of food products including jellies, jams, peanut butter, cheeses, and dairy products. Many different glass companies produced the glasses: Federal, Libbey, Jeannette, Hazel Atlas, Brockway, and others. Many of the glasses are hard to identify because there are no glass makers' marks. However, in many cases, the style of the glass helps to identify the producer.

The pitcher on the left in Plate 45: Row 1 goes with the glasses on Plate 46: Row 1. The glasses came in packs of four or six and are all the same. We've turned the glasses so that each of the three panels can be seen. All three scenes appear on the pitcher.

The pitcher on the right end of Plate 45: Row 1 matches the first two glasses in Plate 46: Row 3. The glasses have been turned to show the different scenes. You will notice that these two glasses differ in coloring. The first one is darker and has a little more frosted area, but the scenes do remain the same and are identical to the scenes on the pitcher. Both pitchers are the same size (8¼") and have the date 1955 printed at the base of the scene. The glass set in the center of Plate 46: Row 1 goes with the second pitcher. All were made by the Jeannette Glass Company. The glass in the center of Plate 45: Row 2 is a variation of the glasses in Plate 46: Row 1. It has white scenes on a clear background, and there may be a matching pitcher.

The first glass in Plate 46: Row 2 is forest green with a white design. It's probable that the set consisted of six or eight glasses. The third glass in Plate 46: Row 2 is very thin, probably Federal or Libbey. The scene is nicely done in green, brown, and black.

The last two glasses in Plate 46: Row 3 are the same glass turned to show the entire design. Notice that this glass is tapered, and the color plate has only two lines: "Davy Crockett 1786 – 1836." This glass is not a part of the Color Plate Series of glasses which have straight sides and three lines on the color plate.

With the exception of glasses one and three in the Plate 46: Row 2, all of the glasses shown on this page were made by Jeannette Glass. All are from the mid-1950s.

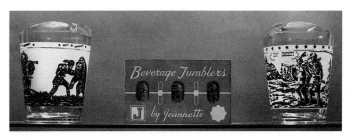

PLATE 45

Row 1: Davy Crockett pitchers and matching tumblers
1. Pitcher, three scenes, 1955, Jeannette Glass . . .$20.00 – 30.00
2. Boxed set of six, 1955, Jeannette Glass . . . . . .$30.00 – 40.00
3. Pitcher, single scene, 1955, Jeannette Glass . . .$20.00 – 30.00

PLATE 46

Row 1: Jeannette glass, 1955
Glasses to accompany pitcher on left in Plate 45 . . . .$4.00 – 6.00
Davy fighting bear; Davy on horse; Davy with Indian

Row 2: Davy Crockett glasses
1. Forest green, no manufacturer's mark . . . .$8.00 – 10.00
2. White on clear, same design as row 2 glass . . . . .$3.00 – 5.00
3. Brown, black, green; Davy firing rifle, no
   manufacturer's mark . . . .$5.00 – 7.00

Row 3: Davy Crockett glasses
1 & 2. 1955 glasses to accompany pitcher above right . .$4.00 – 6.00
3 & 4. Tapered color plate glass; green, yellow, brown, Davy on
   horse/Davy in canoe . . . .$3.00 – 5.00

Davy Crockett, continued

Row 1: Davy Crockett juice glasses

The first two glasses are the same. The second glass is shown with the original Torino grated cheese label still intact. This small juice glass is one of the most commonly encountered Davy Crockett glasses. The scene on this glass (Davy fighting an Indian) is found more frequently than any other scene and was used on glasses of every size (you will see a scale of sizes elsewhere in this section). The center glass in this row is the same shape and size as the Kraft swanky swigs of this era. It is possible that Kraft products came in this juice glass. The last two glasses in Row 1 are the same. This glass came with a panel which could accommodate commercial or souvenir messages up to four lines. The ones pictured here have *Merion Sport Shop* (Merion, PA) and *Shiloh National Military Park* printed on them. This short glass may have been intended as a toothpick holder.

1 & 2. Red, green, clear plate; Indian Fighter; Hazel
  Atlas . . . .$3.00 – 5.00
3. Yellow, brown, green; green solid plate; no manufacturer's
  mark   . . . .$3.00 – 5.00
4 & 5. Brown, orange; Merion Sport Shop; Shiloh National
  Military Park; Hazel Atlas . . . .$8.00 – 10.00

Row 2: Davy Crockett mugs

Milk glass mugs are pictured. There are three different mugs here with front and back views. Hazel Atlas produced the first and third mugs; Fire King produced the middle one. It was common for these mugs to come in sets which had the same scene but different colors.

1 & 2. Red, *Davy Crockett, Indian Fighter*; Hazel Atlas . .$5.00 – 7.00
3 & 4. Brown, *Davy Crockett*; Fire King . . . .$4.00 – 6.00
5 & 6. Green, *Davy Crockett, Famous Frontiersman*; unmarked
  Hazel Atlas (?) . . . .$5.00 – 7.00

Row 1: Complete set of 18 Welch's Davy Crockett glasses

There are six different glasses in the set. Three of the glasses come in either pink, blue, or orange; the other three come in either green, white, or yellow. Since there are no character embossments on the bottoms of these glasses and each scene comes in three different colors, the collector who wants a complete set needs to find only 18 glasses.

1 – 3. *Davy fought this war you see/So Texas people could be free,*
  pink, blue, orange . . . .$7.00 – 10.00
4 – 6. *Davy was a happy boy/With flintlock rifle for a toy,* green,
  white, yellow . . . .$7.00 – 10.00

Row 2: Welch's Davy Crockett glasses, continued

1 – 3. *Davy had a creed that said/Be sure you're right then go
  ahead,* pink, blue, orange . . . .$7.00 – 10.00
4 – 6. *Steady nerves and trigger squeeze/Davy wins it in a breeze,*
  green, white, yellow . . . .$7.00 – 10.00

Row 3: Welch's Davy Crockett glasses, continued

1 – 3. *Ol' Grumpy Bear made his mistake/A fight with Davy sealed
  his fate,* pink, blue, orange . . . .$7.00 – 10.00
4 – 6. *When Davy met an Indian foe/He dealt him just one mighty
  blow,* green, white, yellow . . . .$7.00 – 10.00

PLATE 47

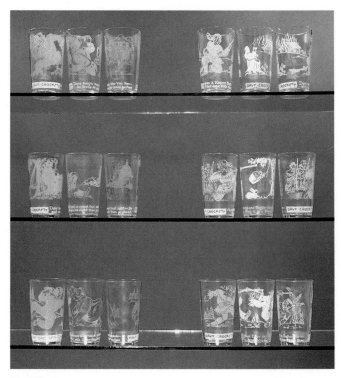

PLATE 48

PLATE 49

Davy Crockett, continued

Row 1: Feathered Banner set
The three glasses in Row 1 belong to a set, perhaps a set of 4. There could be as many as six or eight glasses to this set since the scenes depicted are usually from the movies or TV series. We refer to this set as the Feathered Banner set because of the feathered ends on the banner (see center glass). These glasses are very colorful and have wonderful artwork.
1. Davy Crockett (white banner) Goes to Washington, (orange banner) . . . .$10.00 – 15.00
2. Davy Crockett (yellow banner) Fights Alligator, (blue banner) . . . .$10.00 – 15.00
3. Davy Crockett (orange banner) Indian Fighter, (red banner) . . . .$10.00 – 15.00

Row 2: In a Jam set
Row 2 features a set called *In a Jam*. These glasses have a musical scale type band around the top with words instead of notes. Each one is different. There is no glass maker's mark, but these glasses are in the Jeannette style. ©OVP appears at the base of each scene and may be a reference to Ovaltine Products, since Ovaltine had many premium offers in the 1950s. This is another very attractive set.
1. In a Jam at the Alamo, green/white . . . .$6.00 – 8.00

2. In a Jam with an Indian, red/black . . . .$6.00 – 8.00
3. In a Jam with a Bear, yellow/brown . . . .$6.00 – 8.00
4. In a Jam at Congress, pink/black . . . .$6.00 – 8.00

Row 3: Davy Crockett's Life Events
Row 3 shows a set of four with events in Davy's life in yellow, brown, and green. The set shown here was a store set and did not contain food products. There is no maker's mark on these thick-bottom glasses. Another slightly taller set (not pictured) with different colors (green, yellow, red), the same scenes and designs and a thick lip on the rim was made by Owens Illinois Glass Company (there is no maker's mark; glasses identified from original box). These probably contained a food product. And there is a small set made by Libbey (not pictured) with the colors yellow, red, and green. These glasses have a rim lip and may have contained food. The center glass (white with red lettering) is yet another variation and probably comes in other sizes as well. It has a thick lip, indicating a food container.
1. The Backwoods Boy/Born 1786 — Limestone, Tennessee . . . .$7.00 – 9.00
2. American Pioneer/Grew Up in the Forests . . . . .$7.00 – 9.00
3. American Pioneer, tall variation of #2 above . . .$8.00 – 10.00
4. Coonskin Congressman/Went to Washington — 1827 . .$7.00 – 9.00
5. Great American/Defended the Alamo — 1836 . . .$7.00 – 9.00

PLATE 50

Davy Crockett, continued
Row 1: Three Davy Crockett glasses
Row 1, glasses 1 & 3 are the same with front and back shown. This is a Federal glass. The glass in the center appears to be a single, but we would not presume to say for certain.
1 & 3. *Davy Crockett 1786 – 1836/Remember
   the Alamo 1836* . . . .$7.00 – 9.00
2. Davy the scout . . . .$6.00 – 8.00

Row 2: Ribbed Base set
Row 2 shows what we call the Ribbed Base set. It comes in the three sizes pictured and in at least four colors. The scene is the same on all the glasses. The thick rim lips suggest that these were food containers.
1. Tall, ribbed base . . . .$4.00 – 6.00
2, 3, 4. Short, ribbed base . . . .$4.00 – 6.00

Row 3: Davy Crockett Color Plate Series
Row 3 shows what we call the Color Plate series. Each plate, which takes the form of a stretched hide with a rifle and powder horn at the left and a coonskin cap at the right, has three lines of print, and each color comes with a particular scene. These glasses come in several sizes and glass styles. Some contained food products; others didn't. The first four pictured here are the same size, and there may be two more colors to this set. The fifth glass is the same as number four, but it has an unusual white and brown coloration instead of the more common yellow and brown. The sixth glass is a bit smaller than the others with the same front scene as the first glass but a different back scene. This glass is signed Hazel Atlas. We assume that all of these glasses, regardless of size or style, come in sets of at least six.
1. Blue plate: Indians smoking peace pipe/Davy
   on horse . . . .$4.00 – 6.00
2. Red plate: Davy fighting soldier at Alamo/Davy
   fighting soldier . . . .$4.00 – 6.00
3. Green plate: Indian on rock/Davy fighting bear . .$4.00 – 6.00
4. Orange plate: Indians in canoe/Davy in canoe
   chasing Indians . . . .$4.00 – 6.00
5. Same as #4 but different colors . . . .$5.00 – 7.00
6. White plate: Davy with Indians smoking pipe/Davy with
   rifle waving . . . .$5.00 – 7.00

PLATE 51

Davy Crockett, continued
Plate 51: Rows 1 – 3 and Plate 52: Row 1 show what we refer to as Clear Plate glasses. The plate consists of a stretched hide, rifle, and powder horn to the left, coonskin cap at the right. There are three lines of print (with the second varying depending on the theme of the glass): *Davy Crockett/Hero of the Alamo; Indian Fighter; Frontier Hero,* or *Coonskin Congressman/1786 – 1836.* There is an amazing variety of sizes, colors, and shapes. In Row 3, glass #3 is obviously a food container. Plate 52: Row 1 shows the Indian Fighter theme, the most popular and often found of all the scenes, with glasses graduated from tall to short. Row 2 contains two different Holiday Freeze glasses; a mug with a three-part brown pistol and powder horn plate (this mug also comes in green and perhaps other colors); a white clear plate design with two lines of text and rifle to the left; and a small red Jeannette food container.

Row 1: Davy Crockett Clear Plate Series
1. Green/yellow: *Frontier Hero* . . . .$4.00 – 6.00
2. Red/yellow: *Indian Fighter* . . . .$4.00 – 6.00
3. Yellow/green: *Hero of the Alamo* . . . .$4.00 – 6.00
4. Blue/white: *Hero of the Alamo, Hazel Atlas* . . . .$4.00 – 6.00
5. Yellow/green: *Frontier Hero, Hazel Atlas* . . . .$4.00 – 6.00

Row 2: Davy Crockett Clear Plate Series
1. Red/yellow: *Indian Fighter,* paneled *Hazel Atlas* . .$6.00 – 8.00
2. White/green: *Coonskin Congressman,* paneled
   Hazel Atlas . . . .$6.00 – 8.00
3. Yellow/green: *Hero of the Alamo,* paneled *Hazel Atlas* .$6.00 – 8.00

Row 3: Clear Plate Variations
1. White/green (reverse): *Indian Fighter, Hazel Atlas* .$6.00 – 8.00
2. White/green (reverse): *Coonskin Congressman,* spiral design,
   Hazel Atlas . . . .$7.00 – 9.00
3. Yellow/green (reverse): *Hero of the Alamo* (note rim) . .$6.00 – 8.00
4. White/yellow (front): *Hero of the Alamo* . . . .$6.00 – 8.00

PLATE 52

Davy Crockett, continued

Plate 52

Row 1: Clear Plate variations of *Indian Fighter*
1. White/green, 6⅜" . . . .$5.00 – 7.00
2. Yellow/white, 5½" . . . .$5.00 – 7.00
3. Brown/white, 5" . . . .$5.00 – 7.00
4. Red/black, 4¾" (note base) . . . .$7.00 – 9.00
5. Red/green, 4¹⁄₁₆" . . . .$4.00 – 6.00

Row 2: Miscellaneous Davy Crockett glasses
1. Holiday Freeze, 6⅝" . . . .$10.00 – 15.00
2. Holiday Freeze, 6¹⁵⁄₁₆" . . . .$10.00 – 15.00
3. Mug, red/brown plate, 5⁵⁄₁₆", Davy and friend in canoe, Davy Crockett, Indian Fighter, Statesman, Hero of Alamo, 1786 – 1836 on stretched hide . . . .$10.00 – 15.00
4. White, 5⅝", Davy and friend in canoe/Davy on horse, Davy Crockett, Indian Fighter, Statesman, Hero of Alamo, 1786 – 1836 on stretched hide . . . .$4.00 – 6.00
5. Red, 4⅞", Indian Fighter, Frontier Hero, 1786 – 1836 Jeannette Glass . . . .$6.00 – 8.00

Holly Hobbie

American Greetings Corporation's little girl with the bonnet and calico dresses has been around now for over twenty-five years. The earliest glasses were either unmarked or had American Greetings Corporation's copyrights sometimes with dates and sometimes without. Dating many of these glasses is obviously a problem, if not impossible. However, the decorative bands around the bottoms of the glasses help collectors to identify which glasses belong to which sets. Sometimes the dates are in Roman numerals, and on other glasses they appear in Arabic numerals. Coca-Cola sponsorship characterizes the later glasses of the seventies and eighties. The most recent Holly Hobbie glasses (early nineties) leave the more familiar designs behind, forsaking the classic appearance of the seventies and eighties. A collector of Holly Hobbie glasses will find it difficult to get them all since some are infrequently encountered, and to the untrained eye the sheer variety will be quite bewildering. To complicate matters further, collectors will find unmarked Holly Hobbie look alike glasses put out by a variety of American glass manufacturers.

Holly Hobbie glasses provoke mixed reactions among collectors who either love them or love to hate them. The simplistic sayings common to these glasses irritate some people, but the uplifting goodness and optimism appeal to those who look on the bright side. Coca-Cola sponsorship has helped their popularity among Coca-Cola collectors who might otherwise ignore them. The values of Holly Hobbie glasses tend to be fairly low except for some of the sets which are hard to find and to complete. The low values seem to be a function of overproduction and relatively easy availability. In any case, these glasses have loyal audiences who search for them for a variety of reasons.

Plate 53

Row 1: Holly Hobbie Happy Talk, set of six (Coca-Cola, undated)
1. *A good example is the best teacher* . . . .$2.00 – 5.00
2. *Friendship makes the rough road smooth* . . . . . .$2.00 – 5.00
3. *Happiness is meant to be shared* . . . .$2.00 – 5.00
4. *Love is the little things you do* . . . .$2.00 – 5.00
5. *The easiest tasks are those done with love* . . . . . .$2.00 – 5.00
6. *The happiest times are those shared with friends* .$2.00 – 5.00

Row 2: Holly Hobbie and Friends, Set of 6 (Coca-Cola, undated)
1. *A little smile says a lot* . . . .$5.00 – 8.00
2. *Being yourself is the best way to be* . . . .$5.00 – 8.00
3. *Friends are for thinking and caring about* . . . . . .$5.00 – 8.00
4. *Good friends make the best company* . . . .$5.00 – 8.00
5. *Make every day a sunshine day* . . . .$5.00 – 8.00
6. *Take delight in the little things* . . . .$5.00 – 8.00

Row 3: Holly Hobbie Simple Pleasures, set of six (Coca-Cola, undated)
1. *Fill your day with happiness* . . . .$4.00 – 7.00
2. *Good friends are like sunshine* . . . .$4.00 – 7.00
3. *Good times are for sharing* . . . .$4.00 – 7.00
4. *Make every day a picnic* . . . .$4.00 – 7.00
5. *Simple pleasures are the sweetest* . . . .$4.00 – 7.00
6. *Treat your world with tenderness* . . . .$4.00 – 7.00

PLATE 53

PLATE 54

PLATE 55

The time to be happy is now, in six pack carrier (1967) $3.00 – 5.00 ea.

PLATE 56

Holly Hobbie, continued
Row 1: Set of four (1978)
1. *The world is full of happy surprises* . . . .$2.00 – 4.00
2. *Fun is doubled when you share it* . . . .$2.00 – 4.00
3. *Special friends give the heart a lift* . . . .$2.00 – 4.00
4. *Lighthearted ways make happy days* . . . .$2.00 – 4.00

Row 2: Miscellaneous Holly Hobbie
1. *Life's a picnic . . . enjoy it* (1969) . . . .$2.00 – 4.00
2. *Start each day in a happy way* (1972) . . . .$2.00 – 4.00
3. *Life is filled with sweet surprises* (1977) . . . .$2.00 – 4.00
4. *The smile of a friend is as warm as the sun* (1980) $2.00 – 4.00

Row 3: Miscellaneous Holly Hobbie
1. *You can't be poor if you have a friend* (World Wide Arts
    look-alike glass) . . . .$2.00 – 4.00
2. *Start each day in a happy way* (World Wide Arts) $2.00 – 4.00
3. *Happiness is just being yourself* (1 of 6 in the Bouquet of Joy
    series, Coca-Cola) . . . .$5.00 – 7.00
The others are (not pictured):
Love makes the world a beautiful place . . . .$5.00 – 7.00
Let joy blossom in your heart . . . .$5.00 – 7.00
Today can be the start of something . . . .$5.00 – 7.00
Make every day a fine bouquet . . . .$5.00 – 7.00
Life is filled with sweet surprises . . . .$5.00 – 7.00
4. *Treat yourself to a happy day* (1 of 4 in the Country Kitchen
    series, Coca-Cola) . . . .$5.00 – 7.00
The others are (not pictured):
Don't forget to add love . . . .$5.00 – 7.00
Nice surprises are the spice of life . . . .$5.00 – 7.00
Life is simply delicious . . . .$5.00 – 7.00

Holly Hobbie Christmas Glasses

Row 1: Miscellaneous
1. *Christmas is a time for happy dreams*
    (Coca-Cola, no date) . . . .$2.00 – 4.00
Two others (not pictured) in this set are:
Happy ways bless Christmas days . . . .$2.00 – 4.00
Holidays are the happiest times . . . .$2.00 – 4.00
2. *. . . are filled with happy. . .* (perhaps the 4th glass
    in this set?) . . . .$2.00 – 4.00

Row 2: Set of three (Coca-Cola, no date)
1. *Christmas is a gift of joy* . . . .$2.00 – 4.00
2. *Christmas is the nicest time of all* . . . .$2.00 – 4.00
3. *Christmas is love with all the trimmings* . . . .$2.00 – 4.00

Row 3: Set of three (Coca-Cola, no date)
1. *Have A Happy Holiday!* . . . .$2.00 – 4.00
2. *There's A Special Glow At Christmas* . . . .$2.00 – 4.00
3. *It's Time For Christmas* . . . .$2.00 – 4.00

PLATE 57

PLATE 58

Holly Hobbie Christmas, continued
Row 1: Concave Christmas glasses (American Greetings Corp.)
1. *Christmas is the nicest time of all!* . . . .$2.00 – 4.00
2. *Happy Holidays!* . . . .$2.00 – 4.00
3. *'Tis the season to be merry* . . . .$2.00 – 4.00

Row 2: Concave Christmas glasses (American Greetings Corp.)
1. *Happy ways brighten the holidays* . . . .$2.00 – 4.00
2. *Holiday pleasures are life's sweetest treasures* . . . .$2.00 – 4.00
3. *Christmas is fun for everyone* . . . .$2.00 – 4.00
4. *Love is the magic of Christmas* . . . .$2.00 – 4.00

Holly Hobbie Christmas, continued
Row 1: 1977 Christmas, set of four (American Greetings Corp., Coca-Cola)
1. 1 of 4, *Christmas is fun for everyone* . . . .$3.00 – 5.00
2. 2 of 4, *Christmas brings a world of happy things* . .$3.00 – 5.00
3. 3 of 4, *Christmas is here . . . the nicest time of the year* $3.00 – 5.00
4. 4 of 4, *Christmas is for kids of every age* . . . .$3.00 – 5.00
There is also a dated, unnumbered set of these glasses with a different base.

Row 2: 1978 Christmas: Holly Hobbie and Robby (American Greetings Corp., Coca-Cola)
1. 2 of 4, *Christmas is magic in your heart* . . . .$3.00 – 5.00
2. 3 of 4, *Dreams come true at Christmas* . . . .$3.00 – 5.00
Not pictured:
1 of 4, *Holidays are the happiest days* . . . .$3.00 – 5.00
4 of 4, *Christmas is a gift of love* . . . .$3.00 – 5.00

Row 3: 1979 Christmas: Holly Hobbie and Robby (American Greetings Corp., Coca-Cola)
1. 1 of 4, The Twelve Days Of Christmas, Days 1 – 3 . .$3.00 – 5.00
2. 2 of 4, The Twelve Days Of Christmas, Days 4 – 6 . .$3.00 – 5.00
3. 3 of 4, The Twelve Days Of Christmas, Days 7 – 9 . .$3.00 – 5.00
4. 4 of 4, The Twelve Days of Christmas, Days 10 – 12 . .$3.00 – 5.00

PLATE 59

Holly Hobbie Christmas, continued
Row 1: 1980 Christmas: Holly Hobbie and Robby (American Greetings Corp., Coca-Cola)
1. 1 of 4, *Christmas Is Sharing* . . . .$3.00 – 5.00
2. 2 of 4, *Wrap Each Christmas Gift In Love* . . . . . .$3.00 – 5.00
3. 3 of 4, *Share A Little Christmas Spirit* . . . .$3.00 – 5.00
4. 4 of 4, *Deck The Halls With Joy And Gladness* . . .$3.00 – 5.00

Row 2: 1981 Christmas, set of three (American Greetings Corp., Coca-Cola)
1. *The Holidays have a magic all their own* (Reverse: Holly feeding birds) . . . .$2.00 – 4.00
2. *'Tis the season for fun!* (Reverse: Holly and Robby bringing in tree) . . . .$2.00 – 4.00

3. *A gift of love . . . especially for you* (Reverse: Holly with gift) . . . .$2.00 – 4.00

Row 3: 1982 Christmas, set of three (American Greetings Corp., Coca-Cola)
1. *Wishing you the happiest of holidays!* (Reverse: Holly Hobbie Picking Christmas Holly) . . . .$2.00 – 4.00
2. *Share in the fun of the season!* (Reverse: Holly and Robby Sledding) . . . .$2.00 – 4.00
3. *Holidays are meant to be shared* (Reverse: Holly Telling a Story) . . . .$2.00 – 4.00

PLATE 60

Pac-Man

Bally's Pac-Man video arcade games of the early 80s were immensely popular, and people were lining up to drop quarters into the machines to watch the voracious Pac-Men gobble up fleeing ghosts in an electronic maze. There were many commercial spinoffs — lunch boxes, board games, novelties, clothing, etc. Pac-Man glasses hit the market in the early 80s in such quantity that they are now almost passé. There are so many that they don't command high prices. It might be a good idea, however, to put a couple sets of eight of the Arby's rocks tumblers aside for the future just in case they make a comeback in 2020. Hint: the black on these glasses fades easily, so any glasses that you find with glossy black are probably worth keeping. The AAFES set is not as common as the Arby's and generic Bally Pac-Men glasses, so it is definitely worth seeking and keeping. Not quite as common as the Pac-Men glasses, Ms. Pac-Man glasses were issued in 1981 – 1982, an early example of political correctness and gender equality.

Row 1: Arby's Collector Series (1980)
1. Rocks glass, front view . . . .$2.00 – 4.00
2. Rocks glass, reverse view

Row 2: Miscellaneous Bally Midway Mfg. Co. (1982)
1. Pac-Man, tall 6" flare top (Libbey) . . . .$2.00 – 4.00

2. Pac-Man, short 5⅜" flare top (Libbey) . . . .$2.00 – 4.00
3. Pac-Man, mug . . . .$2.00 – 4.00
Not pictured: Miscellaneous Bally Pac-Man
Ms. Pac-Man, 1981, 6" flare top (Libbey) . . . .$3.00 – 5.00
Ms. Pac-Man, 1982, 3⅜" flare top (Libbey) . . . . . .$3.00 – 5.00
Pac-Man, 1982, 3⅜" flare top (Libbey)
   (similar in design to glasses in Row 2) . . . .$2.00 – 4.00
Pac-Man, 32 oz. mug, 1982
   (same design as mug in Row 2) . . . .$4.00 – 6.00
Pac-Man, mug, ©Midway Mfg. Co.
   no date, 5½" (signed *Houze*) . . . .$3.00 – 5.00
Pac-Man, ceramic mug, ©Midway Mfg. Co., no date (signed
   Houze, Grindley England on bottom) . . . .$4.00 – 6.00

Row 3: AAFES (Army and Air Force Exchange Service)
Pac-Man, Bally Midway Mfg. Co., 1980 (Libbey)
1. *Shadow — nicknamed "Blinky" is always close behind* .$4.00 – 6.00
2. *Bashful — nicknamed "inky" is real
   shy and may run away* . . . .$4.00 – 6.00
3. *Pokey — nicknamed "Clyde," is slow but tries his
   best* . . . .$4.00 – 6.00
4. *Speedy — nicknamed "Pinky" is pink and he's fast* .$4.00 – 6.00

Popeye

The Popeye family of characters has long been part of our popular culture, and glasses featuring the Popeye characters appeared as early as 1929.

Row 1: Popeye Kollect-A-Set of six glasses
This set was sponsored by Coca-Cola and came out in 1975. (Several other glasses exist — Castor Oil, Alice the Coon, Sea Hag, Eugene the Jeep, Pappy and Geezel — but they never made it past the prototype stage. There is also a version of some of these characters in pirate outfits. And recently an unusual shorter 5⅛" set of the original six characters came to light. These glasses are quite uncommon, and collectors are unlikely to encounter them. If found, their value would easily be around $100.00 each.)

1. Wimpy . . . .$3.00 – 5.00
2. Olive Oyl . . . .$3.00 – 5.00
3. Popeye . . . .$5.00 – 7.00
4. Brutus . . . .$3.00 – 5.00
5. Swee' Pea . . . .$3.00 – 5.00
6. Rough House . . . .$3.00 – 5.00

Row 2: Popeye's Pals
A set of four, sponsored by Popeye's Famous Fried Chicken, 1979. Each glass contains a panel of four cartoon frames which feature the Popeye characters and promote Popeye's Fried Chicken.

1. Olive Oyl . . . .$10.00 – 20.00
2. Popeye . . . .$10.00 – 20.00
3. Brutus . . . .$10.00 – 20.00
4. Swee' Pea . . . .$10.00 – 20.00

A Popeye Character Interaction, set of four, sponsored by Popeye's Famous Fried Chicken, was issued in 1978 (not pictured here). Dramatic, humorous interaction, as in the comic strip, is the focus on these colorful glasses.

1. Olive Oyl: Popeye, Brutus, and Olive Oyl in a roller skate race; Popeye holding a drumstick — the only glass on which a piece of chicken appears . . . .$15.00 – 25.00
2. Popeye: Popeye running with a kite, Brutus with a pair of scissors trying to cut the string . . . .$15.00 – 25.00
3. Brutus: Brutus kicking a football, Popeye running, Olive Oyl cheering for Popeye . . . .$15.00 – 25.00
4. Swee' Pea: Swee' Pea sitting with a pin wheel, Olive Oyl and Popeye building a sand castle, Brutus with shovel and pail, helping . . . .$15.00 – 25.00

Row 3: Popeye Thru the Years 10th Anniversary Collectors Series
Sponsored by Popeye's Famous Fried Chicken and Pepsi-Cola, 1982. Each glass depicts the character historically and contemporarily and has a cartoon scene from both past and present.

1. Olive Oyl, in 1919 and 1982 . . . .$10.00 – 15.00
2. Popeye, in 1929 and 1982 . . . .$10.00 – 15.00
3. Brutus, in 1933 and 1982 . . . .$10.00 – 15.00
4. Swee' Pea, in 1933 and 1982 . . . .$10.00 – 15.00

In addition to the glasses listed above and shown on the following page, there are two other interesting sets, one American and one Canadian. The American set with a King Features Syndicate copyright line was issued in the late 1930s. Individual glasses in the set of 8 have either 1929 or 1936 copyright dates. Each glass has a picture of Popeye and one other character. These glasses are highly prized by Popeye collectors and not frequently encountered.

The Canadian set of Popeye glasses are a bit more modern, probably dating from the 1950s. These glasses are 4¾" tall and have a capital *D* on the bottom. The heavy beaded rim suggests that these glasses may have been food containers. It is difficult to get reliable information on these glasses because they seem to be quite elusive. Each glass is numbered and has a wraparound single color line drawing depiction of the Popeye characters in action with a small arrow pointing to the name of the featured character on each glass. At the bottom of each glass there is a KFS©. We believe there are eight in the set, though at present we know of only six.

Late 1930s King Features Syndicate Popeye, set of eight
1. Popeye/Bluto . . . .$30.00 – 60.00
2. Popeye/Goon . . . .$30.00 – 60.00
3. Popeye/Jeep . . . .$30.00 – 60.00
4. Popeye/Olive Oyl . . . .$30.00 – 60.00
5. Popeye/Oscar . . . .$30.00 – 60.00
6. Popeye/Sea Hag . . . .$30.00 – 60.00
7. Popeye/Swee' Pea . . . .$30.00 – 60.00
8. Popeye/Wimpy . . . .$30.00 – 60.00

1950s Canadian King Features Syndicate set of Popeye glasses
#1 Popeye at helm of boat holding can of spinach with Sweet-Pea and Eugene the Jeep looking on, Eugene saying "Jeep," black . . . .$25.00 – 40.00
#2 Olive Oyl watching Popeye pick flowers for her, turquoise . . . .$25.00 – 40.00
#3 Popeye at barbecue cooking hamburgers for Wimpy, Wimpy's name on glass, dark green . . . .$25.00 – 40.00
#4 Popeye and Olive Oyl at beach with Sweet-Pea, Sweet-Pea's name on glass, white . . . .$25.00 – 40.00
#5 Popeye running with hose towards Eugene the Jeep with Sweet-Pea in background, Eugene — the Jeep's name — on glass, yellow . . . .$25.00 – 40.00
#6 Brutus chasing Popeye towards a tree, Brutus' name on glass, red . . . .$25.00 – 40.00

PLATE 61

PLATE 62

Comic Strip, Television, and Film Personalities

Row 1: Animal Crackers, a set of six glasses featuring Rog Bellen's Animal Crackers comic strip characters, ©1978 by The Chicago Tribune and New York News Syndicate, Inc. Louis (the baby lion) is not shown here because it is quite difficult to find. This is evidenced by one collector who, during the late 1980s, found several cases of the other five characters. Louis is the only character he did not find. So when one does turn up, the price becomes over-inflated by all the collectors who would like to complete their set.

1. Lyle (side view) . . . .$7.00 – 10.00
2. Dodo . . . .$7.00 – 10.00
3. Gnu . . . .$7.00 – 10.00
4. Lana . . . .$7.00 – 10.00
5. Eugene . . . .$7.00 – 10.00
6. Lyle (front view) . . . .$7.00 – 10.00

Not pictured:

Louis . . . .$50.00 – 75.00

Row 2: Battlestar Galactica, a set of four glasses, ©1979 Universal City Studios, Inc. These iced tea glasses show the popular early 1980s futuristic TV series' main characters. There's a brief account of each character on the reverse of each glass.

1. Cylon Warriors (*The dreaded enemy of the human race*) . . . .$7.00 – 10.00
2. Apollo (*The son of Battlestar Galactica's commander*) . . . .$7.00 – 10.00
3. Starbuck (*The light-hearted...aerial combat pilot*) . .$7.00 – 10.00
4. Commander Adama (*...a colossal man of war*) . .$7.00 – 10.00

Row 3: James Bond 007 Collector Series, set of four, featuring Roger Moore as Agent 007 in four of the Bond movies. There's a brief synopsis of the movie on the back of each glass and a scene on the front. These glasses were distributed by Taco Bell in some locations and were part of a Pepsi-Cola promotion even though they do not have the Pepsi-Cola logo on them. Each glass bears a different copyright date. The set appeared in 1985.

1. *A View to a Kill* (1985 Danjaq S. A.) . . . .$10.00 – 15.00
2. *Moonraker* (1979 Danjaq S. A.) . . . .$10.00 – 15.00
3. *The Spy Who Loved Me* (1977 Danjaq S. A.) . .$10.00 – 15.00
4. *For Your Eyes Only* (1981 Danjaq S. A.) . . . . . .$10.00 – 15.00

PLATE 63

Ad for Ghostbusters II Glasses from Sunoco.

Comic Strip, Television, and Film Personalities, continued
Row 1: Ghostbusters II, a set of six glasses issued by Sunoco of Canada in 1989, ©1989 by Columbia Pictures. A French/English promotional flyer that came within each glass cautioned: "Limit one per customer with min. 25 litre fill-up" and urged customers to "Collect all six before they disappear, at participating Sunoco stations!" Shown on these glasses are the car and some ghosts from Ghostbusters II. The Ghostbusters II logo appears on the reverse of each glass.
1. Six Eyes is trapped . . . .$5.00 – 7.00
2. Tony Scoleri sees the sights . . . .$5.00 – 7.00
3. Smiling Slimer . . . .$5.00 – 7.00
4. Slimer takes the wheel . . . .$5.00 – 7.00
5. The unsinkable Nunzio Scoleri . . . .$5.00 – 7.00
6. Ecto 1-A to the rescue . . . .$5.00 – 7.00

Row 2: The Goonies Collector Series, ©1985 by Warner Bros. Inc. A set of four glasses distributed by Godfather's Pizza featuring characters and scenes from the film The Goonies. No sponsor indicated on glasses, but some glasses have a sticker on the bottom which reads: "Free Pitcher of Coca-Cola when you buy a medium or large Godfather's Pizza now through 9/30/85."
1. Data on the waterslide . . . .$3.00 – 5.00
2. Goonies in the organ chamber . . . .$3.00 – 5.00
3. Sloth and the Goonies . . . .$3.00 – 5.00
4. Sloth comes to the rescue . . . .$3.00 – 5.00

Row 3: Happy Days Collector Series, ©1977 Paramount Pictures, a set of six glasses featuring characters from the popular television series. Actually, there are two sets of these glasses: one sponsored by Dr Pepper (the primary sponsor) and one bearing both Dr Pepper and Pizza Hut logos. The latter set is less frequently encountered. Dr Pepper/Pizza Hut set

	Dr Pepper	Dr Pepper/ Pizza Hut
1. Ralph	$6.00 – 8.00	$8.00 – 10.00
2. The Fonz (on motorcycle) . . .	$8.00 – 12.00	$12.00 – 15.00
3. The Fonz	$7.00 – 10.00	$10.00 – 15.00
4. Richie	$8.00 – 12.00	$12.00 – 15.00
5. Joanie	$6.00 – 8.00	$8.00 – 10.00
6. Potsie	$6.00 – 8.00	$8.00 – 10.00

In addition to the sets listed above, there is another much rarer and mysterious set of these glasses that has a LP record on the reverse and Arnold's Restaurant or Fonz's office (the restroom) on the front. Little is known about this set's origins or sponsors, but we have seen a few of them and know that they have this information on them: ©1977 by Paramount Pictures Corporation, Dr Pepper Collector Series. According to a dealer we know who has some of these glasses in his collection, there are 8 glasses altogether: a regular set of six, plus two extra Fonz glasses. We also know that on some of the glasses, the center of the record is blue, and on some it is red. These glasses have sold at auction for as much as $500.00 a few years ago.

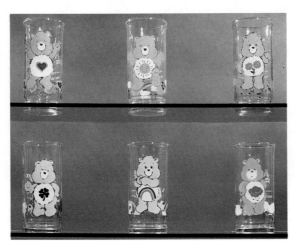

PLATE 64

PLATE 65

Comic Strip, Television, and Film Personalities, continued
Row 1: The Care Bears Limited Edition Collector's Series, 1983. A set of six glasses distributed by Pizza Hut featuring American Greetings' bear characters and comforting sayings. Friend Bear and Good Luck Bear were distributed only in the greater St. Louis area and are therefore much harder to find than the other four. Collectors will also find a set of four 5¹⁄₁₆" Care Bear glasses issued in 1986 with a ©*1986 Those Characters from Cleveland, Inc.* on them ($2.00 – 3.00 ea.). There's also a colorful set of six bilingual Canadian glasses issued in 1984 ($4.00 – 5.00 ea.).
1. Tenderheart Bear (*Share some love*) . . . .$1.00 – 2.00
2. Funshine Bear (*Feeling funtastic!*) . . . .$1.00 – 2.00
3. Friend Bear (*Friends bring fun!*) . . . .$7.00 – 10.00

Row 2: Pizza Hut Care Bears, continued
1. Good Luck Bear (*Luck to you!*) . . . .$7.00 – 10.00
2. Cheer Bear (*Enjoy!*) . . . .$1.00 – 2.00
3. Grumpy Bear (*Hugs welcome*) . . . .$1.00 – 2.00

Comic Strip, Television, and Film Personalities, continued
Row 1: Winnie-the-Pooh and Friends. A set of four glasses sponsored by Sears and ©Walt Disney Productions, probably dating from the 1970s and sold at Sears Stores.
1. Winnie-the-Pooh and Friends — Piglet & Tigger with pots of hunny . . . .$7.00 – 10.00
2. Winnie-the-Pooh for President — Winnie giving speech . . . .$7.00 – 10.00
3. Winnie-the-Pooh and Friends — planting a tree $7.00 – 10.00
Not pictured:
Winnie-the-Pooh and Friends chasing butterfly . . . .$7.00 – 10.00

Row 2: LK's Pierre the Bear Series, 1977. A set of four glasses with the four seasons and seasonal activities as the theme. On the reverse of each glass is a five-line poem which comments on the front scene and resembles a limerick. LK's, we have been told, is the name of a small family restaurant chain in Ohio and some of the southeastern states.
1. Spring — Pierre and kids flying a kite . . . .$3.00 – 5.00
2. Summer — Pierre and kids building sand castles .$3.00 – 5.00
3. Fall — Pierre carrying kids to school . . . .$3.00 – 5.00
4. Winter — Pierre and child building snowman . . .$3.00 – 5.00

Row 3: LK's Pierre the Bear Series, 1979. A set of four glasses showing Pierre the Bear and kids involved in seasonal activities. Generally resemble the 1977 issue, but there are no verses on these glasses.
1. Spring — Pierre picking flowers with children . . .$2.00 – 4.00
2. Summer — Pierre netting a fish, children watching . .$2.00 – 4.00
3. Fall — Pierre sitting under a tree, children raking leaves . . . .$2.00 – 4.00
4. Winter — Pierre and children in snowball fight . .$2.00 – 4.00

PLATE 70   *Comic Strip, Television, and Film Personalities, continued*

Row 1: King Kong, ©1976 Dino De Laurentiis Corporation
This set of four glasses was sponsored by Coca-Cola and presents highlights from the 1976 film revival of King Kong. In 1977, a single King Kong Limited Edition Cinema Glassics tumbler appeared (©1977 Dino De Laurentiis Corporation). This glass, also sponsored by Coca-Cola, has a gray and black film strip encircling its top, and is thought to be more colorful and attractive than the previous issues.
1. Straddling the Twin Trade Towers, the intrepid King Kong faces his most relentless enemy — civilization ......$5.00 – 8.00
2. King Kong wreaks havoc on a New York subway train ..$5.00 – 8.00
3. A crazed King Kong destroys the Skull Island wall ...$5.00 – 8.00
4. Mighty King Kong battles a giant serpent for control of Skull Island ....$5.00 – 8.00
Not pictured:
King Kong Cinema Glassic:
     One of the "biggest" stars in film fantasy (King Kong in leg irons, breaking through fence) ....$5.00 – 8.00

Row 2: *Avoid the Noid/Call Domino's Pizza*, ©1988 Domino's Pizza, Inc.
This set of four Libbey glasses (#1, 2, 4 & 5) shows the Noid engaged in four of his favorite leisure activities. The Noid glass in

the center (#3) is the rocks version of #4, Noid at the beach. Collectors will also encounter a 1987 *Happy Holidays from Domino's Pizza* rocks glass featuring the Noid as Santa with a bag of presents over his shoulder.
1. Noid playing tennis ....$3.00 – 5.00
2. Noid playing golf ....$3.00 – 5.00
3. Rocks glass: Noid at the beach ....$3.00 – 5.00
4. Noid at the beach ....$3.00 – 5.00
5. Noid skiing ....$3.00 – 5.00
Not pictured:
1987 Noid as Santa — Happy Holidays rocks glass .$3.00 – 5.00

Row 3: Urchins, 1976, 1978, ©American Greetings Corporation
This set of six Limited Edition glasses, sponsored by Coca-Cola, features the play activities of the Urchins along with an uplifting saying about life, fun, friends, etc.
1. *A little fun goes a long, long way* — bicycling (1978) .$3.00 – 5.00
2. *Friends make life more fun* — roller skating (1976) ...$3.00 – 5.00
3. *Good friends score a perfect hit!* — baseball (1976) ..$3.00 – 5.00
4. *Serve up sunshine with a smile* — tennis (1976) .$3.00 – 5.00
5. *Good fun is par for the course* — golf (1976) ....$3.00 – 5.00
6. *Life is fun . . . plunge right in!* — swimming (1978) ..$3.00 – 5.00

PLATE 71

PLATE 72

Comic Strip, Television, and Film Personalities, continued
Row 1: Ziggy, miscellaneous glasses
Tom Wilson's lovable Ziggy can be found on an immense variety of glasses, mugs, tankards, juice glasses, giant fountain glasses, rocks glasses, etc. We show only a small sample here.
1. *Merry Christmess* rocks glass — Ziggy tangled up in lights . . . .$3.00 – 5.00
2. *Christmas Surprises* rocks glass — Ziggy falling off of ladder . . . .$3.00 – 5.00
3. *...It looks like love!!* Ziggy with umbrella, falling hearts (1979) . . . .$3.00 – 5.00
4. *Hello world!* (1979) Ziggy standing amongst heart flowers . . . .$3.00 – 5.00
5. *Merry Christmas, Happy New Year,* milk glass mug $2.00 – 4.00

Row 2: Ziggy/7-UP Here's to Good Friends Collector Series, ©Universal Press Syndicate 1977
A set of four glasses showing Ziggy with his animal friends. On the reverse of each glass, Ziggy and his friends are standing under an umbrella on which *7up Collector Series* appears.
1. Ziggy on swing with puppy which is covering its eyes $4.00 – 7.00
2. Ziggy walking his toy duck, seagull showing affection for it . . . .$4.00 – 7.00
3. Ziggy and goldfish in bowl showing affection . . . .$4.00 – 7.00
4. Ziggy and cat on bicycle, cat looking apprehensive $4.00 – 7.00

Row 3: Ziggy, ©1979 Universal Press Syndicate
This is a set of four glasses which, because of various sponsors and logos, comes in four different versions: (1) a Hardee's set, (2) a Pizza Inn set, (3) a no-sponsor set, and (4) a Pizza Inn/Coca-Cola set. There is one other technicality to note: the Pizza Inn and Pizza Inn/Coca-Cola sets have *Time for a Pizza Break* instead of *Time for a Food Break* which appears on the Hardee's and no-sponsor glasses.
1. *Try to have a nice day* — Ziggy looking out window at sun . . . .$5.00 – 8.00
2. *Be nice to little things* — Ziggy under umbrella with friends . . . .$5.00 – 8.00
3. *Smile...it's good for your complexion* — Ziggy smiling . . . .$5.00 – 8.00
4. *Time for a Pizza Break* — Ziggy eating pizza, or *Time for a Food Break* — Ziggy eating hamburger $5.00 – 8.00

Charles Schulz's Peanuts Characters

The characters of Charles Schulz — Snoopy, Lucy, Charlie Brown, Linus and Woodstock — appear on hundreds, perhaps even thousands of drinking and food container glasses. The variety is so immense that a separate book could be devoted to the subject. The characters have been so successful, and so many different glassware items have been produced in such quantity that the value of each is minimal. True devotees can take heart, however, since the sheer quantity available translates into reasonable prices. For space reasons, we show only a small selection here.

Row 1: Peanuts Characters, Kraft Jelly, set of four (1988)
1. Snoopy in swimming pool . . . .$1.00 – 2.00
2. Lucy on swing . . . .$1.00 – 2.00
3. Snoopy on surfboard . . . .$1.00 – 2.00
4. Charlie Brown flying a kite . . . .$1.00 – 2.00

Row 2: Snoopy for President, set of four, sponsored by Dolly Madison Bakery
1. *Vote for the American Beagle* . . . .$4.00 – 6.00
2. *The People's Choice* . . . .$4.00 – 6.00
3. *Back the Beagle* . . . .$4.00 – 6.00
4. *Put Snoopy in the White House* . . . .$4.00 – 6.00

Row 3: Snoopy Sports Series, set of four, sponsored by Dolly Madison Bakery
1. Tennis . . . .$4.00 – 6.00
2. Golf . . . .$4.00 – 6.00
3. Football . . . .$4.00 – 6.00
4. Baseball . . . .$4.00 – 6.00

PLATE 73

Charles Schulz's Peanuts Characters, continued

Plate 73

Row 1: Miscellaneous Peanuts characters glasses
1. Snoopy and Woodstock rocks glass . . . .$2.00 – 3.00
2. Snoopy sitting on lemon, 4" juice glass . . . .$2.00 – 3.00
3. Lucy's lemonade stand, comes in several sizes . . .$2.00 – 3.00
4. Snoopy sitting by apple, 4" juice glass . . . .$2.00 – 3.00
5. Reverse of #1 . . . .$2.00 – 3.00

Row 2: Miscellaneous Peanuts characters glasses
1. Snoopy's kitchen, several sizes, Snoopy . . . .$2.00 – 3.00
2. Snoopy and Woodstock, *Too much root beer*, front view, black
   and white . . . .$2.00 – 3.00
3. *Too much root beer*, back view of #2 . . . .$2.00 – 3.00
4. *Too much root beer*, blue and white, front view . .$2.00 – 3.00
5. Snoopy's Kitchen, same as #1, Charlie Brown & Lucy . .$2.00 – 3.00
Note: there is an accompanying Snoopy's kitchen
   9½" decanter . . . .$4.00 – 6.00

Row 3: Miscellaneous Peanuts characters glasses
1. Super Star, Snoopy pedestal
   (one of four; see note to #4 below) . . . .$2.00 – 3.00
2. Charlie Brown and gang flying a kite . . . .$2.00 – 3.00
3. Lucy skipping rope (a companion glass to #2 above) . . .$2.00 – 3.00
4. Love, Lucy and Charlie Brown, pedestal . . . .$2.00 – 3.00
Note: There are two others in this set: *Cheers* and *Surprise*.

Charles Schulz's Peanuts Characters, continued

Plate 74

Row 1: Miscellaneous Peanuts glasses
1. Snoopy with large hamburger and hot dog . . . . . .$2.00 – 3.00
2. Snoopy eating spaghetti, several sizes . . . .$2.00 – 3.00
3. *Never underestimate the effects of a pretty face!* Peanuts
   characters in love . . . .$3.00 – 5.00
4. Mug: *It never fails…three root beers and Woodstock falls sound
   asleep!* . . . .$3.00 – 5.00

Row 2: Large Peanuts characters pedestals
1. *Hee hee hee, Ha Ha,* Peanuts characters laughing $3.00 – 5.00
2. Snoopy as singing cowboy . . . .$3.00 – 5.00
3. *Get well soon!* Snoopy with foot in cast . . . .$3.00 – 5.00
4. *How nice!* Woodstock giving Snoopy flowers . . . .$3.00 – 5.00

PLATE 74

PLATE 75

Charles Schulz's Peanuts Characters, continued

Row 1: Peanuts Characters plastic cups
1. Charlie Brown and Woodstock, *I have a strange team* . .$5.00 – 8.00
2. Snoopy and Woodstock, *Let's break for lunch!* . . .$5.00 – 8.00
3. Lucy, *I got it! I got it!* . . . .$5.00 – 8.00

Row 2: Miscellaneous Peanuts
1. McDonald's Camp Snoopy (1983) plastic cup,
   Lucy saying "There's no excuse for not being
   properly prepared" . . . .$5.00 – 8.00
2. Snoopy and Woodstock, *Gee, somebody cares!* . .$5.00 – 8.00

3. Snoopy drinking from dish/water fountain, *Very Nice!* . .$5.00 – 8.00
4. McDonald's Camp Snoopy (1983) plastic cup, Snoopy saying
   "Civilization is Overrated!" . . . .$5.00 – 8.00

Row 3: Snoopy milk glass mugs
1. Snoopy . . . .$2.00 – 4.00
2. Snoopy and Woodstock dancing, on reverse: *At Times Life is
   Pure Joy!* . . . .$3.00 – 5.00
3. *Vote for the American Beagle,* #1 from a set of four numbered
   and dated mugs which share the same design as the
   Dolly Madison tumbler companion set . . . .$5.00 – 8.00
4. *Back the Beagle,* #3 in the set of four . . . .$5.00 – 8.00

Fast-Food Restaurants

PLATE 76

PLATE 77

Arby's

Plate 76
Row 1: Arby's Stained Glass Carafe and Glasses
This set was sold at the restaurants in the late 1970s. The glasses come in both 5" & 6" sizes.
5" & 6" glasses . . . .$2.00 – 4.00 ea.
Carafe . . . .$6.00 – 8.00

Row 2: Arby's Bicentennial Series, set of 10 (1976)
This set of ten glasses issued in the mid-1970s is quite popular with collectors. It features a number of different cartoon characters by Walter Lantz, P.A.T. Ward, Leonardo TTV, and Harvey Cartoons. The promotion was coordinated by the same advertising group that did the Pepsi-Cola glass promotions in the 1970s. These Brockway glasses come in both 5" (12 oz.) and 6" (16 oz.) versions. The 5" version also comes with and without the Arby's logo. The version without the logo could be purchased at department stores and has some slight color variations. These glasses, in general, experienced quality control problems. The registration of the colors on many examples is poor. Truly mint examples that retain all their original gloss and are correctly registered are unusual. It seems that finding a 6" version of Casper and Nightmare's Midnight Ride with excellent registration is close to impossible! The 6" variety, in general, is harder to find, while both 5" versions are encountered with similar frequency. (Continued in plate 77.)

	5" with or without logo	**6"**
1. Bullwinkle crossing the Delaware	$10.00 – 12.00	$15.00 – 18.00
2. Bullwinkle to the defense	$10.00 – 12.00	$15.00 – 18.00
3. Casper and Nightmare's midnight ride	$10.00 – 12.00	$15.00 – 20.00
4. Dudley Takes tea at sea	$10.00 – 12.00	$15.00 – 18.00
5. George by Woody	$10.00 – 12.00	$15.00 – 18.00

Plate 77
Row 1: Arby's Bicentennial Series, set of 10 (1976), continued

1. *Hot Stuff Makes it Hot for the Redcoats*	$10.00 – 12.00	$15.00 – 18.00
2. *Never Fear — Underdog is Here*	$10.00 – 12.00	$15.00 – 18.00
3. *Rocky in the Dawn's Early Light*	$10.00 – 12.00	$15.00 – 18.00
4. *Underdog Saves the Bell*	$10.00 – 12.00	$15.00 – 18.00
5. *Woody has the Spirit*	$10.00 – 12.00	$15.00 – 18.00

Row 2: Arby's Actors Series, set of six (1979)
Issued in 1979, this set of smoke-colored glasses features some of the greatest actors and actresses of all time. The black paint in the center oval is highlighted by a silver band. The silver is the first portion that wears off as the glass is washed and used. Mint examples should retain all the original silver color. The reverse of the glass shows a film slate, and each of the different glasses is numbered ("Take 1 of 6," "Take 2 of 6," etc.).
1. Charlie Chaplin, Take: 1 of 6, The Gold Rush, 1925 . .$5.00 – 7.00
2. Abbott & Costello, Take: 2 of 6, In the Foreign Legion, 1949 . . . .$5.00 – 7.00
3. Laurel & Hardy, Take: 3 of 6, *Wrong Again*, 1929 . . .$5.00 – 7.00
4. Mae West, Take: 4 of 6, *I'm No Angel*, 1933 . . . . .$5.00 – 7.00
5. Spanky, Alfalfa, Stymie, Porky, Dickey, and Pete the Pup; Take: 5 of 6, *The Little Rascals*, 1920s . . .$5.00 – 7.00
6. W.C. Fields, Take: 6 of 6, *My Little Chickadee*, 1940 . .$5.00 – 7.00

PLATE 78

PLATE 79

Arby's, continued

Arby's Currier and Ives (1978, 1981)

These are two of the three (actually four — see note below) sets of Brockway Currier and Ives rocks glasses distributed by Arby's restaurants from the mid 1970s to the early 1980s. The third set, which is not shown here, depicts the same scenes as Row 2 but is unnumbered and dated 1981 instead of 1978. All three sets have good quality reproductions of the prints. The value for all three commonly encountered sets is approximately the same.

Row 1: Arby's Currier and Ives Collector Series, set of four (undated; however, we have solid evidence that this set was produced and distributed in 1975 – 1976)
1. The Sleigh Race . . . .$3.00 – 5.00
2. American Homestead in Winter . . . .$3.00 – 5.00
3. Christmas Snow . . . .$3.00 – 5.00
4. Winter in the Country — Getting Ice . . . .$3.00 – 5.00

Row 2: Arby's Currier and Ives Collector Series, numbered set of four (1978)
1. Winter Pastime, 2 of 4 . . . .$3.00 – 5.00
2. The Road in Winter, 1 of 4 . . . .$3.00 – 5.00
3. Frozen Up, 4 of 4 . . . .$3.00 – 5.00
4. American Farm in Winter, 3 of 4 . . . .$3.00 – 5.00

(Note: We recently discovered a fourth, undated set of four Arby's Currier and Ives rocks glasses. This is the only set we know of, so we must assume that it is rare and had very limited production/distribution. The four prints shown in this undated, unnumbered set are: *Railroad Scene — Snowbound, Currier and Ives*; *Winter Sports — Fishing, Currier and Ives*; *American Farm Scene, Currier and Ives*; and *Winter Evening, Currier and Ives*. The overall design of this set suggests a 1974 – 1975 date. We can't comment on value until more of these glasses appear and change hands.)

Arby's, continued

Row 1: Arby's Gary Patterson Thought Factory Collector Series
This 1982 set of four glasses features satiric cartoon potshots at skiers, golfers, pool players, and tennis players by cartoonist Gary Patterson.
1. Luck Out (Tennis) . . . .$2.00 – 4.00
2. Dedication (Golf) . . . .$2.00 – 4.00
3. Pool Shark (Pool) . . . .$2.00 – 4.00
4. First Flake (Skiing) . . . .$2.00 – 4.00

Row 2: Arby's B.C. Ice Age Collector Series, set of six (1981)
Issued in 1981, this set of six glasses features the B.C. characters of cartoonist Johnny Hart in characteristic poses or humorous activities. These tankard-shaped glasses have an unusual rippled effect that was specially created for this promotion. Other non-Arby's Johnny Hart B.C. glassware can be found including: three sizes of tumblers, three pitchers, two cookie jars and two bowls (none of these items was sponsored by Arby's).
1. BC . . . .$3.00 – 5.00
2. Grog . . . .$3.00 – 5.00
3. Wiley . . . .$3.00 – 5.00
4. Anteater . . . .$3.00 – 5.00
5. Thor . . . .$3.00 – 5.00
6. Fat Broad . . . .$3.00 – 5.00
Not pictured: Pitchers, $10.00 – 20.00; unsponsored glasses, $2.00 – 4.00; cookie jars, $25.00 – 40.00; large bowl, $4.00 – 6.00; small bowl, $2.00 – 4.00

Row 3: Arby's Wizard of Id Collector Series, ©Field Enterprises, Inc., set of six (1983)
A set of six tankard-shaped, rippled glasses very similar to the 1981 Ice Age Collector Series. The glasses in this series are intensely rippled, and as a result they are quite fascinating and eye-catching. This set was not as widely distributed as the Ice Age set and therefore is much more difficult to complete.
1. Larsen E. Pettifogger . . . .$7.00 – 10.00
2. King . . . .$7.00 – 10.00
3. Sir Rodney . . . .$7.00 – 10.00
4. Bung . . . .$7.00 – 10.00
5. Spook . . . .$7.00 – 10.00
6. Wizard . . . .$7.00 – 10.00

PLATE 80

PLATE 81

Burger Chef

Row 1: Burger Chef Presidents and Patriots, set of six (1975)
Each glass in this set has a president's or patriot's likeness on the front with a brief biographical sketch below it. On the reverse is a humorous exchange between Burger Chef and Jeff, which makes reference to the president or patriot. The fronts and reverses are shown.
1. George Washington . . . .$3.00 – 5.00
2. Abraham Lincoln . . . .$3.00 – 5.00
3. John Kennedy . . . .$3.00 – 5.00

Row 2: Burger Chef Presidents and Patriots, continued
1. Benjamin Franklin . . . .$3.00 – 5.00
2. Thomas Jefferson . . . .$3.00 – 5.00
3. Paul Revere . . . .$3.00 – 5.00

Rows 1 and 2: reverse of Plate 80

Row 3: Burger Chef Endangered Species Collector's Series, set of four (1978)
This set of four is not only beautiful but deserves our respect because it is probably the first example of fast-food glasses being used to educate the public and to focus attention on an environmental issue of great importance. The front of each glass features an endangered animal, and the reverse has at the top the words "Endangered Species, 1978 Collector's Series" followed by both the Latin and common names of the animal, a paragraph of information on the animal from the World Wildlife Fund, and the Burger Chef logo at the very bottom. It is thought that the Giant Panda glass is the hardest to find. This set can also be found with a Dunkin' Donuts logo; these glasses are much harder to find than the Burger Chef versions, and they command significantly higher prices.
1. Tiger . . . .$5.00 – 7.00
2. Orang-Utan . . . .$5.00 – 7.00
3. Giant Panda . . . .$7.00 – 9.00
4. Bald Eagle . . . .$5.00 – 7.00

PLATE 82

PLATE 83

Burger Chef, continued

Row 1: Burger Chef and Jeff

Burger Chef and Jeff were the early mascots of the Burger Chef chain. The two glasses in Row 1 feature these two characters and are relatively difficult to find. Glass #2 below may be one of Burger Chef's earliest promotional glasses because of its reference to "glassification." The full text reads: "Just think Jeff, now we're glassified!" "Leapin' liquids Burger Chef, I hope everybody wants one!" The gist of this message has led some collectors to conclude that this was a glass given only to managers to help the promotion of another glass, perhaps the Burger Chef and Jeff glass above. We don't think so. We believe this glass was a regular over-the-counter promotional glass.

1. Burger Chef and Jeff (1975) . . . .$8.00 – 10.00
2. Burger Chef and Jeff, . . . *Now we're glassified!* . .$15.00 – 25.00

Row 2: Burger Chef Friendly Monster, set of six, (1977)

In 1977 Burger Chef introduced and distributed a set of glasses with Friendly Monster characters in humorous interaction with Burger Chef and Jeff. These glasses had very limited distribution and are difficult to locate. The set is hard to complete, but its attractiveness makes the effort worthwhile.

1. *Burger Chef & Jeff Go Trail Riding* . . . .$25.00 – 35.00
2. *Burgerilla Falls Head Over Heals in Love* . . . . .$25.00 – 35.00
3. *Burgerini's Rabbit Hops Away* . . . .$25.00 – 35.00
4. *Crankenburger Scores a Touchdown* . . . .$25.00 – 35.00
5. *Fangburger Gets a Scare!* . . . .$25.00 – 35.00
6. *Werewolf Goes Skate Boarding* . . . .$25.00 – 35.00

Burger King

Row 1: Mark Twain Country Series (1985)

A set of four glasses commemorating Mark Twain and the novels he wrote in Elmira, New York. Each glass has a colorful scene on the front, and they originally came in a cardboard Burger King carrying case with *Mark Twain Festival Summer 1985* printed in black. On the reverse of each glass is a brief explanation of the front illustration, and near the bottom of each glass in black are the words, *Mark Twain Country, Series 1985*. This Libbey set was definitely a special limited regional promotion.

1. Mark Twain . . . .$8.00 – 10.00
2. Tom Sawyer . . . .$8.00 – 10.00
3. Huck Finn . . . .$8.00 – 10.00
4. Octagonal Study . . . .$8.00 – 10.00
   (cardboard carrier $10.00 – 15.00)

Row 2: 1776 – 1976 Have it Your Way Collector's Series, set of four (1976)

A set of four pedestal glasses featuring well-known symbols of the American Revolution. The Three Patriots Glass, inspired by Archibald Willard's well-known 1870s painting, *The Spirit of '76*, is shown reversed.

1. Three Patriots . . . .$4.00 – 6.00
2. Crossed Flags . . . .$4.00 – 6.00
3. Liberty Bell . . . .$4.00 – 6.00
4. Eagle & Shield . . . .$4.00 – 6.00

Row 3: 1979 Burger King Corporation Collectors Series, set of five

This set of five round-bottom glasses introduces Burger King's answer to McDonald's promotional characters. Each glass features characters in a sequence of three actions and clever Burger King product-related rhymes. The appeal of these characters was relatively brief.

1. Marvelous Magical Burger King . . . .$4.00 – 6.00
2. Duke of Doubt . . . .$4.00 – 6.00
3. Burger Thing . . . .$4.00 – 6.00
4. Sir Shake-A-Lot . . . .$4.00 – 6.00
5. Wizard of Fries . . . .$4.00 – 6.00

PLATE 84

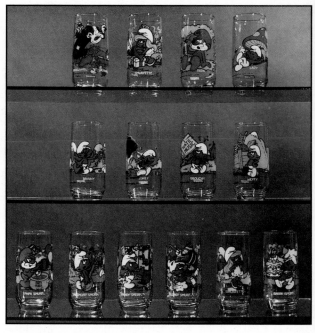

PLATE 86

Burger King, continued
Plate 84
Row 1: Burger King
1. Mardi Gras mug (1988) . . . .$8.00 – 10.00
2. Mardi Gras mug (1989) . . . .$8.00 – 10.00
3. *Put a Smile in Your Tummy* . . . .$8.00 – 10.00
4. Puerto Rico . . . .$10.00 – 15.00
5. Stemware . . . .$8.00 – 10.00
6. Londonderry, New Hampshire, Grand Opening . .$25.00 – 30.00

Row 2: 1978 Burger King characters, set of four, and two Burger King Coca-Cola Collegiate Crest glasses
The character set was the forerunner of the 1979 set above. It was distributed less widely and is more difficult to find. There are probably well over two hundred Coca-Cola Collegiate Crest glasses, but these are the only two we know of that go one step further to include the Burger King logo.
1. Onion Rings . . . .$12.00 – 15.00
2. French Fries . . . .$12.00 – 15.00
3. Milk Shakes . . . .$12.00 – 15.00
4. Hamburgers . . . .$12.00 – 15.00
5. Memphis State University Tigers . . . .$15.00 – 20.00
6. University of New Hampshire . . . .$15.00 – 20.00

Plate 85
Burger King: Where Kids Are King pitcher . . . .$35.00 – 40.00
Not pictured: Matching glasses . . . .$3.00 – 5.00

PLATE 85

Hardee's

Row 1: 1982 Smurfs
A set of eight round-bottom glasses featuring the popular Smurf cartoon characters. Although these glasses do not carry the Hardee's logo, they were distributed by Hardee's. The scenes on these glasses are essentially action scenes with Smurfs engaged in various characteristic activities.
1. Gargamel/Azrael . . . .$2.00 – 4.00
2. Smurfette . . . .$2.00 – 4.00
3. Papa . . . .$2.00 – 4.00
4. Lazy . . . .$2.00 – 4.00

Row 2: 1982 Smurfs, continued
1. Brainy . . . .$2.00 – 4.00
2. Jokey . . . .$2.00 – 4.00
3. Grouchy . . . .$2.00 – 4.00
4. Hefty . . . .$2.00 – 4.00

Row 3: 1983 Smurfs, set of six
This set was a follow-up to the 1982 issue, but this time there were only six glasses. This set seems more colorful, and the action is more complex. The glasses can be easily distinguished from the 1982 set because the word "Smurf" appears after each character's name (with the exception of Smurfette).
1. Papa Smurf . . . .$2.00 – 4.00
2. Harmony Smurf . . . .$2.00 – 4.00
3. Handy Smurf . . . .$2.00 – 4.00
4. Clumsy Smurf . . . .$2.00 – 4.00
5. Smurfette . . . .$2.00 – 4.00
6. Baker Smurf . . . .$2.00 – 4.00

PLATE 87

PLATE 88

McDonald's

Hardee's, continued

Row 1: The Chipmunks, set of four (1985)
A set of four glasses featuring the three original Chipmunks — Alvin, Theodore, and Simon — and the more recent Chipettes. These musical creatures are represented in ovals on the fronts of the glasses, and their names appear underlined in black. On the reverse, these harmonious rodents are pictured in musical action scene roles. These were distributed by Hardee's although they do not bear the Hardee's logo.

1. Chipettes . . . .$2.00 – 4.00
2. Theodore . . . .$2.00 – 4.00
3. Alvin   . . . .$2.00 – 4.00
4. Simon . . . .$2.00 – 4.00

H. Salt

Row 2: H. Salt Historic Ships
A set of six Brockway tumblers commemorating some of the world's most successful ship designs. The front of each glass features a vessel in color, and the reverse has a brief description of the ship type, as well as reference to a specific example of it. These are a mid to late 1970s issue that are not commonly found.

1. Chinese Lorcha . . . .$7.00 – 10.00
2. The Frigate . . . .$7.00 – 10.00
3. James Watt . . . .$7.00 – 10.00

Row 3: H. Salt Historic Ships, continued

1. The Prince Royal — 1610 . . . .$7.00 – 10.00
2. The Flying Cloud . . . .$7.00 – 10.00
3. The Caravel *Nina* . . . .$7.00 – 10.00

Row 1: Garfield mugs, set of four (1987)
A set of four undated mugs featuring Jim Davis's Garfield character. On each mug, Garfield is depicted in an action scene with one or more other characters, and there is a white bubble containing one of his philosophical sayings. The copyright dates say 1978, but the glasses were distributed nationally in 1987. These mugs are plentiful and inexpensive.

1. *I'm not one who rises to the occasion* . . . .$1.00 – 3.00
2. *Use your friends wisely* . . . .$1.00 – 3.00
3. *It's not a pretty life but somebody has to live it* . . .$1.00 – 3.00
4. *I'm easy to get along with when things go my way* . . .$1.00 – 3.00

Row 2: Garfield checkerboard mugs, set of four (1987)
This set of undated mugs, which has been dubbed the "checkerboard" set because of the colored grid backgrounds, received a much smaller distribution than the other set of Garfield mugs (above). They bear a 1978 copyright date and are definitely more regional and uncommon. Each mug has two related sayings by Garfield. The Ronald McDonald figure in the center is a Happy Meal premium.

1. *The early cat gets the hotcake/This is the only alarm clock I*
   need to set . . . .$8.00 – 10.00
2. *Whoever invented evenings probably invented teddy bears*
   too/I'd like mornings better if they started later . .$8.00 – 10.00
3. *I never met a dinner I didn't like/And what will you fellas have*
   for breakfast? . . . .$8.00 – 10.00
4. *I've never seen a sunrise…I'm waiting for the movie/Such a*
   beautiful sunset…and me without a horse . . . . . .$8.00 – 10.00

Row 3: Garfield tumblers, set of four (1987 – 1988?)
This set of undated glasses was never sold through the restaurants to our knowledge. They do have the McDonald's logo and were available briefly through the outlet stores. This may have been a rejected design in favor of the mugs. We assume that these tumblers were made available at about the same time as the Garfield mugs — 1987 – 1988.

1. Poetry in Motion . . . .$8.00 – 10.00
2. Are we having fun yet? . . . .$8.00 – 10.00
3. Just me and the road . . . .$8.00 – 10.00
4. Home, James . . . .$8.00 – 10.00

PLATE 89

PLATE 90

McDonald's, continued

Row 1: Olympic mugs, set of four (1984)
A set of four dated glass mugs commemorating the 1984 Olympic Games. With the handle on the right, the glasses are identical from the front. The side shown here features four cubes depicting individual Olympic sports in four colors. These mugs are normally described by the color of the cube.
1. White: Baseball, Volleyball, Basketball, Soccer . . .$5.00 – 7.00
2. Yellow: Weightlifting, Wrestling, Track, Archery . .$5.00 – 7.00
3. Red: Steeplechase, Fencing, Ice Skating, Cycling . .$5.00 – 7.00
4. Blue: Sailing, Kayaking, Sculling, Swimming . . . . .$5.00 – 7.00

Row 2: Coffee mug set
This is a set of four ceramic mugs with office motifs and the standard jokes about how tough it is to function on the job early in the morning, especially before that first cup of coffee. These were made in Japan and distributed at the restaurants in the mid-1980s.
1. a.m. . . . .$3.00 – 5.00
2. Warning: First Cup . . . .$3.00 – 5.00
3. Leave a Note . . . .$3.00 – 5.00
4. Gone for the morning! . . . .$3.00 – 5.00

Row 3: Smoked glass mugs
This is a set of four embossed mugs with the McDonaldland characters in action. These mugs are undated, but were probably issued in 1977. Each character's name is embossed at the bottom of the mug. The front and back designs are identical and a large embossed McDonald's logo appears on the bottom of each mug. These are unusual limited issues that were probably part of a regional promotion.
1. Ronald McDonald throwing a football . . . .$8.00 – 10.00
2. Hamburglar as a hockey goalie . . . .$8.00 – 10.00
3. Grimace shooting a basketball . . . .$8.00 – 10.00
4. Captain Crook hitting a baseball . . . .$8.00 – 10.00

McDonald's, continued

Row 1: 1982 Knoxville World's Fair
The front and reverse of this flare glass commemorating the World's Fair are shown. Coca-Cola co-sponsored this widely distributed issue.
1. front . . . .$3.00 – 5.00
2. (reverse)

Row 2: McVote, set of three (1986)
This is a set of three glasses which have as their theme a mock election, urging McDonald's patrons to vote for the finest McDonald's hamburger. These barrel-shaped glasses are colorful and have wraparound campaign action. This series was distributed in the Northeast and as a result they are unusual in other parts of the country. Northeasterners have been keeping collectors supplied with them though, and prices are still relatively inexpensive. We have found two glasses from this set with significant color differences, leading us to believe that another set of darker colors was tried and then abandoned.
1. Big Mac . . . .$6.00 – 8.00
2. Quarter Pounder . . . .$6.00 – 8.00
3. McD.L.T. . . . .$6.00 – 8.00

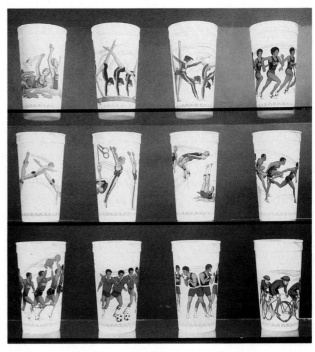

PLATE 91

Plates 91 & 92 — McDonald's Olympics, LA Plastics. $1.00 – $2.00

PLATE 92 (reverse of Plate 91) **PLATE 93**

McDonald's, continued
Plate 93
Row 1: McDonald's Canadian Character, set of four
This set of four undated glasses was co-sponsored by Coca-Cola. It came out in the late 80s, early 90s. Collectors will notice that the character line-up is odd: no Captain Crook, Mayor McCheese, or Big Mac. The easiest way to differentiate Canadian McDonald's glasses from U.S. McDonald's glasses is to look at the arches logo. The Canadian sets have a small maple leaf under the logo. This set is no exception. It was only distributed in Canada and is quite colorful. This is the only set that you will find with the Birdie character featured.
1. Ronald McDonald and rainbow . . . .$5.00 – 7.00
2. Hamburglar at sunrise with farm background . . . . .$5.00 – 7.00
3. Birdie the Early Bird . . . .$5.00 – 7.00
4. Grimace playing baseball . . . .$5.00 – 7.00

Row 2: *The Great Muppet Caper*, set of four (1981)
The Great Muppet Caper movie provided the inspiration for this set of four glasses featuring Jim Henson's Muppet characters. Complex wraparound action characterizes each glass. These glasses are plentiful due to successful national distribution. A Canadian version of this set exists too (look for the small maple leaf under the logo). The Canadian glasses bring about 50% more than the American version. Also be on the lookout for the manager's version of this glass. Prior to the promotion, the managers at each McDonald's restaurant were

sent a glass that asked them to commit to the program. These glasses have sold for over $250.00 (see Plate 79: Row 1).
1. Miss Piggy . . . .$2.00 – 4.00
2. Kermit . . . .$2.00 – 4.00
3. Kermit, Fozzie Bear, The Great Gonzo . . . .$2.00 – 4.00
4. Happiness Hotel . . . .$2.00 – 4.00

Row 3: Camp Snoopy, set of five (1983)
A set of five glasses featuring the Peanuts gang. This must have been the most successful of all the McDonald's glass promotions. It was nationally distributed, and these glasses can be found at almost any flea market. Don't pay more than a dollar for any of them, and don't let naive fleamarketers tell you that the 1965 copyright date means they were issued in the 1960s. This set also has a manager's glass; the characters on this glass say "Good Grief McDonald's Camp Snoopy glasses are coming" and "Hurry! Commit by March 15, 1983." The glass looks very similar to the rest of the set and has sold for over $250.00 (see Plate 97: Row 1).
1. *There's No Excuse For Not Being Properly Prepared* . .$1.00 – 2.00
2. *Rats! Why Is Having Fun Always So Much Work?* .$1.00 – 2.00
3. *Civilization is Overrated!* . . . .$1.00 – 2.00
4. *Morning People Are Hard To Love* . . . .$1.00 – 2.00
5. *The Struggle For Security Is No Picnic!* . . . .$1.00 – 2.00

PLATE 94

McDonald's, continued

Row 1: McDonald's Hawaii

A set of four heavy smoke-tinted, etched rocks glasses celebrating Hawaii's culture, occupations, and attractions. These glasses are fairly difficult to find and were available from McDonald's stores in Hawaii during the mid to late 1980s. They came in a gift box describing them as *Hawaiians And Their Sea Glassware/A Souvenir From Hawaii*.

1. Sunset with Catamaran and Outrigger . . . .$6.00 – 8.00
2. Fishermen Bringing in Their Nets . . . .$6.00 – 8.00
3. Surfers . . . .$6.00 – 8.00
4. Outrigger Races . . . .$6.00 – 8.00

Row 2: Miscellaneous McDonald's mugs and tumblers

1. Good Morning milk glass mug . . . .$1.00 – 2.00
   A common mug promotion from the late 1970s. Some Good Morning mugs had the name of a city on them (*Good Morning, Pittsburgh*) or the name of a country (*Good Morning, Canada*). These mugs are worth considerably more than those without placenames.
2. Tall Milk Glass Mug . . . .$2.00 – 4.00
   A more unusual version or the morning mug promotion.
3. *The Denim Collection from McDonald's* . . . .$5.00 – 7.00
   This glass, co-sponsored by Coca-Cola, was a regional promotion featuring a denim jeans look.
4. All-American Team mug. . . . .$6.00 – 8.00
   An in-house promotion for employees.
5. Arches and Flowers . . . .$2.00 – 4.00
   A relatively common juice glass promotion.

Row 3: Two Types of McDonald's Collectors Series glasses

1. Ronald McDonald with red lettering . . . .$4.00 – 6.00
   This is a variation of the more usual Ronald McDonald Collector Series glass.
2, 3 & 4. 12 oz. Brockway Collector Series, set of six
   This set of six thick 5⅛" Brockway glasses may have been the first set of promotional glasses that McDonald's produced. They were issued in 1975 or 1976, and they pre-date the more common Collector Series. At the time of this promotion, there was some concern that the paint on the images might have contained some lead. This may account for their relatively short-lived presence and the subsequent issuing of the second Collectors Series set.
2. Ronald McDonald . . . .$10.00 – 14.00
3. Captain Crook . . . .$10.00 – 14.00
4. Grimace . . . .$10.00 – 14.00
Not pictured:
Big Mac, Hamburglar, Mayor McCheese . . . . .$10.00 – 14.00 ea.
5. Grimace — blue . . . .$3.00 – 5.00
   A color variation of the purple Grimace in the Collector Series. The finish on this glass is rough and dull, and the design is clearly different from the standard Grimace glass (see Plate 95: Row 1, #2, page 61).

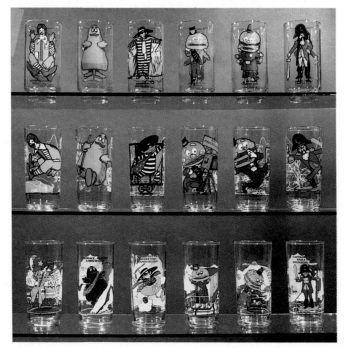

PLATE 95

PLATE 96

McDonald's, continued
Row 1: Collector Series
A set of six undated glasses featuring the popular McDonaldland characters. These glasses were widely distributed in the mid-70s (probably 1976 – 1977) and are readily available. Two variations, noted above, probably occurred because of the heavy demand for these glasses. Since they were not all produced at one location, variations like these were unavoidable.
1. Ronald McDonald . . . .$2.00 – 4.00
2. Grimace . . . .$2.00 – 4.00
3. Hamburglar . . . .$2.00 – 4.00
4. Mayor McCheese . . . .$2.00 – 4.00
5. Big Mac . . . .$2.00 – 4.00
6. Captain Crook . . . .$2.00 – 4.00

Row 2: McDonaldland Action Series, set of six (1977)
This set was the follow-up to the Collector Series, showing the characters in action. It can be found in two glass sizes. The more common set is 5⅝" tall, and the more unusual set (shown) is 6¼" high. The taller version brings about 25% more than the price shown.
1. Ronald McDonald . . . .$3.00 – 5.00
2. Grimace . . . .$3.00 – 5.00
3. Hamburglar . . . .$3.00 – 5.00
4. Mayor McCheese . . . .$3.00 – 5.00
5. Big Mac . . . .$3.00 – 5.00
6. Captain Crook . . . .$3.00 – 5.00

Row 3: McDonaldland Adventure Series, set of six (1980)
The third — and most sophisticated — set in the character trilogy. This set received sporadic distribution across the country and is the most difficult of the three to complete.
1. Ronald McDonald Saves the Falling Stars . . . .$10.00 – 12.00
2. Grimace Climbs A Mountain . . . .$10.00 – 12.00
3. Hamburglar Hooks the Hamburgers . . . .$10.00 – 12.00
4. Mayor McCheese Rides a Runaway Train . . . . . .$10.00 – 12.00
5. Big Mac Nets the Hamburglar . . . .$10.00 – 12.00
6. Captain Crook Sails the Bounding Main . . . . . .$10.00 – 12.00

McDonald's, continued
Row 1: Toledo Zoo Panda Mugs, set of three (1988) and Baylor University
This set of three Libbey mugs was available at the Toledo, Ohio, McDonald's restaurants for a limited time. The back of each mug has interesting scientific information about pandas.
1. Pandas . . . .$8.00 – 10.00
2. Nan-Nan . . . .$8.00 – 10.00
3. Le-Le . . . .$8.00 – 10.00
4. Baylor University, Waco, Texas — mascot . . . .$12.00 – 15.00

Row 2: McDonald's Classic 50s, (1993,) set of four, and University of Texas Longhorns
The McDonald's classic 50s glasses give the impression of being original fountain glasses, but only the designs are old; they were distributed in the greater Akron, Ohio, area during the summer of 1993 by a small group (about 20) of McDonald's franchises.
1. Speedy on the arches with 15¢ sign . . . .$3.00 – 5.00
2. Speedy holding "I'm Speedy" sign . . . .$3.00 – 5.00
3. The Original Shake, Burger & Fries . . . .$3.00 – 5.00
4. McDonald's Restaurant Circa 1957 . . . .$3.00 – 5.00
5. Hook'em Horns — Univ. of Texas . . . .$12.00 – 15.00

PLATE 97

PLATE 98

McDonald's, continued

Row 1: McDonald's managers' glasses

The three glasses in this row were all pre-promotion distributions to managers at McDonald's restaurants. They were sent as incentives or reminders for managers to sign on for upcoming glass promotions. These glasses are in very limited supply (one glass per McDonald's restaurant?) and are highly sought by McDonald's and other glass collectors. The Olympic Eagle glass in Row 1 may have paved the way for the 1984 Olympic mugs.

1. Sam the Olympic Eagle glasses (1984) . . . . . .$200.00 – 300.00
2. *Good Grief! McDonald's Camp Snoopy Glasses Are Coming!* (1983) . . . .$200.00 – 300.00
3. *Extra! The Muppets Are Coming!* . . . .$200.00 – 300.00

Row 2: McDonald's Espana, set of four (1982)

This set of four colorful and busy glasses — co-sponsored by Coca-Cola and Naranjito — promoted the World Cup soccer games of 1982. The four glasses show the flags of all participating nations. It is believed that distribution was in Spain.

1. Fans on the bus going to games . . . .$15.00 – 20.00
2. Fans in the stands . . . .$15.00 – 20.00
3. Fans on the field . . . .$15.00 – 20.00
4. Players and fans celebrating . . . .$15.00 – 20.00

McDonald's, continued

Row 1: Miscellaneous foreign McDonald's

The first two items in this row are from a set of three Japanese McDonald's glasses. The original box is shown next to the glass. The Donald Duck glass has a hologram on it.

1. Mickey Mouse . . . .$50.00 – 60.00
2. Donald Duck . . . .$50.00 – 60.00
Not pictured: Alice in Wonderland
3. Cordial Glass, Paris, Jan. 27, 1984 . . . .$20.00 – 25.00
4. Australian, Pewter, 10th Anniversary . . . .$25.00 – 30.00

Row 2: Foreign McDonald's Mugs

1. Mug: Keys to quality with compliments, Pfungstadter Brewery, West Germany . . . .$25.00 – 30.00
2. Munchen, Germany, celebrating the opening of the 6,000th restaurant worldwide. November 29, 1980 . . . .$45.00 – 60.00
3. Japanese mug celebrating the 100th store opening in 1976 . . . .$65.00 – 80.00
4. Hamburglar mug, Phillipines . . . .$35.00 – 50.00

PLATE 99

PLATE 100

McDonald's Plastic Tumblers

Row 1: *Honey, I Shrunk the Kids* (1989)
A set of three plastic tumblers issued during the release of the Disney film.
1. Dog's nose . . . .$1.00 – 2.00
2. Bee . . . .$1.00 – 2.00
3. Magnifying glass . . . .$1.00 – 2.00

Row 2: *Roger Rabbit* (1988)
A set of three plastic tumblers issued during the release of the Disney film.
1. Man in black outfit . . . .$1.00 – 3.00
2. Man, woman, and car . . . .$1.00 – 3.00
3. Man driving car . . . .$1.00 – 3.00

McDonald's Plastic Tumblers, continued
Row 1: McDonald's plastic issues
1. Early Ronald McDonald cup . . . .$5.00 – 6.00

McDonald's Adventureland (1980)

Like many of the McDonald's sets, the 1980 Adventureland issue can be found in plastic. The plastic version is much harder to find than the glass, especially in fine condition.
2. Ronald McDonald saves the falling stars . . . .$4.00 – 7.00
3. Grimace climbs a mountain . . . .$4.00 – 7.00
4. Hamburglar hooks the hamburgers . . . .$4.00 – 7.00
5. McKids cup (Sears) . . . .$1.00 – 2.00
  This cup came with a clothing purchase at the Sears McKids department.

Row 2: Birthday cups . . . .$1.00 – 2.00 ea.
Plastic tumblers like these were standard at McDonald's kids' birthday parties.

Row 3: Action Series
These are the plastic versions of the popular 1977 Action Series. The tumblers came in both white and yellow.
1. Ronald McDonald . . . .$3.00 – 5.00
2. Grimace (white) . . . .$3.00 – 5.00
3. Grimace . . . .$3.00 – 5.00
4. Hamburglar . . . .$3.00 – 5.00
5. Hamburglar (white) . . . .$3.00 – 5.00
6. Captain Crook . . . .$3.00 – 5.00

PLATE 101

PLATE 102

Pizza Pete

Pizza Pete is (or was) a relatively small pizza franchise with locations in the Pacific Northwest and the Midwest. Its name recognition problem notwithstanding, it has the distinction of having produced some pretty unusual glasses. As far as we know, the two glasses in Row 1 are a set of 2. Dating them is a problem. We don't know of any other glasses shaped like these. Our guess is the mid 70s. These glasses — especially the orange one — can be found in the Pacific Northwest with not too much trouble, but the yellow and red one is not often encountered. The set of six we show in Row 2 is unnamed and undated, but it has a very high standing among collectors who prize the unusual. It can best be described as an insider's set, because this is a small franchise, and there's not much helpful information on the glasses to provide outside collectors with any meaningful context. We put the issue date between 1976 and 1978 because of the shape of the glasses which is identical to the 1976 Star Trek issue, the 1977 Happy Days issue, and the 1978 Star Trek issue. These glasses are not cheap, and they are hard to find in excellent condition. A complete set is difficult to assemble.

Row 1: Petesa Pete
1. *There's a Pete behind every Petesa*, yellow and red .$15.00 – 25.00
2. *There's a Pete behind every Petesa*, orange . . . .$10.00 – 15.00

Row 2: Petesa Pete Character, set of six
1. Boom Boom Mushroom . . . .$25.00 – 35.00
2. Charlie Cheezerella . . . .$20.00 – 30.00
3. Frankie Peperoni . . . .$20.00 – 30.00
4. Olive — *Name Me!* . . . .$25.00 – 35.00
5. Pizza Pete . . . .$25.00 – 35.00
6. Rosie Tomato . . . .$30.00 – 40.00

Miscellaneous Fast-Food Restaurants

Row 1: Gino's, A&W, and TG & Y
1. Gino's Pizza & Spaghetti House . . . .$1.00 – 2.00
2. A & W Root Beer Bear . . . .$2.00 – 4.00
Not pictured:
16 oz. Brockway version . . . .$5.00 – 7.00
Matching pitcher . . . .$25.00 – 35.00
3. TG & Y (1981) . . . .$1.00 – 2.00

Row 2: Big Boy Restaurants
1 & 5. Big Boy 50th Anniversary glass (1986) . . . . . .$5.00 – 7.00
  (Both sides of this anniversary tumbler are shown.)
2, 3, 4. Big Boy plastic cups . . . .$1.00 – 2.00

Row 3: Dairy Queen and Howard Johnson tumblers
1. Dairy Queen — Little Miss Dairy Queen . . . .$2.00 – 4.00
2 & 3. Howard Johnson water glasses . . . .$3.00 – 5.00
4. Dairy Queen menu items with filigree design (1989) . .$2.00 – 4.00

PLATE 103

PLATE 104

Plate 103
Miscellaneous Fast-Food Restaurants, continued
Row 1 & 2: Rax Restaurant Squeezees . . . .$1.00 – 2.00 ea. These plastic juice containers were premiums for kids from Rax Restaurants.

Row 3: Wendy's Restaurants
Wendy's is by no means a prolific sponsor of collectible glasses, but it is responsible for some memorable issues. Among them are the Clara Peller glasses shown below. Clara, who died recently at the age of 86, achieved cult status with her booming "Where's the beef?" mid-80s television commercials. Clara can also be found on mugs and a few other other glasses.
1. Clara Peller 5" glass: *Where's the Beef?* (1984) . . .$6.00 – 8.00
2. Clara Peller 6" glass: *Where's the Beef?* (1984) . .$8.00 – 10.00
3. Wendy's Freedom of Choice (1976) . . . .$5.00 – 7.00
4 & 5. Wendy's 1982 World's Fair . . . .$2.00 – 4.00
   This glass was issued by Wendy's to commemorate the 1982 World's Fair. Both sides of this relatively common glass are shown.

Wendy's Plastic Issues

Plate 104
Row 1: Sesame Street
1. Big Bird . . . .$1.00 – 2.00
2. Bert & Ernie . . . .$1.00 – 2.00
3. Super Grover . . . .$1.00 – 2.00
4. Oscar the Grouch . . . .$1.00 – 2.00

Row 2: The Goodstuff Gang and The World of Teddy Ruxpin
1 – 3. The Good Stuff Gang . . . .$1.00 – 2.00 ea.
4 – 5. Teddy Ruxpin . . . .$1.00 – 2.00 ea.

Row 3: Disney Gummi Bears and Willow Magic Cup Series
1 – 2. Gummi Bears . . . .$1.00 – 2.00 ea.
3 – 5. Willow Magic Cups . . . .$1.00 – 2.00 ea.

Wylers

Plate 105 (right)
Row 1: Family Circus color cups
1. Jeffy . . . .$1.00 – 2.00
2. Dolly . . . .$1.00 – 2.00

Row 2: Family Circus
1. Green . . . .$1.00 – 2.00
2. Red . . . .$1.00 – 2.00
3. Blue . . . .$1.00 – 2.00
4. Purple . . . .$1.00 – 2.00

Row 3: Family Circus — full color
1. *Mommy Why...* . . . .$1.00 – 2.00
2. *That's my ball...* . . . .$1.00 – 2.00
3. *Do I hafta?* . . . .$1.00 – 2.00

PLATE 105

Food Containers

PLATE 106

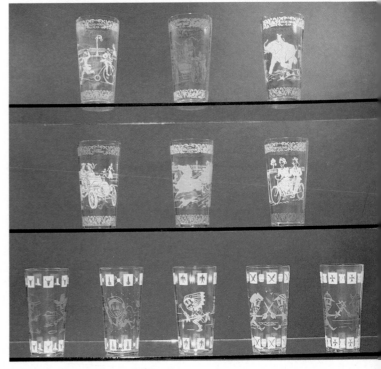

PLATE 107

Armour Peanut Butter Transportation Series

These tumblers were distributed in the early 50s as containers for the company's peanut butter. There are eight in each set, and they come in two lettering colors. Row 1 shows a set with brown lettering, and Row 2 shows a set with black lettering.

Row 1: Armour Peanut Butter Transportation Series, brown lettering
1. The Covered Wagon . . . .$3.00 – 5.00
2. The Pony Express . . . .$3.00 – 5.00

Row 2: Armour Peanut Butter Transportation Series, black lettering
1. The Stagecoach . . . .$3.00 – 5.00
2. The Surrey . . . .$3.00 – 5.00
3. The Automobile . . . .$3.00 – 5.00
Not pictured:
The Hansom Cab . . . .$3.00 – 5.00
The Riverboat . . . .$3.00 – 5.00
The Locomotive . . . .$3.00 – 5.00

Row 3: Native set
These colorful glasses feature gorillas and African natives in humorous activities. We are not sure of their date, and we don't know how many different glasses there are. It does seem obvious, however, that they pre-date our more enlightened views on African culture.
1. Ape dancing . . . .$5.00 – 10.00
2. Ape with broom . . . .$5.00 – 10.00
3. Native dancing . . . .$5.00 – 10.00

Jewel Tea Jelly

Row 1: Jewel Tea Old Time Series
These two sets were packaged with jelly in the 50s for Jewel Tea as well as other manufacturers. The set in Row 3 only has five glasses and also comes in a 5" version.
1. Rush Hour . . . .$2.00 – 4.00
2. Show Boat . . . .$2.00 – 4.00
3. Circus Parade . . . .$2.00 – 4.00

Row 2: Jewel Tea Old Time Series, continued
1. Sunday Afternoon . . . .$2.00 – 4.00
2. Old Times . . . .$2.00 – 4.00
3. Bicycling . . . .$2.00 – 4.00

Row 3: National Tea Company, Fantasy Glasses, set of five
1. Cowboys . . . .$3.00 – 5.00
2. Spacemen . . . .$3.00 – 5.00
3. Indians . . . .$3.00 – 5.00
4. Pirates . . . .$3.00 – 5.00
5. Vikings . . . .$3.00 – 5.00

Big Top Peanut Butter

During the 1950s, Big Top Peanut Butter used a variety of designs and themes to package their peanut butter. Each glass shown below has a song with notes and lyrics on the reverse. The front shows a picture which complements the song. The next three pages show some of the tumblers produced. The most common of these sets is the Old Time Songs, but also available were nursery rhymes, states, college fight songs, and cities. These can also be found in mugs and shot glasses with carafes.

Plate 108: Rows 1 and 2: Nursery Rhymes . . . .$3.00 – 5.00

Plate 109: Rows 1, 2, and 3: Old Time Songs . . . . . .$2.00 – 4.00

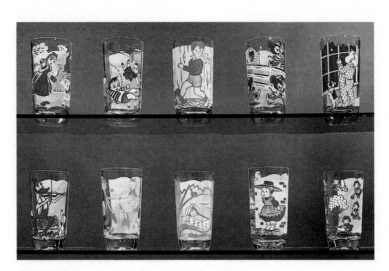

PLATE 108

PLATE 109

Big Top Peanut Butter, continued
Plates 110, 111, 112, and 113: State Songs . . . .$2.00 – 4.00

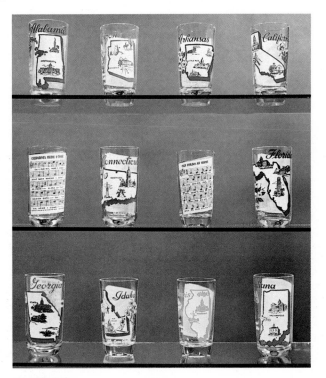

PLATE 110

PLATE 111

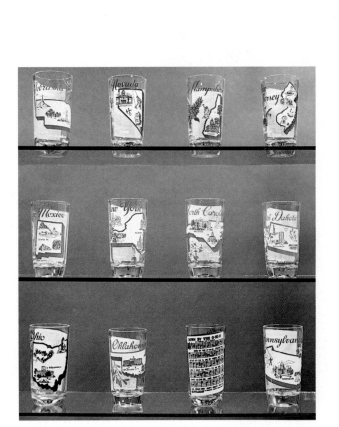

PLATE 112

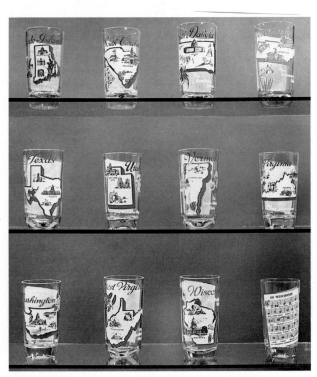

PLATE 113

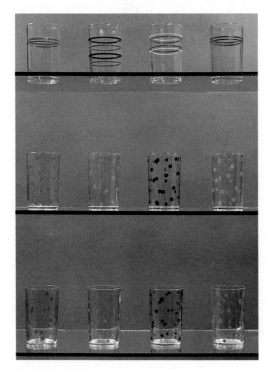

PLATE 114

PLATE 115

Kraft Swanky Swigs

These small glasses were food containers used over a number of years by Kraft and a few other food companies. The number of glasses and designs is practically countless, and collectors will readily find them at flea markets, yard sales, and antique malls.

Row 1: Bands (1933)
1. Red and black hairline . . . .$2.00 – 4.00
2. Black, red, black, red . . . .$2.00 – 4.00
3. White, blue, blue, white . . . .$2.00 – 4.00
4. Blue, blue . . . .$2.00 – 4.00

Row 2: Circles (1934)
1. Blue . . . .$3.00 – 5.00
2. Green . . . .$3.00 – 5.00
3. Black . . . .$3.00 – 5.00
4. Red . . . .$3.00 – 5.00

Row 3: Stars (1935)
1. Blue . . . .$3.00 – 5.00
2. Green . . . .$3.00 – 5.00
3. Black . . . .$3.00 – 5.00
4. Red . . . .$3.00 – 5.00

Kraft Swanky Swigs, continued
Row 1: Checkerboard (1936)
1. White/blue . . . .$15.00 – 20.00
2. White/green . . . .$15.00 – 20.00
3. White/red . . . .$15.00 – 20.00

Row 2: Texas Centennial (1936)
1. Blue . . . .$8.00 – 10.00
2. Black . . . .$8.00 – 10.00
3. Green . . . .$8.00 – 10.00
Sailboat No. 2 (1936) . . . .$8.00 – 10.00
4. Blue . . . .$8.00 – 10.00
5. Green . . . .$8.00 – 10.00
6. Red . . . .$8.00 – 10.00

Row 3: Tulips (1937) and Bachelor's Button (1955)
1. Blue Tulips . . . .$3.00 – 6.00
2. Green Tulips . . . .$3.00 – 6.00
3. Bachelor's Button . . . .$2.00 – 4.00
4. Black Tulips . . . .$3.00 – 6.00
5. Red Tulips . . . .$3.00 – 6.00

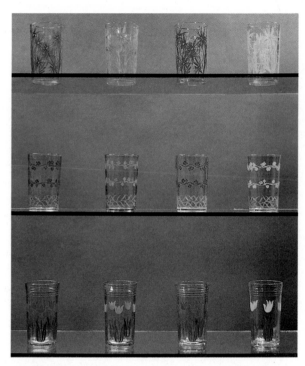

PLATE 117

PLATE 116

Kraft Swanky Swigs, continued
Row 1: Carnival (1939)
These glasses have opaque fired-on color.
1. Blue . . . .$4.00 – 6.00
2. Pale green . . . .$4.00 – 6.00
3. Orange . . . .$4.00 – 6.00
4. Yellow . . . .$4.00 – 6.00

Row 2: Posy Patterns (1941)
The flowers are all one color, and the leaves are green.
1. Jonquil . . . .$3.00 – 5.00
2. Violet . . . .$3.00 – 5.00
3. Tulip . . . .$3.00 – 5.00
4. Cornflower No. 1 . . . .$3.00 – 5.00

Kraft Swanky Swigs, continued
Row 1: Posy Pattern Cornflower No. 2 (1947)
The flowers and leaves are all the same color.
1. Dark blue . . . .$2.00 – 4.00
2. Light blue . . . .$2.00 – 4.00
3. Red . . . .$2.00 – 4.00
4. Yellow . . . .$2.00 – 4.00

Row 2: Forget-Me-Not (1948)
1. Dark blue . . . .$2.00 – 4.00
2. Light blue . . . .$2.00 – 4.00
3. Red . . . .$2.00 – 4.00
4. Yellow . . . .$2.00 – 4.00

Row 3: Tulip No.3 (1950)
1. Dark blue . . . .$2.00 – 4.00
2. Light blue . . . .$2.00 – 4.00
3. Red . . . .$2.00 – 4.00
4. Yellow . . . .$2.00 – 4.00

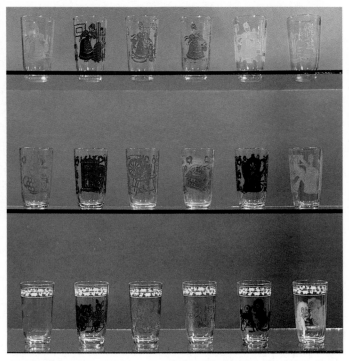

PLATE 118

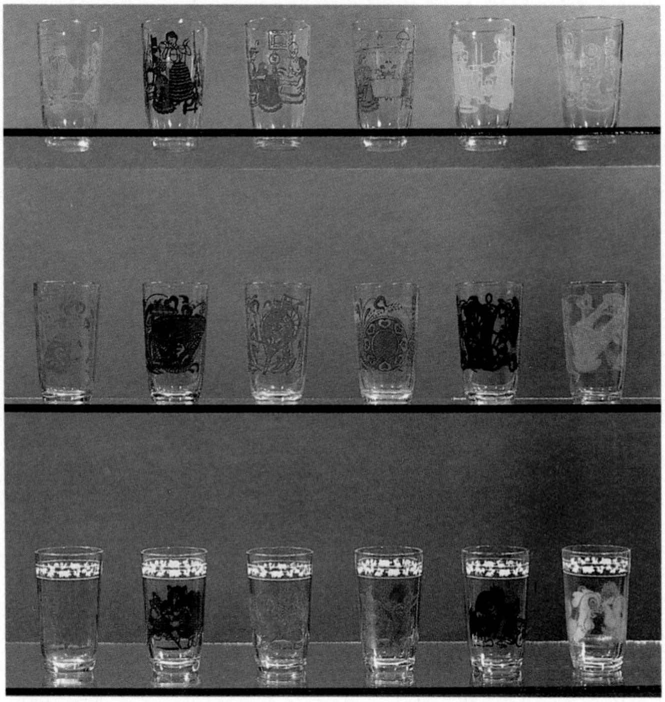

PLATE 119

Kraft Swanky Swigs, continued
Plate 118
Row 1: Bustling Betsy (1953)
Betsy the maid is pictured doing her daily chores.
1. Light blue ....$ 2.00 – 4.00
2. Brown ....$ 2.00 – 4.00
3. Red ....$ 2.00 – 4.00
4. Green ....$ 2.00 – 4.00
5. Yellow ....$ 2.00 – 4.00
6. Orange ....$ 2.00 – 4.00

Row 2: Antique No. 1 (1954)
Row 2 (reverse)
1. Blue ....$2.00 – 4.00
2. Brown ....$ 2.00 – 4.00
3. Red ....$ 2.00 – 4.00

Kraft Swanky Swigs, continued
4. Green ....$ 2.00 – 4.00
5. Black ....$ 2.00 – 4.00
6. Orange ....$ 2.00 – 4.00

Row 3: Kiddie Kup (1956)
Row 3: (reverse)
1. Blue ....$2.00 – 4.00
2. Brown ....$ 2.00 – 4.00
3. Red ....$ 2.00 – 4.00
4. Green ....$ 2.00 – 4.00
5. Black ....$ 2.00 – 4.00
6. Orange ....$ 2.00 – 4.00

Plate 119: Reverse of glasses in Plate 118.

PLATE 120

PLATE 121

Miscellaneous Food Containers

Row 1: 1939 Loews & MGM *Wizard of Oz*; Whataburger 50th Anniversary of the *Wizard of Oz*

Glasses 1 and 3 are from a set of seven glasses from Sealtest cottage cheese. These are very difficult to locate, and a complete set will take some time to put together. The Bad Witch appears to be the most difficult to find and is valued at $150 to $200. It is not known for certain whether a Wizard glass is a part of this set. No. 2 is an etched glass distributed by Whataburger restaurants in 1989 to commemorate the 50th anniversary of the movie.

1. The Good Witch ....$85.00 – 150.00
2. Whataburger 50th Anniversary ....$8.00 – 10.00
3. Tin Woodman ....$85.00 – 150.00
Not pictured:
Dorothy, Scarecrow, Toto,
Cowardly Lion ....$85.00 – 150.00 each
Bad Witch ....$150.00 – 200.00

Row 2: Swift's *Wizard of Oz*, set of six

Swift's peanut butter came in *Wizard of Oz* containers during the late 50s and early 60s. The set shown here has fluted bottoms and is the most difficult of the four Swift sets to complete. It was probably issued later than the other sets. The Wicked Witch of the West is the most difficult of the six to find. Some color and size variations can also be found in this set, and some of the glasses can be found with a starburst embossed on the bottom. The starburst adds 20% to the value of the glass.

1. Flying Monkeys (white or red) ....$15.00 – 20.00
2. Winkies (white) ....$15.00 – 20.00
3. Emerald City (white or green) ....$15.00 – 20.00
4. Witch of the North (white or yellow) ....$25.00 – 40.00
5. Glinda (white or pink) ....$15.00 – 25.00
6. Wicked Witch of the West (white) ....$35.00 – 50.00

Row 3: Coca-Cola/Krystal *Wizard of Oz*, set of six (1989)

For the 50th Anniversary of the *Wizard of Oz* movie, the Krystal chain offered this set of six Libbey glasses. There were available primarily in the southeastern United States and display a Coca-Cola logo. The artwork on these glasses is not particularly attractive, although the prices of these glasses have continued to creep up as supplies have dwindled.

1. Dorothy ....$6.00 – 8.00
2. Good Witch ....$6.00 – 8.00
3. Bad Witch ....$6.00 – 8.00
4. Lion ....$6.00 – 8.00
5. Scarecrow ....$6.00 – 8.00
6. Tin Man ....$6.00 – 8.00

Plate 121

Rows 1, 2, and 3: Swift's *Wizard of Oz*, three different sets of six: fluted bottom, wavy bottom, and plain bottom

The Swift's glasses shown in Plate 120: Row 2, came in three other versions with different characters. These three other sets feature the most popular of the characters. Each set is characterized by collectors according to the shape of the tumbler, specifically the detail on the bottom half-inch of the glass. Plate 121: Row 1 shows the tumbler with the fluted bottom. Row 2 shows the wavy bottom, and Row 3 shows the plain bottom. The characters on all three sets are the same with some minor variations in design and color. All of these glasses are equally difficult/easy to obtain.

1. Dorothy ....$12.00 – 18.00
2. Toto ....$12.00 – 18.00
3. Scarecrow ....$12.00 – 18.00
4. Cowardly Lion ....$12.00 – 18.00
5. Tinman ....$12.00 – 18.00
6. The Wizard ....$12.00 – 18.00

PLATE 122

PLATE 123

Welch's

Row 1: Kagran Howdy Doody, set of six
All eighteen of the Kagran Howdy Doody variations are shown in the first three rows. Three of the glasses were available in three colors: red, yellow, and green. The other three were available in three other colors: orange, blue, and pink.These glasses are not dated, but they are early 50s and are the most difficult of the Welch's sets to find and complete. The bottom of each glass is embossed with the face of one of the Howdy Doody characters. We believe there are six possible bottom embossings: Howdy Doody, Clarabell, Flub-A-Dub, Phineas T. Bluster, Dilly Dally, and Princess Summerfall Winterspring. A collector who wanted to find all the color variations and different bottom embossings would have to find 108 different glasses — a formidable task! Most collectors settle for a basic set of six without regard to colors or bottom embossings.
1, 2 & 3. *Doodyville Elephant Squirts Clarabell!* . .$15.00 – 20.00
4, 5 & 6. *Clarabell Gets A Kick Out Of Circus Mule!* . .$15.00 – 20.00

Row 2: Kagran Howdy Doody, set of 6, continued
1, 2 & 3. *Drinking Grape Juice Is Seal's Favorite Act.* . .$15.00 – 20.00
4, 5 & 6. *Dilly Dally Is Circus Big Shot!* . . . .$15.00 – 20.00

Row 3: Kagran Howdy Doody, set of 6, continued
1, 2 & 3. *Here Comes Music for Doodyville Circus* . . . .$15.00 – 20.00
4, 5 & 6. *Clarabell Tries Tiger Trick!* . . . .$15.00 – 20.00

Welch's, continued

Row 1: Welch's Howdy Doody, set of 6 (1953)
These are the more familiar of the Welch's Howdy Doody glasses. All 21 of the variations are shown here. Three of the glasses are available in three colors: pink, blue, and orange. The other three are available in four colors: white, red, green, and yellow. The bottoms of these glasses are embossed with the faces of six Howdy Doody characters: Flub-A-Dub, Clarabell, Howdy Doody, Phineas T. Bluster, Dilly Dally, and Princess Summerfall Winterspring. A collector wanting to get all of these glasses with their variations would have to find 126 different glasses — possible, but expensive and time-consuming!
1, 2 & 3. *Hey Kids! Come on along. Your Welch's sure helps make you strong* . . . .$10.00 – 15.00
4, 5, 6 & 7. *Hey Kids! What a shot. Just like Welch's it hits the spot* . . . .$10.00 – 15.00

Row 2: Welch's Howdy Doody, set of 6, continued
1, 2 & 3. *Hey Kids! Ding Dong Dell. Ring for Welch's, You'll like it swell* . . . .$10.00 – 15.00
4, 5, 6 & 7. *Hey Kids! On land or sea/Welch's tastes best. We all agree* . . . .$10.00 – 15.00

Row 3: Welch's Howdy Doody, set of 6, continued
1, 2 & 3. *Hey Kids! Hip hip hooray. Welch's leads the parade each day* . . . .$10.00 – 15.00
4, 5, 6 & 7. *Hey Kids! Wherever we eat, Welch's is our favorite treat* . . . .$10.00 – 15.00

PLATE 124

Welch's, continued

During the early 1970s, Welch's found a new theme for their jam glasses: The Archie Comics. The Saturday morning cartoon featuring the Archies was a big hit. Two different sets were produced and widely distributed. The bottom of each glass is embossed with one of eight of the Archie characters (Archie, Veronica, Betty, Reggie, Hot Dog, Mr. Weatherbee, Jughead, and Sabrina), making a total of 48 variations that can be found for each set. As plentiful as these glasses are, it would be a difficult task to complete a set of 96. The 1973 set can occasionally be found in a colorful six-pack carrier that adds $10.00 to $15.00 to the value of the set.

Row 1: Welch's Archies, set of six (1971)
1. *Reggie Makes the Scene* . . . .$1.00 – 2.00
2. *Hot Dog Goes to School* . . . .$1.00 – 2.00
3. *Archie Taking the Gang For a Ride* . . . .$1.00 – 2.00
4. *Betty and Veronica Fashion Show* . . . .$1.00 – 2.00
5. *Sabrina Cleans Her Room* . . . .$1.00 – 2.00
6. *Archies Having a Jam Session* . . . .$1.00 – 2.00

Row 2: Welch's Archies, set of six (1973)
1. *Archie Gets a Helping Hand* . . . .$1.00 – 2.00
2. *Friends Are For Sharing* . . . .$1.00 – 2.00
3. *Sabrina Calls the Play* . . . .$1.00 – 2.00
4. *Mr. Weatherbee Drops In* . . . .$1.00 – 2.00
5. *Betty and Veronica Give A Party* . . . .$1.00 – 2.00
6. *Jughead Wins the Pie Eating Contest* . . . .$1.00 – 2.00

PLATE 125   *Welch's, continued*

Row 1: Welch's Warner Brothers Action Series, set of eight (1974)
Welch's tied in with Warner Brothers after the Archies glasses. Eight different glasses were produced with eight different characters embossed on the bottoms (Road Runner, Yosemite Sam, Porky Pig, Tweety, Bugs Bunny, Daffy Duck, Elmer Fudd, and Foghorn Leghorn), making a total of 64 different glasses.
1. *Th-Th-Th-That's All Folks!* . . . .$2.00 – 4.00
2. *What's Up, Doc — Fresh Carrots?* . . . .$2.00 – 4.00
3. *Bugs Leads a Merry Chase* . . . .$2.00 – 4.00
4. *Speedy Snaps Up the Cheese!* . . . .$2.00 – 4.00
5. *Thufferin' Thuccotash!* . . . .$2.00 – 4.00
6. *I Tawt I Taw A Puddy Tat!* . . . .$2.00 – 4.00
7. *Wile E. Heads For A Big Finish!* . . . .$2.00 – 4.00
8. *Foghorn Switches Henery's Egg* . . . .$2.00 – 4.00

Row 2: Welch's Warner Brothers, set of eight (1976 – 1977)
These characters in static poses are among the most attractive of the Welch's sets and are popular with Warner Brothers collectors. Their value tends to be a little higher than other Welch's glasses due to their popularity with Warner Brothers collectors. The characters embossed on the bottoms are the same as those on the 1974 action set, so there are 64 different glasses to collect. We have an Elmer Fudd glass with the original Grape Jelly label which has a one-inch circle on it with Bugs Bunny's head and these words: *1977 Welch's Collector Series Looney Tunes Glass*. So while the glasses are copyright dated 1976, Welch's thought of them as a 1977 set.
1. Road Runner . . . .$5.00 – 7.00
2. Yosemite Sam . . . .$5.00 – 7.00
3. Porky Pig . . . .$5.00 – 7.00
4. Tweety . . . .$5.00 – 7.00
5. Bugs Bunny . . . .$5.00 – 7.00
6. Daffy Duck . . . .$5.00 – 7.00
7. Elmer Fudd . . . .$5.00 – 7.00
8. Foghorn Leghorn . . . .$5.00 – 7.00

Row 3: Welch's Dinosaurs, set of four (1988)
A more recent Welch's promotion is the dinosaur glasses. Four different glasses were issued. There are two variations to this set — an undated and a dated set. The types of jam that came in each glass are listed below so that collectors can match lids with jars.
1. Brontosaurus (strawberry jam) . . . .$1.00 – 2.00
2. Stegosaurus (raspberry-apple jam) . . . .$1.00 – 2.00
3. Pterodactyl (concord grape jam) . . . .$1.00 – 2.00
4. Tyrannosaurus Rex (concord grape jelly) . . . .$1.00 – 2.00

PLATE 127

PLATE 126

Welch's, continued

Welch's Flintstones (1962, 1963, 1964)

In the early 1960s, Welch's was offering their jelly in Hanna-Barbera Flintstones tumblers. A total of three different sets with 14 glasses was issued. In 1962 there were six different glasses, in 1963 two different glasses, and in 1964 six different glasses. Each set comes in eight different colors (red, yellow, orange, aqua, pink, green, blue, and white) and with seven different embossed bottoms (Fred, Barney, Wilma, Betty, Pebbles, Bamm Bamm, and Dino). That works out to a total of 784 variations in these sets, and it shouldn't be news to anyone that Welch's made a lot of these glasses. There are several collectors who are attempting to find all 784. We haven't heard of anyone succeeding yet!!

Row 1: Welch's Hanna-Barbera Flintstones, set of six (1962)
1. *Fred in His Sports Car* . . . .$4.00 – 8.00
2. *Fred and Barney Play Golf* . . . .$4.00 – 8.00
3. *Having a Ball* . . . .$4.00 – 8.00
4. *Fred and Barney Bowl Duckpins* . . . .$4.00 – 8.00
5. *Fred's Newest Invention* . . . .$4.00 – 8.00
6. *Fred and His Pal at Work* . . . .$4.00 – 8.00

Row 2: Welch's Hanna-Barbera Flintstones, set of two (1963)
1. *Pebbles' Baby Sitters* . . . .$4.00 – 8.00
2. *Flintstones Salt & Pepper shakers*
3. *Fred Builds a Doll Cave* . . . .$4.00 – 8.00

Row 3: Welch's Hanna-Barbera Flintstones, set of six (1964)
1. *Pebbles Lands a Fish* . . . .$4.00 – 8.00
2. *Fred and Barney Play Baseball* . . . .$4.00 – 8.00
3. *Bedrock Pet Show* . . . .$4.00 – 8.00
4. *Fred Goes Hunting* . . . .$4.00 – 8.00
5. *Pebbles' Birthday Party* . . . .$4.00 – 8.00
6. *Pebbles at the Beach* . . . .$4.00 – 8.00

Mister Magoo (1961 – 1964)

Row 1: Mister Magoo
The Mister Magoo glasses — which depict Mister Magoo in comic situations — come in four different shaped containers (4⅝" tumbler, 4⅝" jar-type round bottom, 5½" tumbler, 5½" jar-type round bottom) and in at least four different color combinations. Which product was available in these glasses is still unknown at this time. Perhaps someday one of the glasses will turn up with an original label or lid. At the present time, we are not sure how many different Mister Magoo glasses there are, but we do know that they are hard to find and expensive when they are found.
1. Mister Magoo with shotgun and falling duck . . .$25.00 – 35.00
2. *Mister Magoo Driving — Road Hog!*/riding cow
    backwards . . . .$25.00 – 35.00
3. *What a Crazy Ride* — Mister Magoo parachuting$25.00 – 35.00
4. *Mister Magoo Road Hog*/riding cow backwards .$25.00 – 35.00

Row 2: Mister Magoo, continued
1. Mister Magoo Hailing Taxi/riding horse backwards —
    Giddiyap . . . .$25.00 – 35.00
2. Taxi/riding horse backwards . . . .$25.00 – 35.00
3. *Mister Magoo — Road Hog*/riding cow backwards . . .$25.00 – 35.00
Not pictured:
Mister Magoo skiing backwards/*Where's the beach?* . . . .$25.00 – 35.00
Mister Magoo tipping hat to fire hydrant/holding balloons
    . . . .$25.00 – 35.00

Advertising Glasses

PLATE 128

PLATE 129

The Gulf Collector Series Limited Edition

Plate 128

Rows 1, 2, and 3: The Gulf Collector Series Limited Edition, set of six
This set of Gulf glasses illustrates the early history of the Gulf Oil Company. A fairly detailed historical description of the pictured scene appears on the reverse of each glass. The set comes in three sizes: a tall tumbler (Row 1), a mug (Row 2, reverse view), and a rocks glass (Row 3). They were made by the Indiana Glass Company in Sapulpa, Oklahoma and probably available to customers at Gulf stations in the early 1980s.
1. Old Spindle Top — Gulf's First Gusher, Texas 1901 .$3.00 – 5.00
2. World's First Drive-in Service Station, Pittsburgh, PA
    1913 . . . .$3.00 – 5.00
3. The World War I Years . . . .$3.00 – 5.00
4. The Roaring '20s . . . .$3.00 – 5.00
5. The Great Depression Years . . . .$3.00 – 5.00
6. The Dawning of a New Era . . . .$3.00 – 5.00

Plate 129

H. J. Heinz Company

Row 1: H. J. Heinz Company Product Label, set of six
These glasses were employee premiums given for Christmas or other occasions in the late '70s and early '80s. The glasses came as a set of six with two each of three different products. The front and reverse of each glass are shown.
1 & 2. Green Pea Soup . . . .$4.00 – 7.00
3 & 4. Pork and Beans . . . .$4.00 – 7.00
5 & 6. Tomato Soup . . . .$4.00 – 7.00

The Keebler Company

Row 2: Keebler's Soft Batch Cookie, set of four (1984) and 135th Birthday Glass (1988)

Both of the issues pictured were premium offers. The glasses could be obtained by collecting Keebler's proofs of purchase and mailing them in with an order form found on various Keebler's product packages. The set of four (shown in Rows 1: # 1, 2, 4 & 5) was issued in 1984, and the 135th anniversary glass (#3) was issued in 1988 and cost $4.99 for a box of 4. It never ceases to amaze us what collectors will do to get the glasses they want. One collector was banished from a local grocery store during the 1988 promotion for removing Keebler proof of purchase seals. It seems he was working on his tenth set of glasses!
1. *Ernest, You Don't Bite Into Soft Batch Cookies...You Sorta Sink Into 'Em!* . . . .$6.00 – 8.00
2. *Mom, Soft Batch Tastes Like Cookies Fresh From The Oven...Soft And Chewy!* . . . .$6.00 – 8.00
3. *Keebler's 135th Birthday Glass* . . . .$3.00 – 5.00
4. *Mom, You'd Swear These Soft Batch Cookies Were Home Made...Ernest, This Is Home!* . . . .$6.00 – 8.00
5. *Ernest, Soft Batch Reminds Me Of Cookies I Baked When You Were Little...Mom, I'm An Elf! I've Always Been Little!* . .$6.00 – 8.00

Kellogg's

Row 3: Kellogg's Collector Series, set of six (1977)
This set was another mail-order premium. Collectors could get one glass free by mailing either three Sugar Corn Pops or three Sugar Smacks box tops to the Kellogg's premium center. Each character represents a Kellogg's cereal, but the name of the character does not appear on the glass, nor does the name of the cereal. Kellogg's presumed correctly that lovers of their cereals didn't need to be told what they already knew!
1. Tony the Tiger (Frosted Flakes) . . . .$7.00 – 10.00
2. Toucan Sam (Froot Loops) . . . .$7.00 – 10.00
3. Big Yella (Sugar Pops) . . . .$7.00 – 10.00
4. Snap! Crackle! Pop! (Rice Krispies) . . . .$7.00 – 10.00
5. Dig 'Em (Sugar Smacks) . . . .$7.00 – 10.00
6. Tony Jr. (Frosted Flakes) . . . .$7.00 – 10.00

PLATE 130

PLATE 131

Miscellaneous Milk, Soda, Chocolate, Pet Food, Safety, and Gasoline Glasses

Row 1: Milk-Related Glasses
1. Big Top Soda — advertising glass for Sealtest ice cream . . .$5.00 – 7.00
2. Milk glass with cows . . . .$5.00 – 7.00
3. *How about a Milkshake* generic advertising glass .$5.00 – 7.00

Row 2: Food-Related Glasses
1 & 2. Little Cookie Clown, ©1952 S.B. Co. . . . .$5.00 – 7.00
3. Chef's Custom Bakery — local advertising glass . .$3.00 – 5.00
4. Drummer Boy Fried Chicken . . . .$3.00 – 5.00

Row 3: Miscellaneous Borden glasses
The advertising figures of Elsie the cow and her family have been used by Borden for over half a century. Over the years, the Borden Company has issued a considerable number of glasses both in sets and as singles in many different sizes and shapes.
1. Elsie and Family in the Bicentennial Parade (1976) .$5.00 – 7.00
2. Elsie — '50s advertising glass . . . .$10.00 – 12.00
3. Elsie — '60s advertising glass . . . .$10.00 – 12.00

Miscellaneous Milk, Soda, Chocolate, Pet Food, Safety, & Gaso-line Glasses, continued
Row 1: Three from a Borden set of four and two Squirt glasses
2. Little Lola . . . .$15.00 – 20.00
3. Aunt Elsie . . . .$15.00 – 20.00
4. Celestine . . . .$15.00 – 20.00
Not pictured:
Baby Beulah . . . .$15.00 – 20.00
1. Squirt & Whiskey — glowball glass . . . .$7.00 – 9.00
5. *Just Call Me Squirt* . . . .$12.00 – 15.00

Row 2: Hershey's Chocolate and Morris the Cat
1. *A Kiss for You* . . . .$3.00 – 5.00
2. Hershey's Chocolate . . . .$7.00 – 9.00
This set of two Morris the Cat glasses was a 9-Lives Cat Food mail-order premium. There is no date, but the glass style indicates a late 1970s date.
3. *Morris on Glass Is like Sterling on Silver* . . . .$5.00 – 7.00
4. *There's Something Irresistible About This Glass* . .$5.00 – 7.00

Row 3: Safety Award and Gasoline glasses
1 & 5: West Penn Power — Safety Award glasses . . .$1.00 – 3.00
Esso (now Exxon) Gasoline: Esso issued a variety of glasses over the years, and many of them featured their tiger.
2 & 3: Esso Tiger with multiple languages saying *Put a Tiger in Your Tank* . . . .$3.00 – 5.00
4. *Put a Tiger in Your Tank* . . . .$3.00 – 5.00

PLATE 132

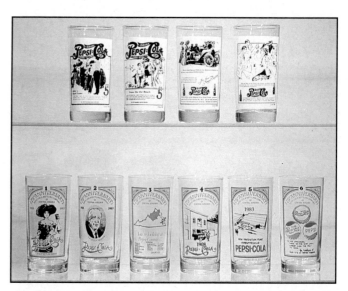

PLATE 133

Heavy Equipment and Commercial Trucking

Row 1: Pepsi-Cola Caterpillar, set of two
This set of two glasses was made for distribution in Caterpillar company food services and features four of the heavy equipment machines from Caterpillar Tractor. A historic machine is shown on one side of each glass, and a modern piece of equipment is shown on the reverse. There are only two glasses in the series. The second glass can also also be found with the word "Caterpillar" spelled "Caterpiller" under the picture of the 1931 Auto Patrol. This oddity commands about a 25% premium over the other two glasses.
1. Caterpillar 16-G Motor Grader/Caterpillar Auto Patrol, 1931,
    Second in a Series . . . .$5.00 – 7.00
2. Caterpillar D8L Tractor/Holt 'Caterpillar' 40 Tractor, 1908,
    First in a Series . . . .$5.00 – 7.00
Not pictured:
#1 above with "Caterpiller" instead of "Caterpillar" .$8.00 – 10.00

Row 2: Interpoint Trucking Company, set of four
This set is probably an in-house company giveaway, and it's typical of the kinds of gifts that companies give their employees at special functions or during the holidays.
1. Conventional cab with tanker . . . .$1.00 – 2.00
2. Conventional cab with boxtrailer . . . .$1.00 – 2.00
3. Cabover with flatbed . . . .$1.00 – 2.00
4. Cabover with boxtrailer . . . .$1.00 – 2.00

Historical

Pepsi-Cola Historical Advertising Posters and Central Virginia Pepsi-Cola Bottlers 75th Anniversary

Soft-drink companies, looking for ways to rekindle interest in their products, often look to the past for nostalgic material, and one of the best sources is historical advertising posters. The set of 4 black and white posters on the glasses shown below date from circa 1900. The set of 6 numbered glasses in Row 2 were made by Galaxy Glass and issued by the Central Virginia Pepsi-Cola Bottling Company. These glasses were intended primarily for employees at the Central Virginia plant, so only a limited number were made. Their price reflects their scarcity.

Row 1: Pepsi-Cola Black and White Advertising, Set of four (1979)
1. *After a hard game...* . . . .$8.00 – 10.00
2. *Down on the beach...* . . . .$8.00 – 10.00
3. *Here's what Barney Oldfield...says about*
    Pepsi-Cola... . . . .$8.00 – 10.00
4. *When you want the best drink at the fountain...* .$8.00 – 10.00

Row 2: 75th Anniversary of Central Virginia Pepsi-Cola Bottling Co., 1908 – 1983, set of six (1983)
1. Jessup Bottling Works, 1908 – 1983 . . . .$30.00 – 50.00
2. S. A. Jessup, Founder . . . .$30.00 – 50.00
3. *You're looking at Pepsi Country!* (list of counties) ..$30.00 – 50.00
4. *Jessup Bottling Works in 1908* . . . .$30.00 – 50.00
5. *New Production Plant/Charlottesville* . . . .$30.00 – 50.00
6. *To our customers: Thank you for your loyal support over the*
    past 75 years! . . . .$30.00 – 50.00

Children's, Nursery Rhymes, and Alphabet Glasses

PLATE 134

Some collectors jest that there are probably as many different children's glasses in the world as there are children — which is to say, there are a lot of them! No one knows exactly how many, since they were issued consistently since the 1930s. The earliest of these glasses were fairly small and commonly held foods such as jams, peanut butter, and cottage cheese and were sold by small grocers, dairies, and other food manufacturers — a trend that continues today as evidenced by the many Welch's jam and jelly "jars." Later, of course, these glasses were produced to be sold in packaged sets in dime stores and department stores. The appeal of these glasses is easy to explain: they transport us back in time to our childhood, to innocence, to better times. They help us remember — and they are fun to collect. Kids still like them!

Row 1: The Libbey Classics
The eight glasses in this issue were sold in two boxed sets of four, and two sizes were available, 3¼" 8 oz. and 5¼" 12 oz. The first four glasses listed here comprise one set; the second four listed comprise the other. Glasses found in the original carton command a premium of at least 25%, as does the Wizard of Oz glass which is prized by Oz collectors.

1. Treasure Island . . . .$10.00 – 15.00
2. Moby Dick . . . .$10.00 – 15.00
3. Three Musketeers . . . .$10.00 – 15.00
4. Robin Hood . . . .$10.00 – 15.00

Row 2: Libbey Classics, second group of four
1. Reverse of *Treasure Island*, #1 above
2. *Alice in Wonderland* . . . .$10.00 – 15.00
3. *Tom Sawyer* . . . .$10.00 – 15.00
4. *The Wizard of Oz* . . . .$25.00 – 30.00
Not pictured: *Gulliver's Travels* . . . .$10.00 – 15.00

Row 3: Polite Series
These glasses originally held one pound of "L&S Ol' Fashun Two Fruit Jelly" ("Pure Apple Blackberry" in the labeled glass we found) packed by Lutz and Schramm, Inc. of Pittsburgh. Each glass features two different rhyming four-line jingles of advice for youngsters, and there are at least six different glasses that we know of. We show five of them here. All the glasses share the same red bottom design of children playing.

1. *Skipping rope is lots of fun.../Be polite and wait your turn...* . . . .$3.00 – 6.00
2. *Boys and girls look spic and span.../When traveling on a train or bus...* . . . .$3.00 – 6.00
3. *Don't laugh at kids for their mistakes.../"Thank you" is the thing to say...* . . . .$3.00 – 6.00
4. *All children like to play with toys.../Everyone likes bread and jam...* . . . .$3.00 – 6.00
5. *Dining out.../You won't be called a sissy...* . . . . . .$3.00 – 6.00
6. *Good little girls.../Open the door...* . . . .$3.00 – 6.00

PLATE 135

Children's, Nursery Rhymes, and Alphabet Glasses, continued
Row 1: Miscellaneous Children's Glasses
1. The Cow Jumped Over the Moon . . . .$5.00 – 8.00
2. Jack Spratt, with complete rhyme (Hazel Atlas) . . .$5.00 – 8.00
3. Peter Piper, with complete rhyme (Hazel Atlas) . . .$5.00 – 8.00
4. Charles Dickens' characters: Mr. Winkle, Mr. Pickwick, Ye Ole
   Tavern, Mrs. Bardell, Mr. Weller . . . .$5.00 – 8.00
5. Little Boy Blue . . . .$5.00 – 8.00
6. Little Red Riding Hood . . . .$5.00 – 8.00

Row 2: Milk-glass nursery rhymes (these sturdy, short tumblers have
no writing on them, just images. Kids knew what the story was!) and
three heavy (made to last a lifetime) nursery rhyme glasses.
1. Mary Had a Little Lamb . . . .$7.00 – 10.00
2. Three Little Pigs . . . .$7.00 – 10.00
3. Jack and Jill . . . .$7.00 – 10.00
4. Wee Willie Winkie, with complete rhyme . . . . .$7.00 – 10.00

5. Little Miss Muffet, with complete rhyme . . . . . .$7.00 – 10.00
6. Little Jack Horner, with complete rhyme . . . . . .$7.00 – 10.00

Row 3: Similarly designed nursery rhyme glasses from two different sets. The glasses are all 5" tall, but one set has a mouth diameter of 2¾" (glasses 1, 3, and 5), and the other has a mouth
diameter of 2½" (glasses 2, 4, and 6). These glasses are thick and
have no maker's mark. There are probably eight or more glasses in
each set. Each glass features the complete rhyme.
1. Ring around the Rosy . . . .$7.00 – 10.00
2. Little Boy Blue . . . .$7.00 – 10.00
3. Mistress Mary . . . .$7.00 – 10.00
4. Jack and Jill . . . .$7.00 – 10.00
5. Jack be Nimble . . . .$7.00 – 10.00
6. Old King Cole . . . .$7.00 – 10.00
Known, but not pictured:
Humpty Dumpty, 2½" dia. . . . .$7.00 – 10.00

PLATE 136

Children's, Nursery Rhymes, and Alphabet Glasses, continued

Miscellaneous Circus Glasses

Glasses with circus themes and scenes on them have been popular for many years, especially with children. Some circus glasses were available for purchase at the circus, some were available at department and variety stores, and still others (like the children's nursery rhyme glasses) were sold by dairies and grocery stores with food products in them. Circus glasses were produced in abundance and great variety.

Row 1: Ringling Brothers and Barnum and Bailey Circus set of six issued in 1975 and sponsored by Pepsi-Cola. Here we show two of the six glasses which were, incidentally, available at the circus in sets. These colorful circus poster glasses can still be found in Florida. The 16 oz. glass is a Federal glass, and the glasses can be found either with or without the Federal imprint on the bottom.

1. Ringling Bros and Barnum & Bailey Combined Circus, the
   Greatest Show on Earth . . . .$10.00 – 20.00
2. Ringling Bros & Barnum & Bailey Combined Circus, Felix and 99
   other Famous Clowns . . . .$10.00 – 20.00

Not pictured:

#3 100th Anniversary, The Greatest Show on Earth . .$10.00 – 20.00
#4 Barnum & Bailey Greatest Show on Earth, Bears that
Dance . . . .$10.00 – 20.00
#5 Giant Consolidation, World's Biggest Menagerie . .$10.00 – 20.00
#6 Barnum & Bailey Greatest Show on Earth . . . . .$10.00 – 20.00

Row 2: Ringling Brothers Circus Clowns (1976) numbered set of eight Here we show 3 glasses from the set.

1. #2 Clown with tambourine . . . .$8.00 – 12.00
2. #3 Clown with small dog on large chain . . . . . .$8.00 – 12.00
3. #6 Clown driving truck . . . .$8.00 – 12.00

Not pictured:

#1 Clown as drum major . . . .$8.00 – 12.00
#4 Clown in bath tub with wheels . . . .$8.00 – 12.00
#5 Clown with small umbrella . . . .$8.00 – 12.00
#7 Clown carrying stuffed lion . . . .$8.00 – 12.00
#8 Clown with plunger on head . . . .$8.00 – 12.00

Row 3: Miscellaneous Circus Glasses

1. Three clowns, one with an umbrella, one on stilts, and one using
   an umbrella as a cane. This is a Hazel Atlas, 4" ribbed food
   product glass. There is no writing on it. . . . .$5.00 – 10.00
2. Big Top Parade, showing clowns with drums. This glass belongs
   to a set of Big Top Peanut Butter glasses. . . . . . .$5.00 – 10.00
3. Big Top Circus . . . .$3.00 – 5.00

Not pictured, but part of Big Top set:

Lion on circus ball . . . .$5.00 – 10.00
Dancing Elephant . . . .$5.00 – 10.00
Clown juggling . . . .$5.00 – 10.00
Ringmaster . . . .$5.00 – 10.00
Seal balancing ball . . . .$5.00 – 10.00

PLATE 137

PLATE 138

PLATE 139

Children's, Nursery Rhymes, and Alphabet Glasses, continued

Plate 137

Row 1: Juice Glasses and Carafe with Circus Motifs
1. Monkeys . . . .$3.00 – 5.00
2. Clown on Bicycle . . . .$3.00 – 5.00
3. Caraffe with circus wagon . . . .$8.00 – 12.00
4. Elephant . . . .$3.00 – 5.00
5. Lady on horse . . . .$3.00 – 5.00
6. Seal balancing ball . . . .$3.00 – 5.00

Plate 138

Row 1: Numbers 1, 3, and 5 from set of six circus glasses
1. #1 The Ringmaster . . . .$5.00 – 8.00
2. #3 Seal balancing ball . . . .$5.00 – 8.00
3. #5 Clown holding leg in air . . . .$5.00 – 8.00

Row 2: Numbers 2, 4, and 6 from set of six circus glasses
1. #2 Tiger sitting on drum . . . .$5.00 – 8.00
2. #4 Lion balancing on ball . . . .$5.00 – 8.00
3. #6 Elephant with hoops . . . .$5.00 – 8.00

Plate 139

Alphabet Children's Glasses

Glasses, mugs, and plates with either single letters or complete alphabets have long been popular in many cultures. They served as entertainment, distractions, learning aids and, of course, utilitarian vehicles for food and drink. As is the case with nursery rhyme glasses, circus glasses, and children's glasses in general, there are many different singles and sets of these kinds of glasses. Many of these glasses originally were sold with food in them.

The alphabet glasses in Rows 1, 2, and 3 all share a similar design. All have green grass or flowers or leaves around the bottom. Most of the glasses are 4½" tall with 2⅝" mouth diameter, but a few are 4⅝" tall with a 2⅜" mouth diameter. Finally, some have Hazel Atlas markings on the bottom, and some don't. All have a four-line verse which describes the animal.

Row 1: Three 4½" alphabet glasses
1. *A is for Alligator* . . . .$8.00 – 12.00
2. *B is for Bunny* . . . .$8.00 – 12.00
3. *C is for Cow* . . . .$8.00 – 12.00

Row 2: Four alphabet glasses in two different sizes
1. *D is for Donkey, 4⅝"* . . . .$8.00 – 12.00
2. *E is for Elephant, 4½"* . . . .$8.00 – 12.00
3. *H is for Horse, 4½"* . . . .$8.00 – 12.00
4. *O is for Ostrich, 4½", Hazel Atlas* . . . .$8.00 – 12.00

Row 3: Three alphabet glasses
1. *J is for Jaguar, 4½"* . . . .$8.00 – 12.00
2. *L is for Lion, 4⅝", Hazel Atlas* . . . .$8.00 – 12.00
3. *I is for Ibex, 4½"* . . . .$8.00 – 12.00
Known, but not pictured:
A is for Alligator, 4½" . . . .$8.00 – 12.00
K is for Kangaroo, 4½" . . . .$8.00 – 12.00
P is for Puppy, 4½", Hazel Atlas . . . .$8.00 – 12.00
T is for Teddy Bear, 4⅝", Hazel Atlas . . . .$8.00 – 12.00

PLATE 140

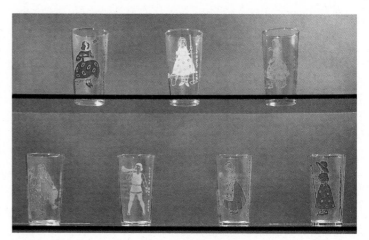

PLATE 141

Children's, Nursery Rhymes, and Alphabet Glasses, continued
Row 1: Milk Glass alphabet glasses, 4¾"
These glasses also come in a 3⅛" version. All have rhyming four-line verses on the reverse side.
1. *C is for Cow* . . . .$5.00 – 8.00
2. *D is for Duckling* . . . .$5.00 – 8.00
3. *D is for Duckling*, reverse showing four-line verse
4. *H is for Horse* . . . .$5.00 – 8.00
5. *L is for Lamb* . . . .$5.00 – 8.00

Row 2: Three heavy alphabet block glasses which go with the three glasses in Row 6 below and presumably belong to a larger set of twenty-six. The glasses shown here were sold in a set in a department store and have the look of quality. They have thick bottoms and heavy walls for longevity. On each glass the letter in question is shown on a child's wooden block, and there is a catchy four-line verse to describe the animal.
1. *B is for Bunny* . . . .$7.00 – 10.00
2. *F is for Fox* . . . .$7.00 – 10.00
3. *H is for Hippo* . . . .$7.00 – 10.00

Row 3: Three heavy alphabet block glasses from same set as Row 2.
1. *O is for Opossum* . . . .$7.00 – 10.00
2. *R is for Raccoon* . . . .$7.00 – 10.00
3. *S is for Skunk* . . . .$7.00 – 10.00
Known, but not pictured:
A is for Alligator . . . .$7.00 – 10.00
I is for Impala . . . .$7.00 – 10.00
K is for Kangaroo . . . .$7.00 – 10.00
T is for Turtle . . . .$7.00 – 10.00
X is for Xema . . . .$7.00 – 10.00

Children's, Nursery Rhymes, and Alphabet Glasses, continued

Nursery Rhyme Glasses
Row 1: Libbey Nursery Rhyme Glasses, 4⅝"
Each has the character's name in vertical letters down the right side of the glass and the well-known rhyme on the reverse. These glasses originally contained food products.
1. Little Miss Muffet . . . .$8.00 – 10.00
2. Mistress Mary . . . .$8.00 – 10.00
3. Mary [had a little lamb] . . . .$8.00 – 10.00

Row 2: Four Libbey Nursery Rhyme Glasses, continued
1. Jack and Jill . . . .$8.00 – 10.00
2. Little Boy Blue . . . .$8.00 – 10.00
3. Old Mother Hubbard . . . .$8.00 – 10.00
4. Little Bo-Peep . . . .$8.00 – 10.00
Known, but not pictured: *Jack is nimble/And Jack is quick,/The milk he drinks/Explains the trick.* This glass comes in green and blue variations, with green being the most common. Made by Libbey, may or may not be part of this set. . . . .$8.00 – 10.00

PLATE 142

PLATE 143

Children's, Nursery Rhymes, and Alphabet Glasses, continued
Row 1: Nursery Rhyme Glasses
In all there may be a dozen glasses or more in this set. They are 4⅝" Federal glasses. Each has a rhyme on the reverse. Originally, they held preserves, as the label we have on a Little Jack Horner glass indicates. The label reads: "Fine Foods, Orchard Park Brand, Contents 12 OZ. AVD, Pure Apricot Preserves, Orchard Park Foods, Inc., Buffalo, N.Y. Distributors."
1. Little Miss Muffet, pink . . . .$8.00 – 10.00
2. Mistress Mary, yellow . . . .$8.00 – 10.00
3. Little Bo-Peep, red . . . .$8.00 – 10.00

Row 2: Nursery Rhyme Glasses, continued
1. Little Boy Blue, blue . . . .$8.00 – 10.00
2. Jack and Jill, orange . . . .$8.00 – 10.00
3. Little Jack Horner, pink . . . .$8.00 – 10.00
Known, but not pictured:
Wee Willie Winkie, turquoise . . . .$8.00 – 10.00
Jack Be Nimble, red . . . .$8.00 – 10.00

Row 3: The glasses in this row have the same designs and rhymes as the glasses in Rows 1 and 2, but they are 5" tall, thick and heavy, and they do not all share the same colors with their name-sakes in the Federal set. This set was the department store version of the Federal preserve set.
1. Wee Willie Winkie, turquoise . . . .$8.00 – 10.00
2. Jack Be Nimble, red . . . .$8.00 – 10.00
3. Little Miss Muffet, yellow . . . .$8.00 – 10.00
4. Little Boy Blue, blue . . . .$8.00 – 10.00
5. Little Bo-Peep, yellow . . . .$8.00 – 10.00
Known, but not pictured:
Little Bo-Peep, lime green . . . .$8.00 – 10.00
Little Jack Horner, maroon . . . .$8.00 – 10.00

Children's, Nursery Rhymes, and Alphabet Glasses, continued

Nursery Rhyme Glasses

The glasses shown in Plate 143: Row 1 – 3 and Plate 144: Row 1 belong to a very large set of 4⅛6" Hazel Atlas ribbed food container jars. At the present time, no one knows how many different nursery rhymes appeared in this series, nor is anyone sure about the number of color variations each jar had. One thing is certain: this is a very appealing series both because of its age (1940s) and because of the designs and verses on the jars. Most nursery rhyme sets consist of the well-known stories and rhymes; this set has both the standard ones as well as older more obscure ones. Collectors might be interested in knowing that these jars seem to be most plentiful in the midwest and north central states. A knowledgeable collector tells us that these jars came with tin lids and were distributed by a dairy in Wisconsin. Listed after each jar pictured are the colors that the jar comes in.

Row 1: Hazel Atlas ribbed nursery rhyme jars
1. Old Mother Hubbard (white) . . . .$10.00 – 15.00
2. Pussy Cat, Pussy Cat (white, blue) . . . .$10.00 – 15.00
3. Little Jack Horner (red) . . . .$10.00 – 15.00
4. Mary Had A Little Lamb (white) . . . .$10.00 – 15.00

Row 2: Hazel Atlas ribbed nursery rhyme jars
1. There Was An Old Woman (green) . . . .$10.00 – 15.00
2. A Frog He Would A-Wooing Go (red, green) . . .$10.00 – 15.00
3. Old Mother Goose (blue, no rhyme) . . . .$10.00 – 15.00
4. Simple Simon (red) . . . .$10.00 – 15.00

Row 3: Hazel Atlas ribbed nursery rhyme jars
1. The Queen Of Hearts (yellow) . . . .$10.00 – 15.00
2. Goosey Goosey Gander (white) . . . .$10.00 – 15.00
3. These Little Pigs (green, orange) . . . .$10.00 – 15.00
4. Old King Cole (white, yellow) . . . .$10.00 – 15.00

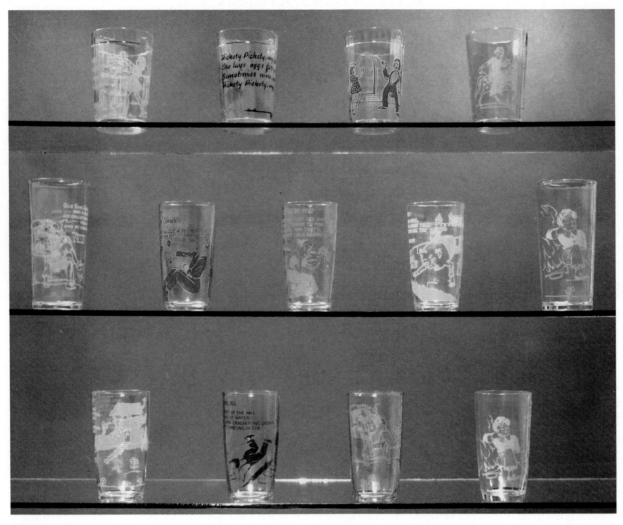

PLATE 144

Children's, Nursery Rhymes, and Alphabet Glasses, continued
Row 1: Hazel Atlas ribbed nursery rhyme jars
1. Hickety Pickety, My Black Hen (yellow, black) .$10.00 – 15.00
2. Hickety Pickety, My Black Hen, view of reverse
   (black) . . . .$10.00 – 15.00
3. Doodle Doodle Doo (red) . . . .$10.00 – 15.00
4. I Had A Little Pony (yellow, light green). Note that the glass
   shown here does not have the ⅝" band around the top that the
   other glasses have. However, we have an example of this glass
   that has the band. The bandless glass is therefore an anomaly and
   probably not common. . . . .$10.00 – 15.00
Known, but not pictured:
Barber, Barber (red) . . . .$10.00 – 15.00
A Jolly Old Pig (white) . . . .$10.00 – 15.00
Cinderella Wed The Prince (orange, yellow) . . . .$10.00 – 15.00
Hark, Hark! The Dogs Do Bark! (black) . . . .$10.00 – 15.00
Jack Spratt . . . .$10.00 – 15.00
Lickety Split . . . .$10.00 – 15.00
Little Bo-Peep Has Lost Her Sheep (blue) . . . .$10.00 – 15.00
Little Boy Blue (blue) . . . .$10.00 – 15.00
Little Miss Muffet (green) name only, no poem . . . .$10.00 – 15.00
Red Riding Hood Meets The Wolf (red) . . . .$10.00 – 15.00
The North Wind Doth Blow (red) . . . .$10.00 – 15.00
To Market, To Market (blue) . . . .$10.00 – 15.00
Tom, Tom, The Piper's Son (white) . . . .$10.00 – 15.00

Handy Spandy, Jack-A-Dandy (yellow) . . . .$10.00 – 15.00
Jack and Jill (blue) . . . .$10.00 – 15.00
Twinkle Twinkle Little Star (blue) . . . .$10.00 – 15.00
Fingers and Thumbs (red) . . . .$10.00 – 15.00
Hey Diddle Diddle (blue) . . . .$10.00 – 15.00

Row 2: Food product nursery rhyme glasses. Glasses 1 and 5 here
are 5¾" tall; the others, including Row 3, are 4¾" tall. The designs
are the same on both heights, but what we have here are glasses
from two different sets since the small set is barrel-shaped, and the
tall set has straight sides. There are also color variations since Old
King Cole is yellow on the tall glass and red on the shorter one. All
the glasses have the appropriate verse mixed in with the design.
1. Old King Cole . . . .$7.00 – 10.00
2. Little Jack Horner . . . .$7.00 – 10.00
3. Little Boy Blue . . . .$7.00 – 10.00
4. Humpty Dumpty . . . .$7.00 – 10.00
5. Little Boy Blue . . . .$7.00 – 10.00

Row 3: Food product nursery rhyme glasses
1. There Was An Old Woman . . . .$7.00 – 10.00
2. Jack and Jill . . . .$7.00 – 10.00
3. Old King Cole . . . .$7.00 – 10.00
4. Little Boy Blue . . . .$7.00 – 10.00

Christmas Glasses

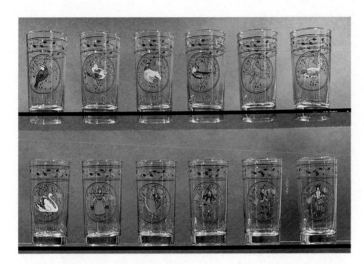

PLATE 145

PLATE 146

The Twelve Days of Christmas

The song *The Twelve Days of Christmas* has been the inspiration for many glass sets. Shown here are two of the sets that are available. You will notice that it is not uncommon to find sets that disagree on the sequence of the lyrics. The set shown in Plate 145: Rows 1 and 2 is a retail department store issue that could be purchased only as a set. The set in Plate 146: Rows 1 and 2 was a 16-ounce fast-food restaurant issue made by the Brockway Glass Company and sponsored by Pepsi-Cola (available one glass at a time in 1976), but the same design can be found in a number of other configurations including (1) a 12-ounce glass sponsored by Pepe's Mexican Restaurant and Dr Pepper, (2) a 16-ounce version without any logos (available as a boxed store set), (3) a 16-ounce round bottom version with a Pepsi-Cola logo, (4) a short round bottom version without any logos (available as a boxed store set), and (5) a short straight-sided non-logo version (available as a boxed store set). Since so many of these glasses were made, they are fairly easy to find and therefore not expensive. However, collectors will find that it takes some hunting to complete some of the sets that they will encounter. Glasses with logos are worth more than those without: add 50% to price for Pepsi-Cola logo and 100% for Pepe's logo.

Row 1: *Twelve Days of Christmas* department store issue
1. Partridge in a pear tree . . . .$1.00 – 3.00
2. Two turtle doves . . . .$1.00 – 3.00
3. Three French hens . . . .$1.00 – 3.00
4. Four calling birds . . . .$1.00 – 3.00
5. Five golden rings . . . .$1.00 – 3.00
6. Six geese a laying . . . .$1.00 – 3.00

Row 2: *Twelve Days of Christmas* department store issue
1. Seven swans a swimming . . . .$1.00 – 3.00
2. Eight maids a milking . . . .$1.00 – 3.00
3. Nine dancers dancing . . . .$1.00 – 3.00
4. Ten lords a leaping . . . .$1.00 – 3.00
5. Eleven pipers piping . . . .$1.00 – 3.00
6. Twelve drummers drumming . . . .$1.00 – 3.00

Row 1: Pepsi-Cola *Twelve Days of Christmas*, 16-Ounce Brockway version (1976)
1. Partridge in a pear tree . . . .$1.00 – 3.00
2. Two turtle doves . . . .$1.00 – 3.00
3. Three French hens . . . .$1.00 – 3.00
4. Four calling birds . . . .$1.00 – 3.00
5. Five golden rings . . . .$1.00 – 3.00
6. Six geese a laying . . . .$1.00 – 3.00

Row 2: Pepsi-Cola *Twelve Days of Christmas*, 16-Ounce Brockway version (1976)
1. Seven swans a swimming . . . .$1.00 – 3.00
2. Eight maids a milking . . . .$1.00 – 3.00
3. Nine drummers drumming . . . .$1.00 – 3.00
4. Ten pipers piping . . . .$1.00 – 3.00
5. Eleven dancers dancing . . . .$1.00 – 3.00
6. Twelve lords a leaping . . . .$1.00 – 3.00

PLATE 147

PLATE 148

Christmas Glasses from Coca-Cola and Pepsi-Cola

The sets pictured on this page are all Coca-Cola or Pepsi-Cola sponsored Christmas glasses. The first four rows are all Coca-Cola sponsored glasses with three glasses in each set. Plate 147: Row 1 features three Norman Rockwell images from illustrations done by the artist for *The Saturday Evening Post* in the 1920s. Rows 2 and 3 feature Haddon Sundblom illustrations of the classical Santa Claus from the Coca-Cola archives. Plate 148: Row 1 shows the characters from *Mickey's Christmas Carol,* a 1982 take-off on Dickens' well-known tale.

Plate 147: Rows 2 and 3 feature Pepsi-Cola Christmas glasses. There are two versions of each of the two sets shown. The glasses in Plate 148, Row 2 feature four verses from *The Night Before Christmas.* They have a 1982 copyright and have what is called a button bottom. They can also be found in a round bottom version (similar in shape to the glasses in Row 3) with a 1983 copyright date. Values for both versions are similar. The Pepsi-Cola glasses in Row 3 feature verses from four popular Christmas carols. The same designs can be found on the same style tumbler with a 1983 or a 1984 copyright date. Again, values on both sets are similar.

Row 1: Coca-Cola Norman Rockwell Saturday Evening Post Santas, set of three
1. December 4, 1920 — Santa with ledger . . . .$4.00 – 6.00
2. December 2, 1922 — Santa with elves in workshop . . .$4.00 – 6.00
3. December 4, 1926 — Santa studying globe . . . . . .$4.00 – 6.00

Row 2: Coca-Cola Haddon Sundblom Historical Santas, Series I, set of three
1. 1961 Santa — One of three . . . .$4.00 – 6.00
2. 1960 Santa — Two of three . . . .$4.00 – 6.00
3. 1947 Santa — Three of three . . . .$4.00 – 6.00

Row 3: Coca-Cola Haddon Sundblom Historical Santas, Series II, set of three . . . .
1. 1943 Santa — One of three . . . .$4.00 – 6.00
2. 1946 Santa — Two of three . . . .$4.00 – 6.00
3. 1948 Santa — Three of three . . . .$4.00 – 6.00

Christmas Glasses from Coca-Cola and Pepsi-Cola, continued
Row 1: Coca-Cola *Mickey's Christmas Carol,* set of three (1982)
1. Scrooge McDuck as Ebenezer Scrooge . . . .$8.00 – 10.00
2. Mickey Mouse and Nephew Morty as Bob Cratchit and
   Tiny Tim . . . .$8.00 – 10.00
3. Goofy as Marley's Ghost . . . .$8.00 – 10.00

Row 2: Pepsi-Cola *Night Before Christmas* Collection, set of four (1982 & 1983)
1. *'Twas the night before Christmas...* . . . .$5.00 – 7.00
2. *Now Dasher! Now Dancer! Now Prancer and Vixen!...* .$5.00 – 7.00
3. *But I heard him exclaim, Ere he drove out of sight...* . . . .$5.00 – 7.00
4. *The stockings were hung By the chimney with care...* . . . .$5.00 – 7.00

Row 3: Pepsi-Cola Christmas Song Collection, set of four (1983 & 1984)
1. *Jingle Bells* . . . .$5.00 – 7.00
2. *O Christmas Tree* . . . .$5.00 – 7.00
3. *Toyland* . . . .$5.00 – 7.00
4. *We Wish You a Merry Christmas* . . . .$5.00 – 7.00

PLATE 149

PLATE 150

Miscellaneous Christmas Glasses

McCrory's stores and Coca-Cola have co-sponsored an attractive Christmas glass annually since at least 1982. Collectors of this series can get their glasses with a drink purchase at McCrory's stores that have luncheon counters. There is not actually a set of these, but a series of individual glasses. Most, but not all, are dated. Several examples are shown in Rows 1 and 2.

Row 1: Coca-Cola McCrory's Annual Christmas Issues
1. Santa with bags and packages, *McCrory's 100th Anniversary,* 1982 . . . .$2.00 – 4.00
2. Rudolph on ground, Santa driving sleigh in sky, 1983 $2.00 – 4.00
3. Christmas tree and fireplace, Santa with bag of toys, 1984 . . . .$2.00 – 4.00
4. Sleigh with packages, Santa putting star on top of tree, no date (1985) . . . .$2.00 – 4.00

Row 2: Coca-Cola McCrory's Annual Christmas Issues
1. Santa in flying sleigh, comet above his head (no date) (1986) . . . .$2.00 – 4.00
2. Santa in sleigh at North Pole (no date) (1987) . . . .$2.00 – 4.00
3. Christmas Town with Toy Shoppe (no date) (1988) $2.00 – 4.00
4. Santa unpacking bag, putting toys under tree (no date) (1989) . . . .$2.00 – 4.00

Miscellaneous Christmas Glasses, continued
Avon managers gave away Christmas glasses to their representatives in the late 1960s and early 1970s. The first three glasses shown in Plate 150: Row 1 were all made by The Federal Glass Company. The fourth glass is a heavier tumbler from a different maker.

Rows 2 and 3 show several holiday glasses. Some of these glasses have no sponsor and are probably retail store issues, while two are definitely restaurant premiums.

Row 1: Avon Christmas Issues
1. *Holiday Greetings from Avon,* December 1969 . . .$2.00 – 5.00
2. *Holiday Greetings from Avon,* December 1970 . . .$2.00 – 5.00
3. *Holiday Greetings from Avon,* December 1971 . . .$2.00 – 5.00
4. *Holiday Greetings from your Avon Manager,* December 1972 . . . .$2.00 – 5.00

Row 2: Miscellaneous Christmas glasses
1. Decorated tree — Federal Glass (in set with #5 below) $2.00 – 4.00
2. Santa in three different poses . . . .$2.00 – 4.00
3. Santa with elves . . . .$3.00 – 5.00
4. Decorated trees and poinsettias . . . .$2.00 – 4.00
5. Santa and sleigh with hanging stockings — Federal Glass . . . .$2.00 – 4.00

Row 3: Miscellaneous Santas
1. Santa with bag of burgers — *In-N-Out Burger,* Brockway Glass . . . .$4.00 – 6.00
2. *Santa Claus Brings...* . . . .$3.00 – 5.00
3. Santas — *Jack's Restaurants* . . . .$4.00 – 6.00

Americana

PLATE 151

World's Fairs, Expositions, War Victory Celebrations

World's Fair glasses and various Exposition glasses have been popular since at least the mid-1930s, and collectors can still find nice examples from the Great Lakes Expositions, the Golden Gate Exposition, and the 1939 New York World's Fair which spawned the greatest number of commemorative sets and effectively set a precedent for world's fair issues. The sets — usually of six or eight glasses — were sold at the fair and advertised as official. Single glasses showing scenes or themes from the fair were issued too, but they tended to be sold with food products in them in grocery stores; sets, therefore, were less common. Other single and specialized world's fair glasses found their way to the souvenir hungry public, making this area of glass collecting extremely interesting and challenging. In Rows 1 – 3, we show a variety of early and late New York World's Fair glasses.

Plate 151

Row 1: 1939 New York World's Fair glasses
1. *Official Souvenir New York World's Fair, 1939* — view of amusement park rides, fireworks — one of a set of six official glasses sold in a set by Canada Dry for *3¢ each when purchased with big 15¢ bottle.* . . . .$12.00 – 15.00
2. 1939 New York World's Fair, Textile Building Exhibit (one of a set of eight depicting different theme buildings) . .$15.00 – 20.00
3. *New York World's Fair, 1939* — showing 200 foot perisphere and 700 foot trylon. One of a set of six Canada Dry glasses (see #1 above). . . . .$12.00 – 15.00

Row 2: 1939 New York World's Fair glasses by Libbey
1. A Section of the Court of the States . . . .$12.00 – 15.00
2. Twentieth Century Transportation (railroad exhibits) .$12.00 – 15.00
3. Fountain and Lagoon of the Nations . . . .$12.00 – 15.00
4. Flight Around the World (text on glass: *On July 14, 1938 the plane 'New York World's Fair 1939' completed a record breaking three day trip around the world, thereby linking the entire world with the fair*) . . . .$12.00 – 15.00
5. Amusement Area and the Parachute Jump . . . . .$12.00 – 15.00

Row 3: Miscellaneous Modern Seattle and New York World's Fair glasses
1. 1962 Seattle World's Fair water glass . . . .$6.00 – 10.00
2. 1964 – 65 New York World's Fair food container . . .$5.00 – 8.00
3. 1964 – 65 New York World's Fair Unisphere, juice glass, sponsored by U.S. Steel . . . .$5.00 – 8.00

Plate 152

Row 1: Post World War II victory glasses
Rows 1 and 2 feature seven glasses from a set of eight World War II victory cocktail glasses. Alluring ladies, identified with roles crucial to the war effort, pose in the middle of a red, white, and blue V for victory. Glasses like this are difficult to find in excellent condition because the gold decoration tended to fade, and the applied decoration tended to fade, scratch, or chip easily.
1. Messenger . . . .$7.00 – 10.00
2. Air Raid Warden . . . .$7.00 – 10.00
3. Bomb Squad . . . .$7.00 – 10.00

Row 2: Post World War II victory glasses, continued
1. Auxiliary police . . . .$7.00 – 10.00
2. Demolition and cleaning crew . . . .$7.00 – 10.00
3. Decontamination corps . . . .$7.00 – 10.00
4. Auxiliary fireman . . . .$7.00 – 10.00

PLATE 152

PLATE 153

World's Fairs, Expositions, War Victory Celebrations, continued
Row 1: 1939 Golden Gate Exposition — San Francisco, California
1. California Building . . . .$15.00 – 20.00
2. Portals of the Pacific . . . .$15.00 – 20.00
3. Tower of the Sun . . . .$15.00 – 20.00
4. Chinese Village . . . .$15.00 – 20.00

PLATE 154

1962 Seattle World's Fair and 1964 – 65 New York World's Fair Frosted Iced Tea Tumblers

During the 1950s and 1960s the majority of souvenir glasses appeared in a popular tall frosted iced tea format. Sets commemorating the history and natural scenery of many of our states dominated this market. Most of these glasses were gas station premiums available for practically nothing with a minimum purchase, sometimes over a period of weeks, the premise behind the enterprise being repeat business at a particular station or loyalty to a particular oil company. The World's Fair glasses we show below could be purchased in sets at the fairs or at participating Mobil dealers. These glasses were also available by mail order.

Row 1: 1962 Seattle World's Fair frosted iced tea tumblers, set of eight
1. Space Needle . . . .$4.00 – 6.00
2. World of Art . . . .$4.00 – 6.00
3. Hydro-Electric Exhibit . . . .$4.00 – 6.00
4. Coliseum 21 . . . .$4.00 – 6.00

Row 2: 1962 Seattle World's Fair frosted iced tea tumblers
1. World of Entertainment . . . .$4.00 – 6.00
2. United States Science Pavilion . . . .$4.00 – 6.00
3. Monorail . . . .$4.00 – 6.00
4. Boulevards of the World . . . .$4.00 – 6.00

PLATE 155

World's Fair Tumblers, continued
Row 1: 1964 – 65 New York World's Fair frosted iced tea tumblers, set of eight
1. The Unisphere . . . .$4.00 – 6.00
2. William A. Shea Stadium . . . .$4.00 – 6.00
3. World's Fair Circus . . . .$4.00 – 6.00
4. New York State Exhibit . . . .$4.00 – 6.00

Row 2: 1964 – 65 New York World's Fair frosted iced tea tumblers, continued
1. Pool of Industry . . . .$4.00 – 6.00
2. Hall of Science . . . .$4.00 – 6.00
3. Port Authority Building . . . .$4.00 – 6.00
4. The Federal Pavilion . . . .$4.00 – 6.00

PLATE 156

National Flag Foundation Bicentennial 200 Collection

In the late 1960s, in anticipation of America's Bicentennial celebration, the National Flag Foundation based in Pittsburgh, Pennsylvania, commissioned Don Hewitt to execute a series of paintings depicting flags that played a role in America's history. These paintings are in the Heritage Collection at Flag Plaza in Pittsburgh. The glasses shown below bear Hewitt's designs and were marketed by Anchor Hocking as their *Bicentennial 200 Collection.* Anchor Hocking issued the glasses in cardboard six-packs with two each of three different glasses, and each six-pack had a Series name and number as follows: Series I — Early Flags of our Nation; Series II — The Revolution; Series III — Discovering a Continent; Series IV — From Yorktown West; Series V — Revolution at Sea; Series VI — Flags for Freedom; and Series VII — The Continent and Beyond. Completing this set is difficult. The later series (V, VI, and VII) seem to be tougher to find than the earlier ones.

Collectors need to know that in addition to this set of twenty-one glasses, another set of eight glasses was issued by the National Flag Foundation under the sponsorship of the Pittsburgh Press. This set, referred to on the glasses as *The Pittsburgh Press Bicentennial Collection,* uses six of the flags from the Anchor Hocking issue and two new ones: Iwo Jima and Confederate Battle Flag. This set was available for purchase from The Pittsburgh Press, and it was also offered as a prize in contests held by the newspaper. This set contains the following: Bunker Hill Flag, Commodore Perry, Confederate Battle Flag, Flag of the U.S. on the Moon, First Stars and Stripes, Gadsden, Iwo Jima, Star Spangled Banner. Values: $5.00 – 10.00.

Another set of National Flag Foundation glasses must be mentioned. This was the sixteen-glass set issued by Herfy's Restaurants on the west coast in 1975 – 1976. These glasses were co-sponsored by Coca-Cola in a 16-ounce round-bottom shell, and there was also a pitcher that went with this set. In this set, there are two flags that didn't appear in other sets: California Bear Flag and Cowpens. It con-

sists of: Alamo, Bennington, Bunker Hill, California Bear Flag, Commodore Perry, Cowpens, First Stars and Stripes, General Fremont, Grand Union, Green Mountains, Iwo Jima, Promontory Point, Rattlesnake, Star Spangled Banner, Taunton, Washington's Cruisers. Values: glasses, $5.00 – 10.00 each; pitcher, $25.00 – 30.00.

Finally, there's another much lesser known set which uses the NFF designs but a different glass shell. These glasses have a sort of modified pedestal base. We have encountered only half a dozen of them, so we are not sure how many there are in this set. We do know that they are less frequently encountered than any of the other NFF glasses (value: $5.00 – 10.00).

In addition to the sets, there are some singles worth mentioning. One is an Anchor Hocking pedestal with the First Stars and Stripes on it, Archibald Willard's three patriots, Concord Bridge, and Old North Church. On the reverse is a large Fyfe & Drum Beer sign/logo. Except for the back, it looks like it belongs with the Anchor Hocking series (value: $4.00 – 6.00). Another is the same glass but with an advertisement for Fyfe & Drum "Lyte Beer" (value: $4.00 – 6.00). The other single we know of is a 12-ounce glass sponsored by the Pepsi-Cola Bottling Company of Washington, D.C. It features the Bennington Flag, Independence Hall, Betsy Ross, and a Revolutionary War battle scene (value: $15.00 – 20.00).

Row 1: Pittsburgh Press Bicentennial Collection, set of eight, 1974 – 1976
1. Bunker Hill Flag . . . .$5.00 – 7.00
2. Commodore Perry — Don't Give Up the Ship . . . .$5.00 – 7.00
3. Confederate Battle Flag . . . .$7.00 – 10.00
4. First Stars and Stripes . . . .$5.00 – 7.00

Row 2: Pittsburgh Press Bicentennial Collection, continued
1. Gadsden — Don't Tread on Me . . . .$5.00 – 7.00
2. Iwo Jima . . . .$7.00 – 10.00
3. Star Spangled Banner . . . .$5.00 – 7.00
4. The Flag of U.S. on the Moon . . . .$7.00 – 10.00

PLATE 157

PLATE 158

America's Bicentennial (1776 – 1976)

America's Bicentennial celebration in 1976 was the inspiration for unprecedented commemorative glassware production. Everyone, it seemed, got in on the action, and, more often than not, the action consisted of variations on the independence theme — its historic personalities, places, and events. These themes were played over and over again on glass with astounding commercial success. Collectors who decide to focus only on this area of glass collecting will find that they have what appears to be an insurmountable task since there are an almost unlimited number of interesting bicentennial-related glasses to collect. We show three sets here that were inspired by America's most important event. Row 1 shows A & P's Ann Page *Creamy Smooth Peanut Butter,* set of four. Row 2 shows Coca-Cola's 1976 Heritage Collector Series *Spirit 1776,* set of four. There are three panels on each of these glasses, each focusing on a specific aspect of the Revolution. One panel is the same on all four glasses — the one which shows Archibald Willard's famous painting entitled *The Spirit of 1776.* Row 3 shows another Coca-Cola 1976 Heritage Collector Series, set of four. Each of these glasses focuses on one important Revolutionary person/event.

Row 1: National Flag Foundation, set of 21, by Anchor Hocking, 1974 – 1976
Early Flags of our Nation — Series I
1. First Stars and Stripes . . . .$3.00 – 5.00
2. Star Spangled Banner . . . .$3.00 – 5.00
3. Grand Union . . . .$3.00 – 5.00
The Revolution — Series II
4. Bunker Hill Flag . . . .$4.00 – 6.00
5. The Green Mountains . . . .$4.00 – 6.00
6. Taunton . . . .$4.00 – 6.00

Row 2: National Flag Foundation, set of 21, continued
Discovering a Continent — Series III
1. Royal Standard of Spain . . . .$7.00 – 10.00
Not pictured:
British Union . . . .$5.00 – 7.00
French Fleur de Lis . . . .$6.00 – 8.00
From Yorktown West — Series IV
2. Alamo . . . .$6.00 – 8.00
3. Commodore Perry — Don't Give Up the Ship . . . .$4.00 – 6.00
Not pictured:
General Fremont . . . .$4.00 – 6.00
Revolution at Sea — Series V
4. Rattlesnake — Don't Tread on Me . . . .$6.00 – 8.00
5. Washington's Cruisers — An Appeal to Heaven . . .$7.00 – 9.00
6. Gadsden — Don't Tread on Me . . . .$6.00 – 8.00

Row 3: National Flag Foundation, set of 21, continued
Flags for Freedom — Series VI
1. Bennington . . . .$5.00 – 7.00
2. Serapis . . . .$6.00 – 8.00
3. Guilford Courthouse . . . .$6.00 – 8.00
The Continent and Beyond — Series VII
1. Peary Flag . . . .$8.00 – 10.00
Not pictured:
Promontory Point . . . .$8.00 – 10.00
The Flag of U.S. on the Moon . . . .$8.00 – 10.00

Row 1: A & P Ann Page Peanut Butter Bicentennial Celebration, set of four (1976)
1. Militia Men with Fife and Drum . . . .$2.00 – 4.00
2. Paul Revere . . . .$2.00 – 4.00
3. Liberty Bell . . . .$2.00 – 4.00
4. Mt. Vernon . . . .$2.00 – 4.00

Row 2: Coca-Cola Heritage Collector Series "Spirit 1776," set of four
1. Valley Forge/The Minutemen . . . .$4.00 – 7.00
2. Nathan Hale/John Paul Jones . . . .$4.00 – 7.00
3. Declaration of Independence/Paul Revere . . . .$4.00 – 7.00
4. Betsy Ross & Old Glory/Washington Crossing the
   Delaware . . . .$4.00 – 7.00

Row 3: Coca-Cola Heritage Collector Series, set of four (1976)
1. John Paul Jones, *I Have Not Yet Begun To Fight* . . .$3.00 – 6.00
2. Patrick Henry, *Give Me Liberty Or Give Me Death* . . .$3.00 – 6.00
3. George Washington, *Times That Try Men's Souls* . . .$3.00 – 6.00
4. Paul Revere, *The Regulars Are Out!* . . . .$3.00 – 6.00

PLATE 159

United States Presidents

The set of presidential glasses pictured on this page was made by Libbey in the late 1940s or early 1950s. The set was available as a boxed set in retail stores and had a glass for each of the Presidents from George Washington through Harry Truman. The Truman glass has an open-ended date for his term of office (1945 —), which helps us to date the glasses. The John Quincey Adams glass (6th President) is not pictured here. Notice that the glasses have gold rims — a factor you should consider when buying them. The preferred way to get this set is to buy it complete in the box, since the set is quite difficult to put together one glass at a time.

Row 1: Libbey Presidential Series
1. George Washington . . . .$5.00 – 8.00

2. John Adams . . . .$5.00 – 8.00
3. Thomas Jefferson . . . .$5.00 – 8.00
4. James Madison . . . .$5.00 – 8.00
5. James Monroe . . . .$5.00 – 8.00
6. Andrew Jackson . . . .$5.00 – 8.00

Row 2: Libbey Presidential Series, continued
1. Martin Van Buren . . . .$5.00 – 8.00
2. William Harrison . . . .$5.00 – 8.00
3. John Tyler . . . .$5.00 – 8.00
4. James Polk . . . .$5.00 – 8.00
5. Zachery Taylor . . . .$5.00 – 8.00
6. Millard Fillmore . . . .$5.00 – 8.00

PLATE 160

Row 1: Libbey Presidential Series, continued
1. Franklin Pierce . . . .$5.00 – 8.00
2. James Buchanan . . . .$5.00 – 8.00
3. Abraham Lincoln . . . .$5.00 – 8.00
4. Andrew Johnson . . . .$5.00 – 8.00
5. Ulysses S. Grant . . . .$5.00 – 8.00
6. Rutherford Hayes . . . .$5.00 – 8.00

Row 2: Libbey Presidential Series, continued
1. James Garfield . . . .$5.00 – 8.00
2. Chester Arthur . . . .$5.00 – 8.00
3. Grover Cleveland . . . .$5.00 – 8.00

4. Benjamin Harrison . . . .$5.00 – 8.00
5. William McKinley . . . .$5.00 – 8.00
6. Theodore Roosevelt . . . .$5.00 – 8.00

Row 3: Libbey Presidential Series, continued
1. William Taft . . . .$5.00 – 8.00
2. Woodrow Wilson . . . .$5.00 – 8.00
3. Warren Harding . . . .$5.00 – 8.00
4. Calvin Coolidge . . . .$5.00 – 8.00
5. Herbert Hoover . . . .$5.00 – 8.00
6. Franklin Roosevelt . . . .$5.00 – 8.00
7. Harry Truman . . . .$5.00 – 8.00

Space Related

PLATE 161

Star Trek and Star Wars

Collectors are fortunate to have four different sets of Star Trek glasses to collect. The first set, shown in Plate 161: Row 1, was sponsored by Dr. Pepper and was issued in 1976. In 1978, a follow-up set in the same glass style but with better color and more detailed pictures of the same characters was issued. This later set commands slightly higher prices than the earlier one and seems to be more difficult to find. In Row 2 we picture the 1980 *Star Trek the Motion Picture* set which was sponsored by Coca-Cola. In Row 3 we show the 1984 Taco Bell *Star Trek III: The Search for Spock.* The double ring glass design is unique to this interesting set, but because of plentiful production, the price on these glasses languishes.

Row 1: Star Trek, 1976, set of four, sponsored by Dr. Pepper
1. The U. S. S. Enterprise . . . .$15.00 – 20.00
2. Mr. Spock . . . .$15.00 – 20.00
3. Captain James Kirk . . . .$15.00 – 20.00
4. Dr. Leonard McCoy . . . .$15.00 – 20.00
Not pictured: Dr. Pepper, *Star Trek*, 1978, set of four
#1 The U. S. S. Enterprise . . . .$20.00 – 30.00
#2 Mr. Spock . . . .$20.00 – 30.00
#3 Captain James Kirk . . . .$20.00 – 30.00
#4 Dr. Leonard McCoy . . . .$20.00 – 30.00

Row 2: *Star Trek: The Motion Picture*, 1980, set of three
1. Starship U.S.S. Enterprise . . . .$10.00 – 15.00
2. Captain James T. Kirk, Mr. Spock, and Dr. "Bones"
   McCoy . . . .$10.00 – 15.00
3. Commander Willard Decker and Navigator Lieutenant
   Ilia . . . .$10.00 – 15.00

Row 3: Taco Bell, *Star Trek III: The Search for Spock*, 1984, set of 4
1. The Enterprise Destroyed . . . .$3.00 – 5.00
2. Spock Lives . . . .$3.00 – 5.00
3. Lord Kruge . . . .$3.00 – 5.00
4. Fal-Tor-Pan . . . .$3.00 – 5.00

PLATE 162

Star Trek and Star Wars, continued

The Star Wars movie trilogy is amply documented on glass, thanks to Coca-Cola and Burger King. The Star Wars set (Plate 162: Row 1) was issued in 1977 and is thought by many collectors to be the most attractively designed and hardest to find in mint condition. It therefore commands higher prices than the sequel sets. In Row 2, we show The Empire Strikes Back set, which has a couple of interesting variations (not shown here): (1) a Canadian set which is generally the same but has some minor but noticeable design and color differences and (2) a U. S. set which is the same but has a thin applied decal instead of a baked-on enamel coating. In Row 3 we show The Return of the Jedi set, which seems to be more available than the other two and therefore commands relatively lower prices.

Row 1: *Star Wars*, 1977, set of four
1. R2-D2/C-3PO . . . .$5.00 – 9.00
2. Darth Vader . . . .$5.00 – 9.00
3. Luke Skywalker . . . .$5.00 – 9.00
4. Chewbacca . . . .$5.00 – 9.00

Row 2: *The Empire Strikes Back*, 1980, set of four
1. R2-D2/C-3PO . . . .$3.00 – 7.00
2. Lando Calrissian . . . .$3.00 – 7.00
3. Darth Vader . . . .$3.00 – 7.00
4. Luke Skywalker . . . .$3.00 – 7.00

Row 3: *The Return of the Jedi*, 1983, set of four
1. Han Solo in the Tatooine Desert . . . .$2.00 – 5.00
2. Luke and Darth Vader in the Emperor's Throne Room . . .$2.00 – 5.00
3. Intergalactic Gangster Jabba the Hutt . . . .$2.00 – 5.00
4. At the Ewok Village . . . .$2.00 – 5.00

PLATE 163

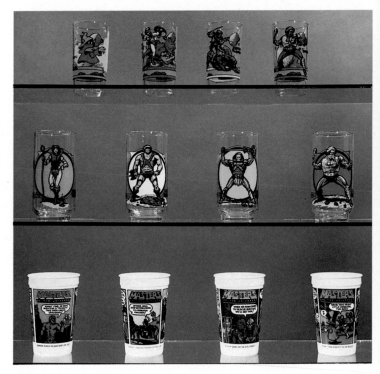

PLATE 164

E.T. (The Extra Terrestrial) and Mattel Masters of the Universe

The glass spinoffs from E.T. have been fairly modest, considering the phenomenal success of the 1982 movie. Nevertheless, there are three pretty nice sets out there for collectors. In Plate 163: Row 1 we picture the 1982 AAFES (Army and Air Force Exchange Service) set of four, which takes the prize for successful design. Row 2 shows the 1988 MCA Home Video Pepsi-Cola set of six which was available from Pepsi-Cola through the mail to anyone who sent in video rental coupons and Pepsi-Cola UPC's. This set is hard to find and relatively expensive, mostly because Pepsi-Cola collectors are driving up the price. From a design-appearance standpoint, there is little to recommend it. Row 3 pictures the overabundant 1982 Pizza Hut E.T. Collector Series set of four.

Row 1: AAFES E.T., set of four (1982)
1. Be good . . . .$5.00 – 10.00
2. E.T. Phone Home . . . .$5.00 – 10.00
3. I'll be right here . . . .$5.00 – 10.00
4. To the spaceship . . . .$5.00 – 10.00

Row 2: Pepsi-Cola/MCA Home Video E.T., set of six, 1988
1. E.T. in Disguise . . . .$15.00 – 25.00
2. E.T. and Elliott say goodbye . . . .$15.00 – 25.00
3. E.T.'s finger glows . . . .$15.00 – 25.00
4. Gertie kisses E.T. . . . .$15.00 – 25.00
5. Elliott hugs E.T. . . . .$15.00 – 25.00
6. E.T. rides with Elliott . . . .$15.00 – 25.00

Row 3: E.T. Collector's Series, Pizza Hut, 1982, set of four
1. Be Good . . . .$2.00 – 4.00
2. Phone home . . . .$2.00 – 4.00
3. I'll be right here . . . .$2.00 – 4.00
4. Home . . . .$2.00 – 4.00

Mattel Masters of the Universe

The early to mid 1980s witnessed a blast of interest in science fiction characters, and some of these made it into the glass format. Plate 164: Row 1 pictures the brightly colored 1986 juice set, and Row 2 features the earlier 1983 set. In Row 3 we show four plastic versions.

Row 1: Mattel Masters of the Universe juice set, 1986, set of four
1. Orko . . . .$3.00 – 5.00
2. He-Man/Battle Cat . . . .$3.00 – 5.00
3. Skeletor/Panthor . . . .$3.00 – 5.00
4. Man-At-Arms . . . .$3.00 – 5.00

Row 2: Mattel Masters of the Universe, 1983, set of four
1. Teela . . . .$5.00 – 10.00
2. He-Man . . . .$5.00 – 10.00
3. Skeletor . . . .$5.00 – 10.00
4. Man-At-Arms . . . .$5.00 – 10.00

Row 3: Masters of the Universe plastic tumblers, set of four
1. He-Man saves the day . . . .$1.00 – 3.00
2. Stalking enemies of Skeltor . . . .$1.00 – 3.00
3. He-Man takes on the Evil Hoarde . . . .$1.00 – 3.00
4. He-Man and Roboto to the rescue . . . .$1.00 – 3.00

PLATE 165

U.S. Space Program Glasses

Many different glasses were issued by various sponsors to chronicle the accomplishments of the United States in its race for space exploration supremacy. Some were available from oil companies who were quick to exploit the connection between rocket fuel and their product; some contained food products and featured rather generic space representations; and others were available through specialty retailers. This is an exciting and important historical collecting niche. The set of four glasses and carafe in Plate 165: Row 1 was sponsored by Marathon Oil Co. and is especially available in Ohio, Indiana, and Illinois. Row 2 shows some serious commemorative type glasses along with an amusing novelty glass with room for "fuel" in either top or bottom. Row 3 shows some food container glasses.

Row 1: Apollo Series with Carafe
1. Apollo 11 (July 1969) . . . .$2.00 – 4.00
2. Apollo 12 (November 1969) . . . .$2.00 – 4.00
3. Apollo 11, 12, 13 carafe . . . .$6.00 – 10.00

4. Apollo 13 (April 1970) . . . .$2.00 – 4.00
5. Apollo 14 (February 1971) . . . .$2.00 – 4.00

Row 2: Miscellaneous Space Program Glasses
1. John Glenn, Friendship 7, Feb. 20, 1962 . . . .$4.00 – 7.00
2. Gemini IV, from *Space Spectacular* set . . . .$5.00 – 8.00
3. Apollo 8, from *Space spectacular* set . . . .$5.00 – 8.00
4. Apollo 11 Moonshot, *Man on the Moon, July 20, 1969* . . . .$5.00 – 8.00
Not pictured:
Harold's [Club] Moon Shot, Reno Nevada (a take-off on #4 above) . . . .$7.00 – 10.00

Row 3: Miscellaneous
1. Spacecraft designs . . . .$3.00 – 5.00
2. Astronauts exploring . . . .$5.00 – 8.00
3. Astronauts working . . . .$5.00 – 8.00
4. U.S. Space Records: Longest Manned Flight, Animal Test Flight . . . .$5.00 – 8.00

Superheroes

PLATE 166

The colorful glasses pictured on this page are all Pepsi-Cola Collector Series Superhero glasses. All were made by the Brockway Glass Company and are 6¼" high. The seven glasses shown in Plate 166: Rows 1 and 2 are known as the D.C. Action Series Set and were issued in 1978, but three of them bear earlier copyright dates which refer to the character's copyright date, not to the issue date of the glass. These date variations frequently mislead people into believing that the glasses are older than they are. There are two color-variation versions of the Wonder Woman glass: the more common one pictured below with red boots, yellow stars on shorts, and red vest/yellow bra; and the rarer colors-reversed version with yellow boots, red stars, and yellow vest/red bra. Another way to put it: everything that is red on the common glass is yellow on the rare one; everything that is yellow on the common glass is red on the rare one. Aquaman can sometimes be found without the date.

Note: This set, minus the Aquaman glass, also comes in a round-bottom 5⅞" tumbler. The designs are identical to those on the Brockway set. On this set the copyright dates are all 1978, except for Batman (1966) and Superman (1975). These glasses are rarer and more valuable than their Brockway counterparts.

Plate 166
Row 1: 1978 D.C. Comics Superheroes
1. Batman (©1966) . . . .$8.00 – 12.00
2. Wonder Woman (©1978), red boots, yellow stars on shorts . . . .$8.00 – 12.00
3. Robin (©1978) . . . .$8.00 – 12.00
Variation of #2, not pictured:
Wonder Woman, colors reversed . . . .$25.00 – 50.00

Row 2: 1978 D.C. Comics Superheroes
1. *Shazam!* (©1978) . . . .$8.00 – 12.00
2. Superman (©1975) . . . .$8.00 – 12.00
3. The Flash (©1971) . . . .$8.00 – 12.00
4. Aquaman (©1978) . . . .$8.00 – 12.00
Not pictured:
1978 D.C. Comics 5⅝" Round-Bottom Superhero, set of six
Batman . . . .$15.00 – 25.00
Wonder Woman . . . .$15.00 – 25.00
Robin . . . .$15.00 – 25.00
Shazam! . . . .$15.00 – 25.00
Superman . . . .$15.00 – 25.00
The Flash . . . .$15.00 – 25.00

D.C. Comics

Plate 167

Row 1: 1976 Pepsi Super Series
The glasses pictured in these three rows, issued in 1976, are called the *Pepsi Super Series.* Collectors sometimes refer to them as the moon superheroes, a reference to the 3" colored circle behind each superhero. The design is the same on both sides of the glass. There are fourteen glasses in the set, and each glass bears either a D.C. Comics Inc. or N.P.P. (National Periodical Publications) Inc. copyright. Thus, there are really two distinct sets to collect. The D.C. glasses are thought to be rarer in general; indeed, several of them command very high, premium prices.

	N.P.P.	D.C.
1. Riddler	$20.00 – 40.00	$40.00 – 60.00
2. Green Lantern	$20.00 – 40.00	$40.00 – 60.00
3. Joker	$20.00 – 40.00	$40.00 – 60.00
4. Green Arrow	$10.00 – 15.00	$20.00 – 30.00
5. Penguin	$20.00 – 40.00	$40.00 – 60.00

Row 2: 1976 Pepsi Super Series, continued
	N.P.P.	D.C.
1. Batman	$10.00 – 15.00	$10.00 – 15.00
2. Batgirl	$10.00 – 15.00	$10.00 – 15.00
3. Robin	$10.00 – 15.00	$10.00 – 15.00
4. *Shazam!*	$10.00 – 15.00	$10.00 – 15.00

Row 3: 1976 Pepsi Super Series, continued
	N.P.P.	D.C.
1. Aquaman	$10.00 – 15.00	$10.00 – 15.00
2. Wonder Woman	$10.00 – 15.00	$10.00 – 15.00
3. Superman	$10.00 – 15.00	$10.00 – 15.00
4. Supergirl	$10.00 – 15.00	$10.00 – 15.00
5. Flash	$10.00 – 15.00	$10.00 – 15.00

PLATE 167

PLATE 168

PLATE 169

Superman in Action, National Periodical Publications, 1964

The glasses shown are jam glasses that originally held Polaner's TV Treat Pure Concord Grape Jam. This jam was marketed by M. Polaner and Son Inc., Newark, New Jersey. These glasses, which are fairly rare and difficult to find, came in two sizes: 4¼" and 5¾". There are at least six different color combinations available and six different scenes, so assembling a complete set in both sizes would be challenging.

The glasses pictured all have the same scene: *Superman in Action* rescuing a bus. We show different views, color combinations, and sizes to convey an idea of the variety of this set.

The titles of the glasses in this set are as follows:
Superman in Action . . . .$20.00 – 35.00
Clark Kent Changes to Superman . . . .$20.00 – 35.00
Superman Uses X-Ray Vision . . . .$20.00 – 35.00
Superman Finds the Spaceship . . . .$20.00 – 35.00
Superman Fighting the Dragon . . . .$20.00 – 35.00
Superman to the Rescue . . . .$20.00 – 35.00

National Periodical Publications

The glasses shown on this page are from the Batman and Superman families with issue dates ranging from the early 1960s to the early 1990s.

Row 1: Two members of the 1960s *Batman with Robin the Boy Wonder* set
These two glasses are from an early 60s National Periodicals Publications set. The two glasses we show here — Batman and Robin — are the two most common members of the set. These two glasses can also be found with three colors, a variation which is rarer, better looking, and pricier. To round the set out, there is a Joker glass and a Penguin glass, but these last two glasses are very rare and command premium prices.
1. Batman (grey and blue) . . . .$10.00 – 15.00
2. Robin (yellow and red) . . . .$10.00 – 15.00
Not pictured:
Batman (grey, blue, and yellow) . . . .$30.00 – 50.00
Robin (yellow, red, and green) . . . .$30.00 – 50.00
Joker . . . .$50.00 – 100.00
Penguin . . . .$50.00 – 100.00

Row 2: Ultramar Petroleum Batman, set of six (1989 – 1990)
The Ultramar Petroleum Batman glasses are Canadian glasses issued at about the same time as the Batman movie. They were priced at 79¢ (Canadian) with a 25 litre purchase of gasoline.
1. Batman Emblem . . . .$3.00 – 6.00
2. Batman's Head . . . .$3.00 – 6.00
3. Batman standing next to Batmobile . . . .$3.00 – 6.00
4. Batman, standing . . . .$3.00 – 6.00
5. Batplane . . . .$3.00 – 6.00
6. Batmobile with Emblem . . . .$3.00 – 6.00

PLATE 170

D.C. Comics

Row 1: Burger King Plastic Superhero figures with detachable mugs, 1988
The plastic superhero figures came from Burger King with a detachable plastic drink container (shown in the middle).
1. Superman ....$2.00 – 4.00
2. Wonder Woman ....$2.00 – 4.00
3. Plastic drink container ....$1.00 – 2.00
4. Dark Side ....$2.00 – 4.00
5. Batman ....$2.00 – 4.00

Row 2: Double Character Pepsi-Cola Superheroes
There is no date, but there are two Pepsi-Cola logos, a D.C. Comic copyright, and Pepsico trademark information. The genesis of these glasses is uncertain, and there is much speculation. It is thought that these glasses are unofficial, unauthorized, freelance items, and totally unconnected with restaurant promotions. But they look good, and they have taken a solid position among Pepsi-Cola collectibles. They probably date from the early 80s. Each glass has a picture of Superman standing with his cape flying behind him. The characters on the other side of these glasses are (1) Superman running towards us with cape flying, (2) Batman swinging on a rope, (3) Robin riding his motorcycle, and (4) Wonder woman twirling her rope.
1. Superman/Superman ....$30.00 – 50.00
2. Batman/Superman ....$30.00 – 50.00
3. Robin/Superman ....$30.00 – 50.00
4. Wonder Woman/Superman ....$30.00 – 50.00

Row 3: Superman the Movie, D.C. Comics, 1978, set of six
This is a very colorful, desirable set which most collectors should be able to complete.
1. From Kal-el the Child to the Man of Steel ....$5.00 – 10.00
2. Kal-el comes to Earth ....$5.00 – 10.00
3. Lois Lane is saved by her hero ....$5.00 – 10.00
4. Superman saves the day ....$5.00 – 10.00
5. The Caped Wonder to the Rescue ....$5.00 – 10.00
6. The Characters ....$5.00 – 10.00

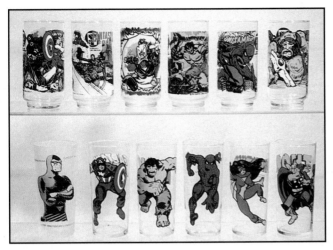

PLATE 171

PLATE 172

7-Eleven Marvel Comics Group Super Heroes (1977)

Row 1: 7-Eleven Marvel Super Heroes, set of six (1977)
This set of six boldly designed and colorful glasses was distributed at 7-Eleven convenience stores in the late 1970s. They are very popular with collectors. The Hulk and Spiderman seem to be the most difficult to find, and they therefore command the highest prices. The complete set is considered a must by most collectors. They just don't make glasses like this anymore.

1. Captain America and The Falcon . . . .$15.00 – 18.00
2. Fantastic Four and Dr. Doom . . . .$15.00 – 18.00
3. Howard the Duck . . . .$15.00 – 18.00
4. The Incredible Hulk . . . .$20.00 – 25.00
5. Amazing Spider-Man . . . .$25.00 – 30.00
6. The Mighty Thor . . . .$15.00 – 18.00

Row 2: The Phantom and 1978 Marvel Comics Group, set of five Super Heroes
The first glass in Row 2 is from Australia and features the *Phantom Ghost who Walks...Man who Cannot Die; Monkeys of Melbourne* also appears on this glass along with *© 1991 King Features Syndicate, Inc.* There is at least one other glass in this set.

1. *The Phantom Ghost who Walks* . . . .$45.00 – 50.00
Not pictured:
Astro Boy . . . .$50.00 – 65.00
The remainder of the glasses in this row are Federal glass tumblers that feature five of the Marvel Comics Group superheroes. These glasses are not marked with a sponsor but were probably distributed by a restaurant or store chain. Quite colorful and hard to find in mint condition, these glasses are considered very desirable by collectors. Collectors seem to agree that Spider-Woman is the most difficult to find in fine condition. This is another set that serious collectors go out of their way to acquire, and acquiring it can take considerable time and money.
Marvel Comics Group, set of five (1978)
2. Captain America . . . .$80.00 – 100.00
3. The Hulk . . . .$80.00 – 100.00
4. Spider-Man . . . .$80.00 – 100.00
5. Spider-Woman . . . .$100.00 – 140.00
6. Thor . . . .$80.00 – 100.00

7-Eleven Marvel Comics Group Super Heroes (1977), continued
Row 1: 1980 Universal Studios, Inc. Monsters, set of five
This colorful set of monster glasses was probably a department store issue from the early 1980s. It has been assumed for some time that there is a sixth glass to the set — possibly The Mummy — but it has not turned up to date and seems to be in the same category as The Sunday Funnies Dick Tracy which also exists only in the imaginations of collectors! This set of five is very desirable because of its scarcity and bold colors and designs. For many collectors, it's another of those must-have sets.

1. Creature From the Black Lagoon . . . .$65.00 – 85.00
2. Dracula . . . .$65.00 – 85.00
3. Frankenstein . . . .$65.00 – 85.00
4. The Mutant . . . .$65.00 – 85.00
5. Wolfman . . . .$65.00 – 85.00
Incidentally, a taller set of four undated monster glasses was available during the 1960s. These 1960s glasses are actually more plentiful than their later counterparts, but they are much less attractive with drab colors and rather commonplace artwork.
Not pictured:
Set of four, 1960s 6" glasses featuring monsters Frankenstein, Wolfman, Creature From the Black Lagoon, Dracula . .$40.00 – 60.00 ea.

Sports

PLATE 173

The glasses on this page feature National Football League teams and players. Wendy's, Burger King, and McDonald's are the sponsors. The Dallas Cowboys glasses in Rows 2 and 3 are undated but probably appeared in 1977 or 1978. There are actually two sets of six — one set with stars and rings around the top, and one set with blue lines only. Collectors will wonder why Roger Staubach isn't represented in these sets. The answer to this question is that Staubach appears on a taller 6¼" straight-sided tumbler which is not sponsored by Burger King/Dr Pepper. He's the only Cowboy on such a glass, which leads us to believe that the glass design was changed after the production of the single Staubach glass.

Plate 173

Row 1: Cleveland Browns, set of four, Wendy's/Dr Pepper, 1981
1. Doug Dieken, #73, Tackle . . . .$5.00 – 8.00
2. Mike Pruitt, #43, Fullback . . . .$5.00 – 8.00
3. Lyle Alzado, #77, Defensive End . . . .$5.00 – 8.00
4. Brian Sipe, #17, Quarterback . . . .$5.00 – 8.00

Row 2: Dallas Cowboys, set of six (two shown), Burger King/Dr Pepper
1. Efren Herrera . . . .$7.00 – 10.00
2. Drew Pearson . . . .$7.00 – 10.00
Not pictured, but part of this set:
#3 Billy Joe DuPree . . . .$7.00 – 10.00
#4 Harvey Martin . . . .$7.00 – 10.00
#5 Charlie Waters . . . .$7.00 – 10.00
#6 Randy White . . . .$7.00 – 10.00

Row 3: Dallas Cowboys, set of six (five shown), Burger King/Dr Pepper
1. D. D. Lewis . . . .$7.00 – 10.00
2. Robert Newhouse . . . .$7.00 – 10.00
3. Cliff Harris . . . .$7.00 – 10.00
4. Pat Donovan . . . .$7.00 – 10.00
5. Bob Breunig . . . .$7.00 – 10.00
Not pictued, but part of this set:
#6 Golden Richards . . . .$7.00 – 10.00
Not shown and not a member of the two sets above:
Roger Staubach . . . .$10.00 – 15.00

Plate 174

Row 1: Atlanta Falcons, Set of Four, McDonald's/Dr Pepper, 1980 – 1981
1. William Andrews, Jeff Van Note, Mike Kenn . . . . .$4.00 – 6.00
2. R. C. Thielmann, Bobby Butler, Lynn Cain . . . .$4.00 – 6.00
3. Steve Bartkowski, Alfred Jackson, Al Jenkins . . . . .$4.00 – 6.00
4. Fulton Kuykendall, Joel Williams, Buddy Curry . . .$4.00 – 6.00

Row 2: Philadelphia Eagles, set of five, McDonald's, 1980
1. Bill Bergey, Linebacker and John Bunting, Linebacker .$4.00 – 6.00
2. Tony Franklin, Kicker and Stan Walters, Tackle . . .$4.00 – 6.00
3. Wilbert Montgomery, Running Back and Billy Campfield, RB . . . .$4.00 – 6.00
4. Harold Carmichael, Wide Receiver and Randy Logan, Safety . . . .$4.00 – 6.00
5. Ron Jaworski, Quarterback and Keith Krepfle, Tight End . . . .$4.00 – 6.00

PLATE 174

PLATE 173

Row 3: 1976 WTAE Stereo 96 Pittsburgh Steeler Players
1. Andy Russell, #34 . . . .$8.00 – 10.00
2. Glen Edwards, #27 . . . .$8.00 – 10.00
3. Ray Mansfield, #56 . . . .$8.00 – 10.00
4. Dwight White, #78 . . . .$8.00 – 10.00

Plate 176

Row 1: McDonald's Pittsburgh Steelers Superbowl 13, set of four (1978)
1. Mike Webster, Terry Bradshaw, L. C. Greenwood .$5.00 – 8.00
2. Donnie Shell, Rocky Bleier, Jack Ham . . . .$5.00 – 8.00
3. John Stallworth, Joe Greene, Mike Wagner . . . . . .$5.00 – 8.00
4. Sam Davis, Jack Lambert, John Banaszak . . . .$5.00 – 8.00

Row 2: McDonald's Pittsburgh Steelers Superbowl 14, set of four (1979)
1. Sam Davis, Terry Bradshaw, Jack Ham . . . .$3.00 – 5.00
2. Rocky Bleier, John Stallworth, Dirt Winston . . . . . .$3.00 – 5.00
3. Sidney Thornton, Joe Greene, Matt Bahr . . . .$3.00 – 5.00
4. Jon Kolb, Jack Lambert, Mel Blount . . . .$3.00 – 5.00

Row 3: McDonald's All-Time Greatest Steelers Team (1982)
1. #1 of 4: Mullins, Brown, Lambert, Harris, Brady, and White . . . .$5.00 – 8.00
2. #2 of 4: Greene, Nickel, Kolb, Bleier, Shell, Ham .$5.00 – 8.00
3. #3 of 4: Gerela, Davis, Wagner, Greenwood, Webster, Swann . . . .$5.00 – 8.00
4. #4 of 4: Blount, Stoutner, Bradshaw, Russell, Stallworth, Butler . . . .$5.00 – 8.00

All of the glasses on this page feature Pittsburgh Steelers players. Plate 175: Rows 1 – 3 shows a complete set of eleven glasses issued in 1976. These 16 oz. Brockway glasses were sponsored by WTAE television and radio in Pittsburgh and were available at Winky's restaurants. However, the Franco Harris and Terry Bradshaw glasses are the only glasses in the set with the *1250/WTAE STEREO 96* logo. There is no player number on the Harris or Bradshaw WTAE glasses. However, the Bradshaw glass can also be found without the WTAE logo but with a player number. The Harris and Bradshaw glasses are the two most difficult to find, and they command higher prices than the others. With the Bradshaw variation, this becomes a set of 12 glasses. Plate 176: Row 1 shows the McDonald's 1978 Superbowl 13 set of four, and Row 2 shows the McDonald's 1979 Superbowl 14 set of four. At 6" with white lettering, the 1978 glasses are a little taller than the 1979 issue which has yellow lettering. Row 3 shows the 1982 McDonald's numbered set of four "All-Time Greatest Steelers Team" 4¾" rocks glasses.

Plate 175

Row 1: 1976 WTAE Stereo 96 Pittsburgh Steelers Players
1. Terry Bradshaw . . . .$15.00 – 25.00
2. Terry Bradshaw (reverse, showing WTAE logo and no #)
Not pictured:
Terry Bradshaw, #12 (no WTAE logo) . . . .$15.00 – 25.00
3. Franco Harris . . . .$15.00 – 25.00
4. Rocky Bleier, #20 . . . .$8.00 – 10.00

Row 2: 1976 WTAE Stereo 96 Pittsburgh Steelers Players
1. Mel Blount, #47 . . . .$8.00 – 10.00
2. Jack Lambert, #58 . . . .$8.00 – 10.00
3. Joe Greene, #75 . . . .$8.00 – 10.00
4. Jack Ham, #59 . . . .$8.00 – 10.00

PLATE 176

PLATE 177

PLATE 178

National Football League Helmets/Logos

Glasses depicting the logos and insignias of National Football League teams have been popular for quite some time, and many types and varieties with various sponsors are available. With the exception of the glasses shown in Plate 177: Row 1, all of the glasses on this page were sponsored by Mobil Oil Co. The four rocks glasses pictured in Row 1 are 3½" high and have football-shaped windows which offer a view of a team's helmet. There is probably a glass for each NFL team at the time of issue. The Mobil helmet glasses were issued from 1985 – 1988 in both short and tall, clear and frosted versions. All 28 team glasses were available only in the 1988 single band set, but even so, the Atlanta, Denver, Kansas City, Pittsburgh, San Francisco, and Seattle glasses had to be specially ordered from Mobil, so collectors will find these team's glasses much harder to find than the others — and more expensive. The 1986 glasses are a similar size to Row 2, but there are no white backgrounds.

Row 1: NFL see-through window rocks glasses.
1. Baltimore Colts . . . .$2.00 – 4.00
2. Houston Oilers . . . .$2.00 – 4.00
3. Pittsburgh Steelers . . . .$2.00 – 4.00
4. Dallas Cowboys . . . .$2.00 – 4.00

Row 2: Frosted panel Mobil NFL helmets, rocks glasses (1987)
1. Washington Redskins . . . .$3.00 – 5.00
2. Buffalo Bills . . . .$3.00 – 5.00
3. Pittsburgh Steelers . . . .$3.00 – 5.00
4. Philadelphia Eagles . . . .$3.00 – 5.00
5. Tampa Bay Buccaneers . . . .$3.00 – 5.00

National Football League Helmets/Logos, continued
Row 1: Mobil NFL helmets, double bands (1989)
1. Washington Redskins . . . .$3.00 – 5.00
2. New York Giants . . . .$3.00 – 5.00
3. Tampa Bay Buccaneers . . . .$3.00 – 5.00

Row 2: Mobil NFL helmets, single bands (1988)
1. Washington Redskins . . . .$3.00 – 5.00
2. New York Giants . . . .$3.00 – 5.00
3. Tampa Bay Buccaneers . . . .$3.00 – 5.00

Row 3: Mobil NFL helmets, single bands
1. Phoenix 1988 Cardinals . . . .$3.00 – 5.00
2. New York Jets . . . .$3.00 – 5.00
3. Miami Dolphins . . . .$3.00 – 5.00
4. Philadelphia Eagles . . . .$3.00 – 5.00

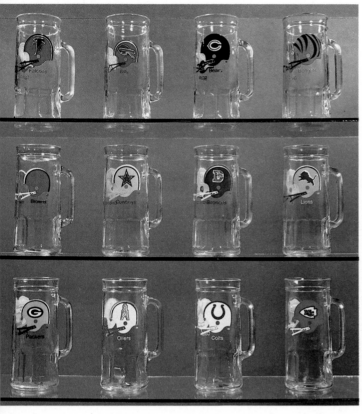

PLATE 179

Fisher Nut Mugs, continued

Plate 180

Row 1: Fisher Nut Mugs
1. Los Angeles Raiders . . . .$2.00 – 4.00
2. Los Angeles Rams . . . .$2.00 – 4.00
3. Minnesota Vikings . . . .$2.00 – 4.00
4. New York Jets . . . .$2.00 – 4.00

Row 2: Fisher Nut Mugs
1. New York Giants . . . .$2.00 – 4.00
2. New England Patriots . . . .$2.00 – 4.00
3. Philadelphia Eagles . . . .$2.00 – 4.00
4. Pittsburgh Steelers . . . .$2.00 – 4.00

Row 3: Fisher Nut Mugs
1. San Francisco 49ers . . . .$2.00 – 4.00
2. San Diego Chargers . . . .$2.00 – 4.00
3. Seattle Sea Hawks . . . .$2.00 – 4.00
4. Washington Redskins . . . .$2.00 – 4.00

Fisher Nut Mugs

Both Fisher and Flavor House promoted their products with mugs of dry-roasted peanuts. These mugs carried the logos of NFL and selected college football teams as well as the logos of recent Super Bowls.

Plate 179

Row 1: Fisher Nut Mugs
1. Atlanta Falcons . . . .$2.00 – 4.00
2. Buffalo Bills . . . .$2.00 – 4.00
3. Chicago Bears . . . .$2.00 – 4.00
4. Cincinnati Bengals . . . .$2.00 – 4.00

Row 2: Fisher Nut Mugs
1. Cleveland Browns . . . .$2.00 – 4.00
2. Dallas Cowboys . . . .$2.00 – 4.00
3. Denver Broncos . . . .$2.00 – 4.00
4. Detroit Lions . . . .$2.00 – 4.00

Row 3: Fisher Nut Mugs
1. Green Bay Packers . . . .$2.00 – 4.00
2. Houston Oilers . . . .$2.00 – 4.00
3. Baltimore Colts . . . .$2.00 – 4.00
4. Kansas City Chiefs . . . .$2.00 – 4.00

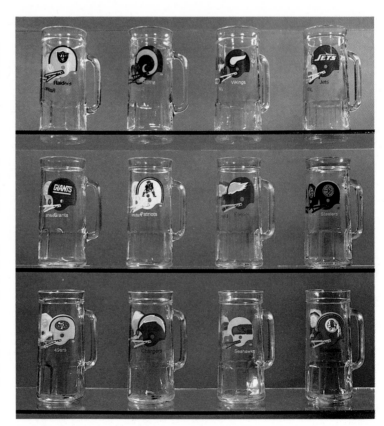

PLATE 180

PLATE 181

PLATE 182

Welch's NFL and Pepsi-Cola/Gary Patterson Sports Issues

The glasses in Row 1 through 3 were issued by Welch's in 1975 and 1976. Originally, they held Welch's jam and had steel lids. Row 1 shows the 1975 set of two NFL team helmet glasses — one glass for the teams of the National Football Conference and one for the American Football Conference. Row 2 shows the 1976 set of three National Football Conference glasses with a separate glass for each division. Row 3 shows the American Football Conference, set of 3. It is still possible to find these glasses with their labels and/or lids intact.

Row 1: Welch's 1975 NFL Collector Series, set of two
1. National Football Conference ....$6.00 – 9.00
2. American Football Conference ....$6.00 – 9.00

Row 2: Welch's 1976 NFC Collector Series, set of three
1. NFC Eastern Division ....$3.00 – 5.00
2. NFC Central Division ....$3.00 – 5.00
3. NFC Western Division ....$3.00 – 5.00

Row 3: Welch's 1976 AFC Collector Series, set of three
1. AFC Eastern Division ....$3.00 – 5.00
2. AFC Central Division ....$3.00 – 5.00
3. AFC Western Division ....$3.00 – 5.00

Rows 1 and 2 show the 1979 Pepsi Thought Factory Sport Collector Series with humorous cartoons by Gary Patterson. Originally, 12 glasses were planned for this set, but only 10 went into production. Two prototypes, which we have copies of, were dropped from the set: *Winner Takes All* (tennis) and *It's Only a Game* (golf). Of the ten, four are harder to find than the others (see values below). Also, in 1980, six of these glasses were issued as a special set for a food services convention in Las Vegas. These glasses bear, therefore, appropriately different date/logo/identification matter, but the basic design of the glasses is the same as the 1979 issue. The Las Vegas glasses are much harder to find than the others and command higher prices. They can sometimes be found in their original six-pack box.

Row 1: 1979 Pepsi Thought Factory Sport Collector Series
1. The Split (Bowling) ....$15.00 – 25.00
2. Heads Up (Soccer) ....$15.00 – 25.00
3. Sportsmanship (Men's Tennis) ....$15.00 – 25.00
4. Backlash (Fishing) ....$15.00 – 25.00
5. Nice Try (Racquetball) ....$5.00 – 8.00
(Nice Try — 1980 Las Vegas issue) ....$20.00 – 30.00

Row 2: 1979 Pepsi Thought Factory Sport Collector Series
1. Birdie (Golf) ....$5.00 – 8.00
(Birdie — 1980 Las Vegas issue) ....$20.00 – 30.00
2. Panic (Women's Tennis) ....$5.00 – 8.00
(Panic — 1980 Las Vegas issue) ....$20.00 – 30.00
3. Line Drive (Baseball) ....$5.00 – 8.00
(Line Drive — 1980 Las Vegas Issue) ....$20.00 – 30.00
4. Leader of the Pack (Bicycling) ....$5.00 – 8.00
(Leader of the Pack — 1980 Las Vegas issue) .....$20.00 – 30.00
5. Psych Out (Downhill Skiing) ....$5.00 – 8.00
(Psyche Out — 1980 Las Vegas issue) ....$20.00 – 30.00

PLATE 183

PLATE 184

Miscellaneous Baseball Teams and Players

The glasses shown on this page suggest the abundant variety of baseball glasses available. Especially since the early 60s, each franchise has offered commemorative, championship, and souvenir glassware, both in sets and as singles. Department stores, food chains, the media, and players have sponsored glasses. Collectors of this kind of glassware had better have extensive shelving for their collections.

Row 1: Set of four Old-Time Baseball Collector Cards-Players, rocks glasses (late 1980s)
1. Honus Wagner . . . .$5.00 – 8.00
2. Christy Mathewson . . . .$5.00 – 8.00
3. Ty Cobb . . . .$5.00 – 8.00
4. Shoeless Joe Jackson . . . .$5.00 – 8.00

Row 2: 50s-60s Team Logos — three from a larger set
1. Braves (Milwaukee) . . . .$5.00 – 8.00
2. Pirates (Pittsburgh) . . . .$5.00 – 8.00
3. Cubs (Chicago) . . . .$5.00 – 8.00

Row 3: 50s-60s Team Logos — four more from Row 2 set
1. Dodgers (Brooklyn) . . . .$5.00 – 8.00
2. Phillies (Philadelphia) . . . .$5.00 – 8.00
3. Giants (New York) . . . .$5.00 – 8.00
4. Cardinals (St. Louis) . . . .$5.00 – 8.00

Miscellaneous Baseball Teams and Players, continued
Row 1: Three 1960s Pittsburgh Pirates glasses
1. Beat 'Em Bucs (black) . . . .$5.00 – 8.00
2. 1960 World Champions Pittsburgh Pirates
   (players' signatures) . . . .$8.00 – 10.00
3. Beat 'Em Bucs (blue) . . . .$5.00 – 8.00

Row 2: Three 1970s Pirates glasses
1. Pirates '75, sponsored by KDKA-TV2 . . . .$3.00 – 5.00
2. Pittsburgh Pirates Logo . . . .$3.00 – 5.00
3. Pirates '76, sponsored by KDKA-TV2 . . . .$3.00 – 5.00

Row 3: Miscellaneous Baseball glasses
1. Philadelphia Phillies, 1980 World Champions,
   rocks glass . . . .$3.00 – 5.00
2. Philadelphia Phillies logo (also shown in Row 3) . .$5.00 – 8.00
3. Gold Star Chili, Pete Rose . . . .$5.00 – 8.00
4. Cincinnati Reds, CHARGE, Home of Professional
   Baseball . . . .$3.00 – 5.00
5. Johnny Bench's Homestretch Restaurant . . . .$5.00 – 8.00

PLATE 185

PLATE 186

Miscellaneous Baseball Teams and Players, continued
Gasoline companies, fast-food restaurants, soft-drink companies, and players' associations have gotten into the glassware business in a big way in the past fifteen or so years. Though not every player and team is represented on glass, collectors will be pleased with the variety of teams and players that is available.

Row 1: United Oil/Pepsi-Cola Baseball Greats, set of four (1988)
1. Roberto Clemente (1973 photo) . . . .$10.00 – 15.00
2. Lou Gehrig (1939 photo) . . . .$10.00 – 15.00
3. Ty Cobb (1936 photo) . . . .$10.00 – 15.00
Not pictured:
#4 Babe Ruth (1936 photo) . . . .$10.00 – 15.00

Row 2: Burger King/Detroit Tigers, set of four (1988)
1. Tiger holding '88 sign . . . .$3.00 – 5.00
2. Tiger batting . . . .$3.00 – 5.00
3. Tiger in stadium waving pennants . . . .$3.00 – 5.00
Not pictured:
#4 Tiger catching ball . . . .$3.00 – 5.00

Row 3: Baltimore Orioles *Make Your Great Comeback In 1985,*
set of six (1984)
1. #8 Cal Ripken, Jr., one in a series of six . . . .$6.00 – 10.00
2. #24 Ric Dempsey, two in a series of six . . . .$6.00 – 10.00
3. #19 Fred Lynn, five in a series of six . . . .$6.00 – 10.00
Not pictured:
#33 Eddie Murray, three in a series of six . . . .$6.00 – 10.00
#34 Storm Davis, four in a series of six . . . .$6.00 – 10.00
#52 Mike Boddicker, six in a series of six . . . .$6.00 – 10.00

Miscellaneous Baseball Teams and Players, continued
Row 1: Milwaukee Brewers/McDonald's, set of four (1982)
1. Rollie Fingers and Ted Simmons . . . .$6.00 – 10.00
2. Gorman Thomas and Cecil Cooper . . . .$6.00 – 10.00
3. Paul Molitor and Pete Vuckovich . . . .$6.00 – 10.00
4. Robin Yount and Ben Oglivie . . . .$6.00 – 10.00

Row 2: Little Caesar's Detroit Tigers "All American Line-Up," set
of four (1984)
1. Lou Whitaker, Dan Petry, Lance Parrish . . . .$6.00 – 10.00
2. Aurelio Lopez, Kirk Gibson, Jack Morris . . . . . .$6.00 – 10.00
3. Willie Hernandez, Chet Lemon, Milt Wilcox . . . .$6.00 – 10.00
4. Dave Rozema, Alan Trammell, Howard Johnson . . .$6.00 – 10.00

Row 3: Elby's Pittsburgh Pirates — Coca-Cola, set of four (1988)
1. Jim Gott and Jose Lind . . . .$6.00 – 10.00
2. Bobby Bonilla and Doug Drabek . . . .$6.00 – 10.00
3. Mike Dunne and Andy Van Slyke . . . .$6.00 – 10.00
4. Mike Lavalliere and Barry Bonds . . . .$6.00 – 10.00

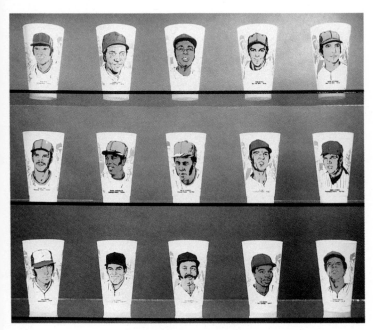

PLATE 187

Baseball Players and Team Logos and Uniforms on Plastic Cups

The low cost, easy storage, light weight, and non-breakable nature of plastic account for its popularity as a promotional item. However, like glass, plastic has its own vulnerabilities: fading and cracking. Like-new examples of older plastic command impressive prices. Plate 187: Rows 1 – 3 show 15 baseball players from a set that was distributed by Isaly's stores in 1976. Plate 188: Rows 1 – 3 show Icee brand cups with Major League Baseball logos and team uniforms from the 1980s.

Plate 187

Row 1: Major League Baseball Stars on 1976 Isaly's Plastic Cups
1. Pete Rose . . . .$6.00 – 9.00
2. Johnny Bench . . . .$6.00 – 9.00
3. Joe Morgan . . . .$6.00 – 9.00
4. Tom Seaver . . . .$6.00 – 9.00
5. Jerry Koosman . . . .$6.00 – 9.00

Row 2: Major League Baseball Stars on 1976 Isaly's Plastic Cups
1. Richie Zisk . . . .$6.00 – 9.00
2. Manny Sanguillen . . . .$6.00 – 9.00
3. Willie Stargell . . . .$6.00 – 9.00
4. Jim Kaat . . . .$6.00 – 9.00
5. Greg Luzinski . . . .$6.00 – 9.00

Row 3: Major League Baseball Stars on 1976 Isaly's Plastic Cups
1. Phil Niekro . . . .$6.00 – 9.00
2. Steve Garvey . . . .$6.00 – 9.00
3. Mike Marshall . . . .$6.00 – 9.00
4. Lou Brock . . . .$6.00 – 9.00
5. Caesar Cedeno . . . .$6.00 – 9.00

Baseball Players & Team Logos & Uniforms on Plactic Cups, continued

Plate 188

Row 1: Icee Baseball Logos and Uniforms on Plastic
1. Minnesota Twins . . . .$2.00 – 5.00
2. California Angels . . . .$2.00 – 5.00
3. Atlanta Braves . . . .$2.00 – 5.00
4. Detroit Tigers . . . .$2.00 – 5.00

Row 2: Icee Baseball Logos and Uniforms on Medium Plastic
1. Pittsburgh Pirates . . . .$2.00 – 5.00
2. Montreal Expos . . . .$2.00 – 5.00
3. Chicago Cubs . . . .$2.00 – 5.00
4. Houston Astros . . . .$2.00 – 5.00
5. Baltimore Orioles . . . .$2.00 – 5.00

Row 3: Icee Baseball Logos and Uniforms on Tall Plastic
1. San Francisco Giants . . . .$2.00 – 5.00
2. Boston Red Sox . . . .$2.00 – 5.00
3. Chicago Cubs (reverse of #3 above) . . . .$2.00 – 5.00
4. New York Yankees . . . .$2.00 – 5.00
5. California Angels . . . .$2.00 – 5.00

PLATE 188

PLATE 189

Kentucky Derby Glasses

Kentucky Derby tumblers were first made available at the concession stands at Churchill Downs in 1938, and they are the most popular of all horse racing glasses collected today. The early tumblers (1939 through 1944) are very expensive and for the most part unavailable to all but the most specialized (and wealthy) collectors. There's a definite lore about these glasses, and a certain knowledgeableness is a must for collectors. For example, there are variations and errors on particular glasses (i.e., 1974 and 1986) which means that a collector would have to get as many as four glasses from 1974 and two glasses from 1986 to complete a collection. And there are other variations that are interesting but which won't affect most collectors. For the details you'll need to know (and there is much more fascinating information on these glasses), we refer you to the latest edition of William D. Falvey and Aaron Chase's excellent book, *The Official Collector's Guide to Kentucky Derby Mint Julep Glasses*, published in 1991by the Louisville Manufacturing Co., 301 S. 30th St., Louisville, KY 40212. There is probably a new edition by now, so you'll probably want to purchase it if you intend to pursue these glasses.

The average Kentucky Derby collector today can hope to begin his or her collection (realistically) with the 1945 Derby glasses and proceed through the 1947 glasses without too much trouble, though these glasses have low production numbers and are pretty expensive. From 1948 on, the glasses are generally available, although you'll spend around $1,000.00 just getting from there through the fifties. In this book, we show a selection of glasses beginning with the year 1948. A note on prices: most Derby glasses can be bought at a slight discount below book prices, but the older glasses tend to hold their book value well, so you'll have to pay something near the average price guide value. More recent glasses — from 1975 to the present — can be purchased quite reasonably, but collectors will soon find that even for these glasses, the magic name Kentucky Derby has resulted in widespread, outlandishly ridiculous asking prices in antique malls and at flea markets. The best solution, therefore, is to be armed with the knowledge that reputable price guides supply.

Row 1: Kentucky Derby Glasses, late 40s and mid-50s
1. 1948 . . . .$120.00 – 150.00
2. 1949 . . . .$125.00 – 150.00
3. 1954 . . . .$100.00 – 150.00
4. 1955 . . . .$80.00 – 110.00
Not pictured:
1950 . . . .$225.00 – 275.00
1951 . . . .$325.00 – 380.00
1952 . . . .$110.00 – 150.00
1953 . . . .$80.00 – 100.00

Row 2: Kentucky Derby Glasses, 1956 – 1959
1. 1956 . . . .$125.00 – 225.00
2. 1957 . . . .$65.00 – 90.00
3. 1958 (referred to as the gold bar 1958 glass) . .$125.00 – 150.00
4. 1959 . . . .$50.00 – 75.00
Not pictured:
1958 Iron Leige (same as 1957 glass, but with *Iron Leige* printed in white just above horse's rump) . . . .$125.00 – 150.00

PLATE 190

PLATE 191

Kentucky Derby Glasses, continued
Row 1: Kentucky Derby Glasses, 1960 – 1964
1. 1960 . . . .$40.00 – 60.00
2. 1961 . . . .$65.00 – 90.00
3. 1962 . . . .$45.00 – 60.00
4. 1963 . . . .$35.00 – 45.00
5. 1964 . . . .$20.00 – 25.00

Row 2: Kentucky Derby Glasses, 1965 – 1968
1. 1965 . . . .$45.00 – 60.00
2. 1966 . . . .$35.00 – 50.00
3. 1967 . . . .$20.00 – 30.00
4. 1968 . . . .$20.00 – 30.00

Row 3: Kentucky Derby Glasses, 1969 – 1973
1. 1969 . . . .$20.00 – 30.00
2. 1970 . . . .$35.00 – 40.00
3. 1971 . . . .$20.00 – 25.00
4. 1972 . . . .$20.00 – 25.00
5. 1973 . . . .$18.00 – 22.00

Kentucky Derby Glasses, continued
Row 1: Kentucky Derby Glasses, 1974 – 1978
1. 1974 (Canonero II) . . . .$10.00 – 12.00
Not pictured:
1974 error (no II) . . . .$8.00 – 10.00
1974 Canonero II with Federal Glass Co. trademark $100.00
1974 error (no II) with Federal Glass Co. trademark $100.00
2. 1975 . . . .$4.00 – 6.00
3. 1976 . . . .$6.00 – 8.00
4. 1977 . . . .$4.00 – 6.00
5. 1978 . . . .$6.00 – 8.00

Row 2: Kentucky Derby Glasses, 1979 – 1984
1. 1979 . . . .$4.00 – 6.00
2. 1980 . . . .$14.00 – 18.00
3. 1981 . . . .$4.00 – 6.00
4. 1982 . . . .$4.00 – 6.00
5. 1983 . . . .$3.00 – 5.00
6. 1984 . . . .$3.00 – 5.00

Row 3: Kentucky Derby Glasses, 1985 – 1989
1. 1985 . . . .$4.00 – 6.00
2. 1986 . . . .$4.00 – 6.00
Not pictured:
1986 with 1985 © . . . .$6.00 – 8.00
3. 1987 . . . .$3.00 – 4.00
4. 1988 . . . .$3.00 – 4.00
5. 1989 . . . .$3.00 – 4.00
Additional Kentucky Derby Glasses Not pictured:
1990 . . . .$3.00 – 4.00
1991 . . . .$3.00 – 4.00
1992 . . . .$3.00
1992 Signature Series, only 1000 produced . . . . .$50.00 – 100.00
1993 . . . .$3.00
1994 . . . .$3.00

PLATE 192

PLATE 193

Miscellaneous Horse Racing Glasses

On this page we show a variety of glasses from The Meadows in Washington, Pennsylvania, Home of the Adios (harness racing); the Jim Beam Stakes; the Belmont; and the Preakness. All of these glasses represent popular collecting categories, but especially the Belmont (glasses issued 1976 to the present) and the Preakness (glasses issued 1973 to the present).

Row 1: Meadows (Harness Racing) Adios Glasses
1. 1969 . . . .$10.00 – 15.00
2. 1970 . . . .$10.00 – 15.00
3. 1971 . . . .$10.00 – 15.00

Row 2: Meadows Adios Glasses, continued
1. Adios Stemware: The Meadows, Pace for the Orchids .$5.00 – 8.00
2. Adios XIII, 1979 . . . .$8.00 – 10.00
3. Reverse of Adios stemware, #1 above

Row 3: Jim Beam Spiral Stakes Glasses
1. Jim Beam Spiral Stakes, 1983 . . . .$5.00 – 8.00
2. Jim Beam Stakes, 1986 . . . .$4.00 – 6.00
3. Jim Beam Stakes, Turfway Park, 1990 . . . .$3.00 – 5.00

Miscellaneous Horse Racing Glasses, continued
Row 1: Belmont Stakes Glasses
1. 1979, 111th Running . . . .$40.00 – 60.00
2. 1980, 112th Running . . . .$90.00 – 110.00
3. 1982, 114th Running . . . .$155.00 – 185.00
4. 1983, 115th Running . . . .$185.00 – 210.00

Row 2: Preakness Glasses
1. 1974, 99th Running . . . .$100.00 – 120.00
2. 1976, 101st Running . . . .$30.00 – 50.00
3. 1978, 103rd Running . . . .$60.00 – 80.00
4. 1980, 105th Running . . . .$20.00 – 30.00

Row 3: Preakness Glasses
1. 1981, 106th Running . . . .$25.00 – 35.00
2. 1983, 108th Running . . . .$30.00 – 50.00
3. 1985, 110th Running . . . .$20.00 – 30.00
4. 1988, 113th Running . . . .$20.00 – 30.00

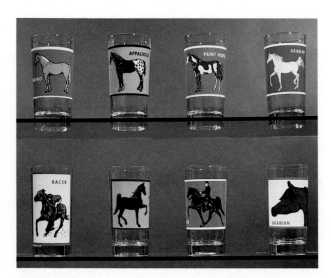

PLATE 194

PLATE 195

Miscellaneous Horse Related Glasses

The glasses on this page are cocktail glasses which normally come in sets of six to eight. Sold in department stores, these glasses are heavy with high quality decoration. The set shown in Row 1 and Plate 195: 2 and 3 dates from the 50s and is the earliest of the sets shown.

Row 1: Breeds of Horses Cocktail set
1. Palomino . . . .$3.00 – 5.00
2. Appaloosa . . . .$3.00 – 5.00
3. Paint Horse . . . .$3.00 – 5.00
4. Arabian . . . .$3.00 – 5.00

Row 2: Breeds of Horses Cocktail set, continued
1. Racer . . . .$3.00 – 5.00
2. Show Horse . . . .$3.00 – 5.00
3. Tennessee Walker . . . .$3.00 – 5.00
4. Arabian . . . .$3.00 – 5.00

Miscellaneous Horse Related Glasses, continued
Row 1: Horse and Rider Country Comic Scenes, set of six
1. Stable hand scrubbing horse . . . .$3.00 – 5.00
2. Rider on jumping horse . . . .$3.00 – 5.00
3. Horse throwing rider over fence . . . .$3.00 – 5.00
4. Horse jumping over fence and throwing rider . . . .$3.00 – 5.00
5. Horse refusing to cross stream . . . .$3.00 – 5.00
6. Horse giving rider bumpy ride . . . .$3.00 – 5.00

Row 2: Horse and Jockey Numbered Cocktail Set
1. #1 . . . .$5.00 – 8.00
2. #2 . . . .$5.00 – 8.00
3. #3 . . . .$5.00 – 8.00

Row 3: Horse and Jockey Numbered Cocktail Set
1. #4 . . . .$5.00 – 8.00
2. #5 . . . .$5.00 – 8.00
3. #6 . . . .$5.00 – 8.00
4. #7 . . . .$5.00 – 8.00
Not pictured:
#8 . . . .$5.00 – 8.00

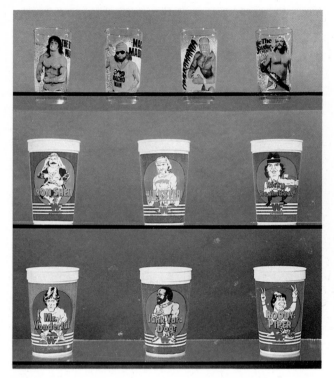

PLATE 196

PLATE 197

World Wrestling Federation and National Hockey League Glasses

Recently, professional wrestling has become almost as popular on glass as it is on television, and many sets and single glasses and plastic cups have been issued in the United States and Canada — but especially in Canada.

In Plate 196: Row 1 we show a Canadian set which originally contained peanut butter. Rows 2 and 3 show a set of six plastic cups.

Row 1: Schwartz's Peanut Butter (1989) World of Wrestling, set of four
1. The Ultimate Warrior . . . .$2.00 – 3.00
2. Macho Man . . . .$2.00 – 3.00
3. Hulkamania . . . .$2.00 – 3.00
4. Jake the Snake . . . .$2.00 – 3.00

Row 2: Plastic Wrestling Cups
1. The Iron Sheik . . . .$2.00 – 3.00
2. The Hulkster . . . .$2.00 – 3.00
3. Ricky Steamboat . . . .$2.00 – 3.00

Row 3: Plastic Wrestling Cups
1. Mr. Wonderful . . . .$2.00 – 3.00
2. Junk Yard Dog . . . .$2.00 – 3.00
3. Roddy Piper . . . .$2.00 – 3.00

Rows 1 and 2 picture two different sets of Elby's Big Boy Pittsburgh Penguins players. The 1989 tumblers in Row 1 feature one player per glass. There are two players on each of the 1990 mugs.

Row 1: Elby's Big Boy Pittsburgh Penguins (1989), set of four
1. #44 Rob Brown . . . .$6.00 – 8.00
2. #66 Mario Lemieux . . . .$6.00 – 8.00
3. #77 Paul Coffey . . . .$6.00 – 8.00
4. #33 Zarley Zalapski . . . .$6.00 – 8.00

Row 2: Elby's Big Boy Pittsburgh Penguins *Make the Team* Mugs (1990), set of four
1. #44 Rob Brown and #11 John Cullen . . . .$6.00 – 8.00
2. #66 Mario Lemieux and # 35 Tom Barrasso . . . . .$6.00 – 8.00
3. #77 Paul Coffey and #10 Dan Quinn . . . .$6.00 – 8.00
4. #33 Zarley Zalapski and #25 Kevin Stevens . . . . .$6.00 – 8.00

Miscellaneous

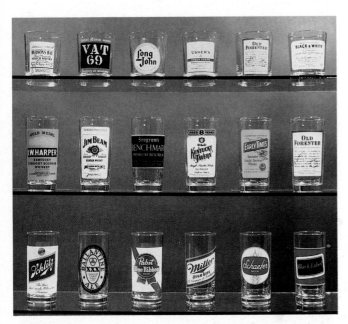

PLATE 198

Liquor, Beer, and Playing Cards Glasses

Party glassware has always been a popular collecting area, and these glasses also get used on appropriate occasions. The kinds of glasses we show here are representative, and they continue to be produced to this day. The glasses in Plate 198: Rows 1 through 3 have *made in France* markings and probably date to the late 60s and early 70s. They were probably sold in department stores in sets of four, six, or eight.

Plate 198

Row 1: Scotch and Whiskey Rocks Glasses
1. Hudson's Bay Scotch . . . .$2.00 – 4.00
2. VAT 69 Scotch . . . .$2.00 – 4.00
3. Long John Scotch . . . .$2.00 – 4.00
4. Usher's Green Stripe Scotch . . . .$2.00 – 4.00
5. Old Forester Kentucky Straight Bourbon Whiskey .$2.00 – 4.00
6. Black and White Scotch . . . .$2.00 – 4.00

Row 2: Bourbon Whiskey Glasses
1. I. W. Harper . . . .$3.00 – 5.00
2. Jim Beam . . . .$3.00 – 5.00
3. Seagram's Benchmark . . . .$3.00 – 5.00
4. Old Kentucky Tavern . . . .$3.00 – 5.00
5. Early Times . . . .$3.00 – 5.00
6. Old Forester . . . .$3.00 – 5.00

Row 3: Beer Glasses
1. Schlitz . . . .$2.00 – 4.00
2. Ballantine Ale . . . .$2.00 – 4.00
3. Pabst Blue Ribbon . . . .$2.00 – 4.00

4. Miller High Life . . . .$2.00 – 4.00
5. Schaefer . . . .$2.00 – 4.00
6. Black Label . . . .$2.00 – 4.00

Plate 199

Row 1: Bridge Glasses
The glasses are marked *Copyright 1942, The Philip Ronald Products Co., Chicago, Ill.* Try to buy these glasses as a set: it would be almost impossible to build a set glass by glass.
1. King of Diamonds . . . .$5.00 – 7.00
2. King of Spades . . . .$5.00 – 7.00
3. King of Hearts . . . .$5.00 – 7.00
4. King of Clubs . . . .$5.00 – 7.00

Row 2: Bridge Glasses, continued
1. Queen of Diamonds . . . .$5.00 – 7.00
2. Queen of Spades . . . .$5.00 – 7.00
3. Queen of Hearts . . . .$5.00 – 7.00
4. Queen of Clubs . . . .$5.00 – 7.00

Row 3: Poker Hand Glasses
This row shows a set of poker glasses with different winning hand combinations. This is another set that would be difficult to build a glass at a time.
1. Royal Flush . . . .$5.00 – 7.00
2. Flush . . . .$5.00 – 7.00
3. Full House . . . .$5.00 – 7.00
4. Three of a Kind . . . .$5.00 – 7.00
5. Two Pair . . . .$5.00 – 7.00
6. Pair . . . .$5.00 – 7.00

PLATE 199

PLATE 200

PLATE 201

Automobile Glasses

Automobiles are abundantly represented on glass, and collectors therefore have a variety of collecting paths to follow. Glasses showing old cars seem to be the most available, but modern classic cars have recently begun to command increased attention. Plate 200: Rows 1 through 3 show glasses from three different sets. Plate 201: Rows 1 and 2 feature reproductions of old car advertisements. Row 3 shows four pedestals from a larger set.

Row 1: Ford Automobile History
1. First Ford 1896/Skyliner Hideaway 500 . . . .$3.00 – 5.00
2. Ford 1908/Fairlaine 500 Club Victoria . . . .$3.00 – 5.00
3. Ford Model T/Ford Thunderbird . . . .$3.00 – 5.00

Row 2: 1908 Maxwell, 1903 Cadillac, 1908 Ford, 1899 Packard
1. Orange and Black . . . .$4.00 – 6.00
2. Aqua and Black . . . .$4.00 – 6.00
3. Red and Black . . . .$4.00 – 6.00
4. Yellow and Black . . . .$4.00 – 6.00

Row 3: Miscellaneous Antique Automobiles
1. Ford 1908/Chevrolet 1913 . . . .$2.00 – 4.00
2. Hudson 1910/Stutz 1914 . . . .$2.00 – 4.00
3. Oakland 1911/Buick 1910 . . . .$2.00 – 4.00
4. Studebaker 1915/Maxwell 1914 . . . .$2.00 – 4.00

Automobile Glasses, continued
Row 1: Antique Automobile Advertising Glasses
1. The 1907 Stearns . . . .$4.00 – 6.00
2. The $850 Fordmobile . . . .$4.00 – 6.00
3. $1,055 Reo the Fifth . . . .$4.00 – 6.00
4. $695 Maxwell "25" . . . .$4.00 – 6.00

Row 2: Antique Automobile Advertising Glasses
1. The Ideal Family Car — Chevrolet . . . .$4.00 – 6.00
2. The Hudson "33" . . . .$4.00 – 6.00
3. The 1914 Dodge . . . .$4.00 – 6.00

Row 3: Historical Oldsmobiles
1. The First Oldsmobile 1897 . . . .$4.00 – 6.00
2. Curved Dash Oldsmobile 1903 . . . .$4.00 – 6.00
3. Oldsmobile Limited 1910 . . . .$4.00 – 6.00
4. Oldsmobile Convertible Coupe 1928 . . . .$4.00 – 6.00

PLATE 202

Automobile Glasses, continued

Plate 202

Row 1: Round Table Pizza, *30 Years of Honest Pizza,* set of four Round Table Pizza is a west coast franchise. These glasses were distributed in the early 90s.
1. '56 Corvette . . . .$4.00 – 6.00
2. '57 Chevrolet . . . .$4.00 – 6.00
3. '57 Thunderbird . . . .$4.00 – 6.00
4. '59 Cadillac . . . .$4.00 – 6.00

Row 2: Bumpers Drive-In, Coca-Cola Classic, set of six classic cars Bumpers is a southern franchise. These glasses came out in the early 90s.
1. 1930 Cadillac . . . .$5.00 – 8.00
2. 1937 Cord . . . .$5.00 – 8.00
3. '46 Town & Country . . . .$5.00 – 8.00
4. '53 Skylark . . . .$5.00 – 8.00
5. '57 Edsel . . . .$5.00 – 8.00
6. '64 Mustang . . . .$5.00 – 8.00

Frosted Iced Teas: Automobiles and American Indians

Tall frosted iced tea glasses were a staple premium from the mid-50s to the mid-60s. They were most widely distributed by gasoline stations where they were available free or for a small fee with a minimum gasoline purchase. Competing oil companies offered different promotions in different parts of the country. Sometimes serving trays or pitchers were available with the glass sets.

Plate 203: Rows 1 and 2 show a set of frosted antique automobiles, while Row 3 shows a set of clear Anchor Hocking automobile glasses with white panels. Plate 204: Row 1 shows a set of 4 Bonded Oil Co. little Indian juice glasses. Rows 2 and 3 feature the Bonded Oil Company's set of eight Famous Ohio Indians (plural, in hard-to-see white letters). Collectors need to know that there is a single glass that *sort of* goes with this set — but not really! It

looks very much like the others, but it is entitled (in brown letters) *Famous Ohio Indian* (singular). The Indian on this glass is *Pontiac — the Red Napoleon.* At the present time it is not known whether this set came with a wooden tray-carrier like the Oklahoma Indians set did. Although there is no artist's signature on any of the pieces in this set, there is speculation that Acee Blue Eagle may have been responsible for it.

The set of eight Famous Oklahoma Indians by the famous American Indian artist Acee Blue Eagle comes in both tall frosted and short clear versions with pitchers and wooden carrier trays. Values for the frosted Oklahoma set without wooden carrier are about the same as the Ohio Indian set, but when the wooden carrier is available for the Oklahoma set, the price increases dramatically. The clear Oklahoma set — especially with wooden carrier — commands a price about 50% above the frosted version.

Plate 203

Row 1: Antique Automobiles — full frosting
1. 1911 Maxwell . . . .$3.00 – 5.00
2. 1909 Nash Rambler . . . .$3.00 – 5.00
3. 1913 Hudson . . . .$3.00 – 5.00
4. 1900 Oldsmobile . . . .$3.00 – 5.00

Row 2: Antique Automobiles — full frosting, continued
1. 1906 Autocar . . . .$3.00 – 5.00
2. 1902 Packard . . . .$3.00 – 5.00
3. 1906 Stanley Steamer . . . .$3.00 – 5.00

Row 3: Antique Automobiles — white panel on clear glass
1. 1908 Buick . . . .$2.00 – 4.00
2. 1906 Stanley Steamer . . . .$2.00 – 4.00
3. 1913 Hudson . . . .$2.00 – 4.00
4. 1902 Packard . . . .$2.00 – 4.00
Not pictured:
1906 Autocar . . . .$2.00 – 4.00
1909 Nash Rambler . . . .$2.00 – 4.00
1900 Oldsmobile . . . .$2.00 – 4.00
1911 Maxwell . . . .$2.00 – 4.00

PLATE 203

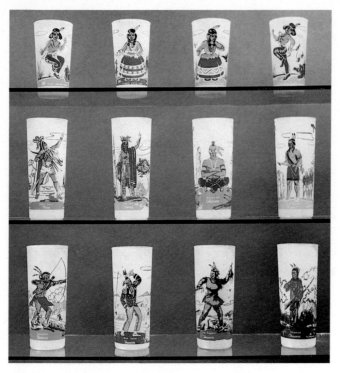

PLATE 204

Automobiles and American Indians, continued

Plate 204

Row 1: Bonded Oil Co., Frosted *Little* Indians, set of four
1. Little Jumping Rabbit . . . .$6.00 – 9.00
2. Princess Little Fawn . . . .$6.00 – 9.00
3. Little Princess Red Wing . . . .$6.00 – 9.00
4. Little Running Bear . . . .$6.00 – 9.00

Row 2: Bonded Oil Co., Frosted *Famous Ohio Indians,* set of eight
1. Chief Logan (Mingo) . . . .$8.00 – 10.00
2. Pontiac (Ottawa) . . . .$8.00 – 10.00
3. White Eyes (Delaware) . . . .$8.00 – 10.00
4. Little Turtle (Miami) . . . .$8.00 – 10.00

Row 3: Bonded Oil Co. *Famous Ohio Indians,* continued
1. Cornstalk (Shawnee) . . . .$8.00 – 10.00
2. Blue Jacket (Shawnee) . . . .$8.00 – 10.00
3. The Prophet (Shawnee) . . . .$8.00 – 10.00
4. Tecumseh (Shawnee) . . . .$8.00 – 10.00
Not pictured:
Pontiac — The Red Napoleon . . . .$10.00 – 12.00

Plate 205

The Famous Oklahoma Indians Frosted, with Pitcher and Wooden Tray-Carrier, set of eight

Acee Blue Eagle, the famous American Creek-Pawnee artist from Okmulgee, Oklahoma, was responsible for the artwork on this set, and his name — Blue Eagle — appears on each of the glasses as well as the pitcher. This set was commissioned by Knox Industries, the makers of "Oklahoma's Most Powerful Gasoline, New Knox-less Super 90 Regular and New Knox-less Super 100 Ethyl." Knox promotional literature stated that "You will receive these tumblers in appreciation of your patronage." This literature also tells us that a "Free Mailing Carton" was available. These glasses date from the late 1950s. Today, putting the entire set together can be expensive, because the trays and pitchers are getting quite difficult to find. We should add that the items in this set are probably most expensive in Oklahoma; it seems to be a clear case of people truly appreciating their own culture.

1. Bacon Rind (Osage) . . . .$8.00 – 12.00
2. Dull Knife (Cheyenne) . . . .$8.00 – 12.00
3. Geronimo (Apache) . . . .$8.00 – 12.00
4. Hen-Toh (Wyandot) . . . .$8.00 – 12.00
5. Hunting Horse (Kiowa) . . . .$8.00 – 12.00
6. Quanah Parker (Comanche) . . . .$8.00 – 12.00
7. Ruling His Sun (Pawnee) . . . .$8.00 – 12.00
8. Sequoyah (Cherokee) . . . .$8.00 – 12.00

PLATE 205

PLATE 206

Plate 206

Bonded Oil Co. Famous Ohio Indians Frosted Pitcher; Knox Gasoline Acee Blue Eagle Frosted Oklahoma Indians Pitcher; and Knox Gasoline Acee Blue Eagle Clear Oklahoma Indians Pitcher

Oklahoma Indians Frosted Pitcher . . . .$40.00 – 60.00
Wooden Tray-Carrier . . . .$75.00 – 125.00
Complete Set of Glasses, Pitcher, and Tray . . . .$175.00 – 275.00
Ohio Indians Pitcher . . . .$30.00 – 45.00
1. Famous Ohio Indians Frosted Pitcher . . . .$30.00 – 45.00
2. Famous Oklahoma Indians Frosted Pitcher . . . .$40.00 – 60.00
3. Famous Oklahoma Indians Clear Pitcher . . . . .$75.00 – 100.00
Not pictured:
8 clear 5¼" Oklahoma Indian glasses . . . .$10.00 – 14.00 each
Wooden Tray-Carrier . . . .$75.00 – 125.00
Complete Set of Clear Oklahoma Indians glasses,
    Tray, and Pitcher . . . .$225.00 – 325.00

Plate 207

Knox Gasoline Acee Blue Eagle Oklahoma Indians Frosted Juice Glasses in Wooden Carrier

This set consists of a wooden carrier with eight 4¾" frosted juice glasses. Since there are only two different juice glasses — Pocahontas and Cochise — the make-up of the set was up to the purchaser. Blue Eagle's name appears on each glass. The glasses can be found, but the tray is extremely difficult to find, and when you find both — together — they will cost you.
1. Pocahontas (Powhatan) . . . .$10.00 – 15.00
2. Cochise (Apache) . . . .$10.00 – 15.00
3. Wooden Tray-Carrier . . . .$100.00 – 150.00
4. Glasses and Tray, set of eight . . . .$180.00 – 270.00

PLATE 207

PLATE 208

Iced Tea Glasses — Frosted and Milk Glass

It has been said that the number of frosted iced tea glasses is without number. While that certainly isn't true, it is true that there is a fascinating variety of them to collect. These glasses are the sole objective of many collectors. Prices on these glasses are still relatively inexpensive, and collectors have not yet been able to identify rarities in the known sets. The prices that have been established are primarily based on the appeal of particular glasses. Considering their age and retro look, general attractiveness, and growing popularity, it will be surprising if in the next few years the prices on these glasses don't begin to accelerate.

Row 1 shows a set of four *Boats of the Ohio River.* Row 2 shows four of a set of six *Michigan Sportsman's Paradise* glasses. Row 3 shows five glasses from a set of six Colorado Centennial glasses. These glasses have great detail and vivid colors along with a gold-washed rim. Plate 209: Row 1 shows 5 glasses from a set of 10 *Wonderful World of Ohio* milk-glass tumblers. This set originally came with a metal tray and milk-glass pitcher, both of which are difficult to find. Row 2 shows six glasses from set of eight American Frontier scenes. And Row 3 shows a set of six tall thin tumblers with carousel animals on them.

Row 1: Boats of the Ohio River, set of four
1. Modern Tow and Barge . . . .$2.00 – 4.00

2. New Orleans . . . .$2.00 – 4.00
3. Great Republic . . . .$2.00 – 4.00
4. Queen City . . . .$2.00 – 4.00

Row 2: Michigan Sportsman's Paradise, set of six
1. Pheasant Hunting . . . .$4.00 – 6.00
2. Fishing . . . .$4.00 – 6.00
3. Duck Hunting . . . .$4.00 – 6.00
4. Bear Hunting . . . .$4.00 – 6.00
Not pictured:
#5 Wolverine . . . .$4.00 – 6.00
#6 Deer . . . .$4.00 – 6.00

Row 3: Colorado *Rush to the Rockies Centennial 1859 – 1959,* set of six
1. Arrival of first passenger train into Denver — June 24, 1870 . . . .$6.00 – 8.00
2. Discovery of gold at Little Dry Creek — Summer of 1858 . . . .$6.00 – 8.00
3. Battle of La Glorieta Pass — March 1862 . . . .$6.00 – 8.00
4. Cattle Drives up Texas Trail — 1866 – 1890 . . . . .$6.00 – 8.00
5. Opera House at Central City — *The Richest Square Mile on Earth* . . . .$6.00 – 8.00
Not pictured:
#6 Kit Carson discussing treaty with Ute Chief Ouray, Ft. Garland, 1866 . . . .$6.00 – 8.00

PLATE 209

PLATE 210

Iced Tea Glasses — Frosted and Milk Glass, continued

Row 1: The Wonderful World of Ohio, set of ten
1. Cleveland Lake Front . . . .$3.00 – 5.00
2. Perry's Victory Memorial, Lake Eire . . . .$3.00 – 5.00
3. Old Man's Cave, Hocking State Park . . . .$3.00 – 5.00
4. Air Force Museum, Fairborn near Dayton . . . .$3.00 – 5.00
5. Fort Recovery State Memorial, Greenville . . . .$3.00 – 5.00
Not pictured:
#6 Pro Football Hall of Fame, Canton . . . .$3.00 – 5.00
#7 Cincinnati Skyline . . . .$3.00 – 5.00
#8 State Capitol, Columbus . . . .$3.00 – 5.00
#9 Memorial at Fallen Timbers, Maumee, Near Toledo . .$3.00 – 5.00
#10 Campus Martius Museum, Marietta . . . .$3.00 – 5.00
Round Metal Tray . . . .$8.00 – 10.00
Pitcher . . . .$30.00 – 45.00

Row 2: American Frontier Scenes, set of eight
1. Cliff Dwellers . . . .$4.00 – 6.00
2. Showdown . . . .$4.00 – 6.00
3. Frontier Society . . . .$4.00 – 6.00
4. Black gold . . . .$4.00 – 6.00
5. Rush for Gold . . . .$4.00 – 6.00
6. Roundup . . . .$4.00 – 6.00
Not pictured:
#7 Iron Horse . . . .$4.00 – 6.00
#8 Gold Strike . . . .$4.00 – 6.00

Row 3: Carousel Animals
1. Zebra . . . .$2.00 – 4.00
2. Elephant . . . .$2.00 – 4.00
3. Tiger . . . .$2.00 – 4.00
4. Pony . . . .$2.00 – 4.00
5. Leopard . . . .$2.00 – 4.00
6. Giraffe . . . .$2.00 – 4.00

Entertainment Glassware

For want of a better label for these kinds of glasses, we call them Entertainment Glassware because the gaiety depicted on them lends itself to the idea of having a good time. The artwork is colorful and exuberant. Glasses like these were extremely popular during the post World War II years. Plate 210: Rows 1 through 3 show dance glasses. Plate 211: Row 1 shows circa 1930 bar glasses of girls in bathing suits. Each glass has a mixed drink recipe on the reverse. Rows 2 and 3 show "girlie" glasses which were enormously popular because of the naked reality behind the more conventional scene that you see pictured here! Condition is especially crucial with these glasses. The artwork usually consists of thin transparent decals which tended to be very vulnerable to practically every kind of wear. It is the exception rather than the rule to find these glasses in fine condition, and as might be expected, you'll have to pay premium prices for the girlie glasses which have survived unscathed.

Row 1: Square Dance Glasses
1. Hoe Down . . . .$3.00 – 5.00
2. Partners All . . . .$3.00 – 5.00
3. Swing Yer Ma . . . .$3.00 – 5.00
4. Do Si Do . . . .$3.00 – 5.00

Row 2: Dance Glasses
1. Minuet . . . .$3.00 – 5.00
2. Waltz . . . .$3.00 – 5.00
3. Charleston . . . .$3.00 – 5.00
4. Conga . . . .$3.00 – 5.00

Row 3: Dance Glasses, continued
1. Lindy Hop . . . .$3.00 – 5.00
2. Samba . . . .$3.00 – 5.00
3. Square Dance . . . .$3.00 – 5.00
4. Jitter Bug . . . .$3.00 – 5.00

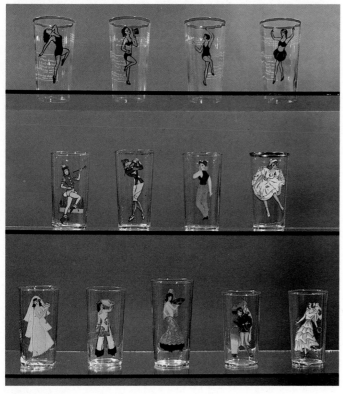

PLATE 211

PLATE 212

Zodiac Glassware

The signs of the Zodiac have always been a popular theme for glassware, and collectors will encounter an enormous variety of beverage containers with these signs on them. Zodiac glassware has always been issued in sets of twelve, so it's quite straightforward to collect. Sometimes you can find boxed sets of twelve, but it's more usual to find singles which makes it frustrating to finish sets.

The set of 4¾" glasses we show here was designed by Beverly and issued as a set in 1976. The same designs appeared on the 16 ounce Brockway version which was distributed by Arby's Restaurants in 1976. Neither set is easy to complete; there's always an elusive sign or two! Because the shorter set does not have a sponsor, it is valued slightly lower than the Arby's set.

Row 1: Beverly Zodiac Glasses
1. Aquarius (the Water Bearer) . . . .$2.00 – 4.00
2. Pisces (the Fishes) . . . .$2.00 – 4.00
3. Aries (the Ram) . . . .$2.00 – 4.00
4. Taurus (the Bull) . . . .$2.00 – 4.00

Row 2: Beverly Zodiac Glasses
1. Gemini (the Twins) . . . .$2.00 – 4.00
2. Cancer (the Crab) . . . .$2.00 – 4.00
3. Leo (the Lion) . . . .$2.00 – 4.00
4. Virgo (the Virgin) . . . .$2.00 – 4.00

Row 3: Beverly Zodiac Glasses
1. Libra (the Balance) . . . .$2.00 – 4.00
2. Scorpio (the Scorpion) . . . .$2.00 – 4.00
3. Sagittarius (the Archer) . . . .$2.00 – 4.00
4. Capricorn (the Goat) . . . .$2.00 – 4.00

Entertainment Glassware, continued
Row 1: Bar Glasses
1. Tarzan . . . .$4.00 – 6.00
2. Happy Daze . . . .$4.00 – 6.00
3. Monkey Gland . . . .$4.00 – 6.00
4. O'Hearn Special . . . .$4.00 – 6.00

Row 2: Girlie Glasses
1. Majorette . . . .$3.00 – 5.00
2. Golfer . . . .$3.00 – 5.00
3. Equestrian . . . .$3.00 – 5.00
4. Dancer . . . .$3.00 – 5.00

Row 3: Girlie Glasses, continued
1. Bride . . . .$3.00 – 5.00
2. Oriental Girl with Fan . . . .$3.00 – 5.00
3. Spanish Girl with Fan . . . .$3.00 – 5.00
4. Girl with Flag . . . .$3.00 – 5.00
5. Girl with Corsage . . . .$3.00 – 5.00

PLATE 213

PLATE 214

Newspaper Headlines Glasses

Many big-city larger circulation newspapers have issued sets of glasses featuring some of their most famous headlines. Such glasses were usually offered in sets of six or eight. Generally, these glasses were marketed as highball glasses, and they are usually pretty heavy, solid glasses, meant for use. Consequently, they are often faded because of repeated washings. When found, they tend not to be very expensive. When used, they often promote lively conversations starting with "I remember…"

Row 1: The Akron Beacon Journal Headlines
1. San Francisco Earthquake ....$2.00 – 4.00
2. The Titanic Sinks ....$2.00 – 4.00
3. Charles Lindbergh's Flight ....$2.00 – 4.00

Row 2: The Akron Beacon Journal, continued
1. Bombing of Pearl Harbor ....$2.00 – 4.00
2. World War II Ends ....$2.00 – 4.00
3. Kennedy Assassination ....$2.00 – 4.00
4. Man Lands on Moon ....$2.00 – 4.00

Newspaper Headlines Glasses, continued
Row 1: The Cincinnati Post Headlines, set of eight
1. San Francisco Earthquake — April 18, 1906 .....$2.00 – 4.00
2. Dirigible Shenandoah Crashes — September 3, 1925 $2.00 – 4.00
3. Stock Market Crash — October 29, 1929 ....$2.00 – 4.00
4. President Hoover's Address — December 2, 1930 .$2.00 – 4.00

Row 2: Cincinnati Post, set of eight, continued
1. Prohibition Ends — April 7, 1933 ....$2.00 – 4.00
2. Ferry Wreck — September 9, 1947 ....$2.00 – 4.00
3. MacArthur to Return — April 11, 1951 ....$2.00 – 4.00
4. Kennedy Assassination — November 22, 1963 ...$2.00 – 4.00

Row 3: Cleveland Plain Dealer, set of six
1. Wright Brothers — Men Are Flying at Last ......$2.00 – 4.00
2. Surrender of Germany ....$2.00 – 4.00
3. Lindbergh Arrives ....$2.00 – 4.00
4. The War is Over — 1945 ....$2.00 – 4.00
5. Indians Win World Title — 1948 ....$2.00 – 4.00
6. Kennedy Assassinated — 1963 ....$2.00 – 4.00

PLATE 215

PLATE 216

Newspaper Comics and Headlines Glasses, continued
In Row 1 we show Wendy's New York Times Limited Edition Glasses which came out in 1981 after the Shuttle Columbia's first successful mission. Rows 2 and 3 show a set of eight Pittsburgh Press headline glasses.

Row 1: Wendy's New York Times Headlines Limited Edition Glasses, set of four (1981)
1. Men Land on Moon/2 Astronauts Avoid Crater/Set Craft On A Rocky Plain (July 21, 1969) . . . .$3.00 – 5.00
2. Nation And Millions In City Joyously Hail Bicentennial (July 3, 1976) . . . .$3.00 – 5.00
3. U.S. Defeats Soviet Squad In Olympic Hockey by 4 – 3 (February 23, 1980) . . . .$3.00 – 5.00
4. Columbia Returns: Shuttle Era Opens (April 15, 1981) . . .$3.00 – 5.00

Row 2: Pittsburgh Press Headlines, set of eight
1. Lindbergh Lands Safely (May 22, 1927) . . . .$2.00 – 4.00
2. Flood Loss Quarter Billion (March 20, 1936) . . . . .$2.00 – 4.00
3. U.S. Declares War on Japan (December 8, 1941) .$2.00 – 4.00
4. Atom Bomb Dropped on Japan (August 7, 1945) . .$2.00 – 4.00

Row 3: Pittsburgh Press Headlines, continued
1. Polio Is Conquered (April 12, 1955) . . . .$2.00 – 4.00
2. Pirates World Champs (October 13, 1960) . . . . . .$2.00 – 4.00
3. President Kennedy Slain (November 22, 1963) . . .$2.00 – 4.00
4. Man on Moon (July 21, 1969) . . . .$2.00 – 4.00

Newspaper Comics Glasses

The Sunday Funnies set of seven glasses pictured in Plate 215: Rows 1 and 2 is one of the most colorful and beautiful sets we know of. The glasses, all of which bear a 1976 copyright, were distributed by a variety of small and midsized chains including The Red Barn during that year. Six of the glasses can be found with some regularity, but the Broom Hilda glass is difficult to find. There is a persistent rumor amongst collectors that a Dick Tracy glass exists, but we have not been able to confirm its existence. Collector Glass News has a standing reward of $25.00 for the first photograph of this glass, but no one has stepped forward to claim the money. If the glass does exist, most serious glass collectors would stand in line to pay several hundred dollars for it.

Row 1: The Sunday Funnies, set of seven (1976)
1. Little Orphan Annie (©1976 New York News Inc.) . .$8.00 – 15.00
2. Broom Hilda (©1976 The Chicago Tribune) . . .$100.00 – 150.00
3. Smilin' Jack (©1976 New York News Inc.) . . . . . .$8.00 – 15.00

Row 2: The Sunday Funnies, continued
1. Moon Mullins (©1976 New York News Inc.) . . . .$8.00 – 15.00
2. Gasoline Alley (©1976 The Chicago Tribune) . . .$8.00 – 15.00
3. Terry and the Pirates (©1976 News Syndicate Co., Inc.) . . . .$8.00 – 15.00
4. Brenda Starr, Reporter (©1976 New York News Inc.) . . .$8.00 – 15.00

PLATE 218

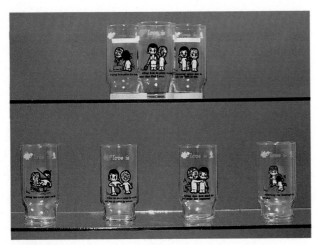

PLATE 217

Newspaper Comics Glasses, continued

The *Los Angeles Times* began running a cartoon in the early 1970s that featured cute answers to the question "Love is?" By the mid 1970s these answers became so successful that they found their way onto at least five different sets of glasses, all in different shapes and sizes with 1975 or 1976 copyrights. The sets consist of four or six glasses, and some of them are numbered. There are even single glasses such as brandy snifters. Most of the glasses have two different cartoons, one on each side. Most of these glasses were retail store issues, but some may have been given away as restaurant premiums. One set can be found with a *Centsible Place* logo.

Row 1: Love is…
1. *helping him paint his boat* . . . .$2.00 – 4.00
2. *telling him he plays tennis better than Rod Laver* . .$2.00 – 4.00
3. *listening again to how he made the hole in one* . . .$2.00 – 4.00

Row 2: Love is…
1. *letting her crew your yacht* . . . .$2.00 – 4.00
2. *when he does what he wants and you do what he wants* . . . .$2.00 – 4.00
3. *telling him how much his golf game has improved* . . .$2.00 – 4.00
4. *adjusting the bindings on her skiis* . . . .$2.00 – 4.00

Newspaper Comics Glasses, continued
Row 1: Love is…
1. giving and forgiving . . . .$2.00 – 4.00
2. an autumn walk through the woods . . . .$2.00 – 4.00
3. telling her she's as lovely as the day you were married $2.00 – 4.00
4. togetherness . . . .$2.00 – 4.00

Row 2: Love is…
1. sharing even the hard times/whatever you make it .$2.00 – 4.00
2. tickling his nose with a long piece of grass/an autumn walk . . . .$2.00 – 4.00
3. watching the sun sink into the sea/the first kiss in the morning . . . .$2.00 – 4.00
4. listening again to how he made the hole in one/telling him how much his golf game has improved . . . .$2.00 – 4.00

Row 3: Love is…
1. togetherness . . . .$2.00 – 4.00
2. the greatest feeling you can feel . . . .$2.00 – 4.00
3. being far away and yet so close . . . .$2.00 – 4.00

Prototype Brockway Company Glassware from the Pepsi-Cola Collectors Series

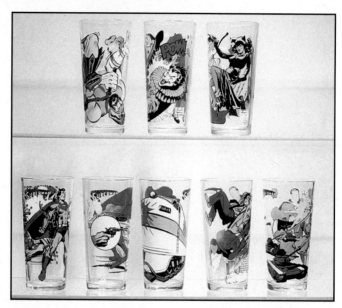

PLATE 219

The glasses on this and the following pages are sample glasses produced by Brockway. Often they have round black and white Brockway Glass Company stickers on their bottoms identifying them, and sometimes they don't. They were prepared for clients and sponsors of the various promotions so that the subjects, graphics, and colors could be evaluated and approved before actual production began. These glasses are also referred to as prototypes by many collectors. It is our understanding that sample glasses were just that: samples of glasses that had been approved, contracted for, and ordered. The assumption was that sample glasses were later going to be produced in large quantities. But in the meantime, Brockway sales representatives would all need to have sample glasses to show prospective customers. So, sufficient glasses were made for these company representatives. Obviously, if the promotion later fell through (and many did), then the samples themselves would — in time — become very scarce or rare because of their limited quantity. At the time these glasses were being produced and considered for production, no one associated with them could have guessed that they would someday become valuable collectibles.

Prototype glasses were a little different. They preceded the sample glasses in the design process, and they were very provisional. Often, only one was made, sometimes two or three — and usually with different colors and designs to show a range of possibilities. Customers would choose their designs from the available prototypes, and then a limited number of uniform sample glasses would be run. If the samples were consistent in quality and approved by the buyer or sponsor, the glass went into production. Left behind, so to speak, in the process would be the prototypes and sample glasses. Again, if something happened along the way and the promotion failed, then the fate of the samples and prototypes was uncertain. Many, perhaps most, were discarded, broken, given away, taken to the dump, or forgotten. (We have talked to people directly involved in Pepsi-Cola glass promotions who say that all of these things have happened!) However, a surprising number of these glasses have survived — stored away for years by former Brockway salespeople and promoters — fortunately, and they are now scattered around the country in various collectors'

collections. In any case, whether they are called prototypes or sample glasses, we do know that they were made in very limited quantities. Some went on to production and mass distribution; others did not. The glasses we show on this page never went into production for reasons best known to promoters, sponsors, restaurant owners, and copyright and license holders. We are told that these glasses are therefore quite rare, and that normally fewer than a dozen copies of a single prototype were ever made while slightly larger runs were normal for sample glasses. As rare as these glasses are, they are still surfacing, and they can still be bought. We bought some from a lady who found a Brockway box full of them at a yard sale! When these glasses are offered for sale by dealers and collectors, they are quite expensive. Essentially, they are worth what a collector is willing to pay for them. On the other hand, if you come across some of these at a flea market or yard sale, the price will probably be much more reasonable. Look for the Brockway sticker!

Row 1: Three Sample Glasses from the 1977 Pepsi-Cola Collector Series, © D.C. Comics, Inc.
1. Wonder Woman roping Roman soldier-type thug
2. Batman in vault subduing bank robber and Joker dressed as clown
3. Batgirl and Robin subduing Catwoman

Row 2: Pepsi-Cola Superman Collector Series, © D.C. Comics, Inc. 1977, set of five
There are no titles on these glasses which describe the action scenes, but it's pretty clear that the scenes on the glasses are intended to correspond to the chronology of Superman's life and his well-known abilities.
1. Superman being sent away from Krypton by his parents in a small rocket/adult Superman breaking chains
2. Superman outrunning and catching bullet fired from a pistol (Faster than a Speeding Bullet)
3. Superman stopping a locomotive (More Powerful than a Locomotive)
4. Superman leaping over tall buildings and collaring thugs (Able to Leap Tall Buildings)
5. Superman battling but not being affected by four tanks (Man of Steel)

PLATE 220

Row 1: Reverse views of 1977 Pepsi-Cola Collector Series D.C. Comics

Row 2: Reverse views of 1977 Pepsi-Cola Superman, set of five

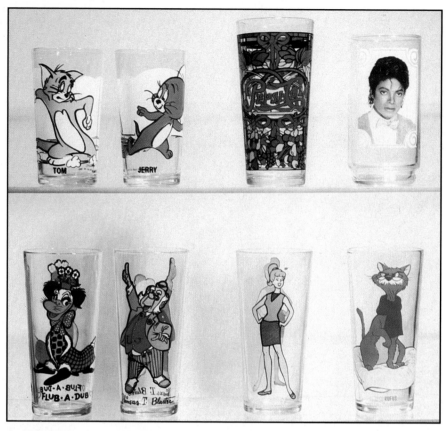

PLATE 221

Prototype Brockway from Pepsi-Cola, continued
Row 1: Miscellaneous Pepsi-Cola Sample Glasses and Prototypes
1. Tom (white background). On the production glass, the white background is yellow.
2. Jerry (white background). On the production glass, the white background is yellow.
3. Pepsi-Cola filigree design, 16 oz. Brockway
4. Michael Jackson. This glass has a large round Pepsi-Cola logo on the reverse, and it is thought that this is a prototype — only one was made. The logo's design, the style of the glass, and Jackson's image all suggest a late 1970s date.

Row 2: Miscellaneous Pepsi-Cola Sample Glasses and Prototypes
A Pepsi-Cola Collector Series featuring the Howdy Doody characters was planned, but it never got into production. We know of 5 glasses that were to be in this ©*1976 National Broadcasting Company, Inc.* set. We show two of them here.

The Archies was another Pepsi-Cola Collector Series that never saw distribution. The glasses have ©*1977 The Archie Company* on them. We show only one here.

The Rufus glass shown below with Rufus sitting on a pillow is an unusual prototype for the Disney/Pepsi-Cola Rescuers Series of 1977. There is little similarity between it and the subsequent Rufus production glass. This glass has the following writing on it: *Pepsi — The Rescuers Collector Series, © Walt Disney Productions, 1977.*

1. Flub-a-Dub, from the 1976 Howdy Doody Pepsi-Cola Collector Series
2. Phineas T. Bluster, from the 1976 Howdy Doody Pepsi-Cola Collector Series
Not pictured:
Howdy Doody, Clarabell, and Dilly Dally
3. Betty, from the 1977 Archies Pepsi-Cola Collector Series
Not pictured:
Archie, Veronica, Reggie, Mr. Weatherbee, Jughead, Big Moose, and Miss Grundy
4. Rufus, a prototype for the 1977 Disney Rescuers Pepsi-Cola Collector Series

PLATE 222

Prototype Brockway from Pepsi-Cola, continued
Row 1: Miscellaneous Pepsi-Cola Sample Glasses and Prototypes Aquaman and Green Arrow from the 1976 Pepsi-Cola NPP and DC Comics Super Series appear here in versions which don't have the colored moon behind the superheroes. These were prototypes for the 1976 Super Series which all have 3" color circles behind the Super Heroes.
1. Aquaman, 1976 NPP — no moon
2. Green Arrow, 1976 NPP — no moon

The Muttley and Frankenstein Jr. glasses shown below were probably intended to be part of the 1977 Hanna-Barbera, set of six, we are familiar with, but they were never produced. These glasses have on them: *Pepsi Collector Series ©1977 Hanna-Barbera Productions, Inc.* There's also a Space Ghost glass which belongs to this Hanna-Barbera grouping.
3. Muttley
4. Frankenstein Jr.

Not pictured:
Space Ghost

Row 2: Pepsi-Cola Collector Series, ©1977 Terrytoons
Mighty Mouse is the only glass in this projected set that ever got distributed, and as we have mentioned before, it was distributed in very limited quantities. The others exist as sample glasses.
1. Deputy Dawg
2. Little Roquefort
3. Lariat Sam
4. Sad Cat
Not pictured:
Heckle & Jeckle, Possible Possum

Collectors should keep in mind the fact that companies other than Brockway made sample glasses and prototypes and that these glasses also are out there somewhere. Many of them can be identified by stickers or labels on their bottoms. Happy hunting, and good luck!!

Index

Schroeder's ANTIQUES Price Guide

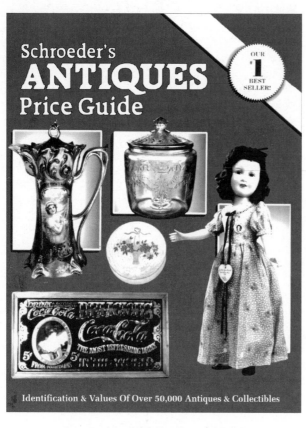

OUR #1 BEST SELLER!

Identification & Values Of Over 50,000 Antiques & Collectibles

8½ x 11, 608 Pages, $14.95

. . . is the #1 best-selling antiques & collectibles value guide on the market today, and here's why . . .

• More than 300 advisors, well-known dealers, and top-notch collectors work together with our editors to bring you accurate information regarding pricing and identification.

• More than 45,000 items in almost 500 categories are listed along with hundreds of sharp original photos that illustrate not only the rare and unusual, but the common, popular collectibles as well.

• Each large close-up shot shows important details clearly. Every subject is represented with histories and background information, a feature not found in any of our competitors' publications.

• Our editors keep abreast of newly developing trends, often adding several new categories a year as the need arises.

If it merits the interest of today's collector, you'll find it in *Schroeder's*. And you can feel confident that the information we publish is up to date and accurate. Our advisors thoroughly check each category to spot inconsistencies, listings that may not be entirely reflective of market dealings, and lines too vague to be of merit. Only the best of the lot remains for publication.

Without doubt, you'll find
SCHROEDER'S ANTIQUES PRICE GUIDE
the only one to buy for
reliable information and values.

COLLECTOR BOOKS
A Division of Schroeder Publishing Co., Inc.